compiled by
patti m. hummel

this is now

a girl-to-girl devotional for teens

THIS IS NOW
published by Multnomah Books

International Standard Book Number: 978-1-59052-605-7
Cover image by Howard Pyle/Zefa/Corbis
Interior design and typeset by Katherine Lloyd

In some instances Scripture versions have been chosen by the publisher and will not necessarily reflect the preference of the contributor.

Published in the United States by WaterBrook Multnomah, an imprint of the Crown Publishing Group, a division of Random House Inc., New York.

Printed in the United States of America

For information:
MULTNOMAH BOOKS
12265 ORACLE BOULEVARD, SUITE 200
COLORADO SPRINGS, CO 80921

Library of Congress Cataloging-in-Publication Data

This is now : a girl-to-girl devotional for teens / compiled by Patti M. Hummel.
p. cm.
ISBN 1-59052-605-8
1. Teenage girls--Prayer-books and devotions--English. 2. Christian teenagers--Prayer-books and devotions--English. 3. Devotional calendars. I. Hummel, Patti M.
BV4860.T45 2006
242'.633--dc22 2006008112

11 12 13 14—10 9 8 7 6 5 4

introduction

Sometimes you just need advice from someone who actually knows how it feels to be you. No parents or preachers or "experts"—just someone your age who understands what you're going through.

Welcome to *This Is Now*, a girl-to-girl 365-day devotional for teens. Each day in the pages of this book you will find stories from girls around the world who want you to know you're not alone, whatever you're going through. They want to encourage you, help you find solutions, and share with you the one thing that's gotten them through it all: the unconditional love of Jesus Christ. Why? Because there's nothing better or more important for all eternity than knowing Jesus *now*.

Blessings,
Patti M. Hummel
Compiler

January 1

happy new year?

He will have no fear of bad news;
his heart is steadfast, trusting in the LORD.

PSALM 112:7

Few people make getting cancer a New Year's resolution. Its presence is never by invitation, and nobody daydreams about the possibility of cancer growing inside a loved one. I had seen it distress families around me, but I never did more than say a halfhearted prayer, share a sympathetic sigh, or lend a listening ear. When the words "Dad has cancer" left my mom's lips, they fashioned the course of my entire year, resulting in a soup of fear, dependence, and relief. I had no idea what gravity the words held until they sunk in moments later as I stumbled into my room. With every step I took toward my bed, new thoughts seared the reality. *Stomp. Dad will have to take chemotherapy. Stomp. I will have to face my peers. Can I handle that? Stomp. Will I cry during my classes?* Plopping onto my bed with these flooding thoughts, the big one hit me: *Will Daddy die?* I cried for hours as this question replayed itself. I began to call out to God, "Stay with him and protect him!" I was not in the mood to offer polite requests. I was screaming at God into my tear-dampened pillow; I wasn't angry at God, but I felt such passion and needed to yell. In the following months, I saw my father's joy. He was weaker in a physical sense, but his spiritual strength inspired everyone. Seeing this helped me cope with all of my questions. I felt that I could make it through anything if I just carried a positive attitude, believed in God's faithfulness, and trusted Him for a happier New Year.

Sonja Mindrebo, 17, Houghton Christian Academy, Houghton, NY

Lord, I want my faith to be strong enough for everyone to see—no matter what my circumstances. Amen.

i promise

"Simply let your 'Yes' be 'Yes' and your 'No' be 'No'; anything beyond this comes from the evil one."

MATTHEW 5:37

Last year I was the student manager for our cross-country team, and I had a lot of fun managing. Coach would give me a bad time every once in a while about how I should run for the team. We laughed about it, and I never really took him seriously. As the season started this year, we were two girls short of a full team, which needs four members. I told Coach that if another girl joined the team, I would run so they could have a full team. Two days later another girl joined the team. I knew that Coach wouldn't hold me to my promise, but I had given him my word. Even in this unimportant situation, that had to mean something. I don't like to run, and I am not anywhere near being in shape, but I am now a member of the girls' cross-country team. To be honest, it is painful, but there is some pride in finishing and doing my best. Also, I get to think a lot about how God uses some things that are painful that we wouldn't choose to do to make us into the people He wants us to be. God is using a simple promise that I made to teach me more about Him. Also, I have been told that some other girls admire me for going out as a senior, especially since I always finish last. I guess that there are some benefits to keeping my word. If only their "Good job!" would make my legs stop hurting!

Lisa A. Osler, 18, Nebraska Christian High School, Kenesaw, NE

I don't want to make promises I won't keep,
especially to You, Father.

January 3

faith—it's how i know

Now faith is being sure of what we hope for
and certain of what we do not see.

HEBREWS 11:1

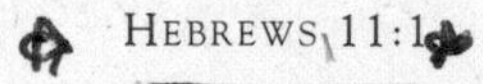

Have you ever sat in an airplane, anxious about take-off, only to get in the sky and have your breath taken away by the most beautiful sight as you fly through the clouds? Have you ever just sat and looked at the rain and seen through the gloom the wonder of the rainbow on the other side? These are reminders of the promises from God! When I have the opportunity to just sit and see these things, my faith is strengthened. I am reminded that God is real. Birds know when to fly south, bears know when to hibernate, the ocean knows where to stop at the shore, and the night knows when to hide as each day arrives. Many times my Mom thinks I don't listen, but I do. She tells me that everything else in life knows its place, that everything else does what God wants, and that we do well when we follow God by faith. She tells me we mess up when we do only what we want to do. I want to find my place; to live for God; to walk by faith. Faith is not an old-fashion, out-of-date, out-of-style idea. Faith keeps us soaring through the clouds. Faith keeps us going through the rain until it parts to reveal the beauty of the day. Faith! It is the substance of things hoped for, the evidence of things not seen. For us to believe that there is no God is foolish. To live for God is faith!

Candace K. Croston, 16, King's Fork High School, Suffolk, VA

Give me enough faith to do Your will in everything,
even when I'm unsure of what will happen.

the breath of life

And he is not served by human hands,
as if he needed anything, because he himself gives
all men life and breath and everything else.

ACTS 17:25

One thing I don't think about every day when I wake up is the fact that I am still breathing. To most people, breathing each day is taken for granted. But sometimes I wonder whether I have enough air to live one more second. I have suffered from asthma since I was two years old. It is a problem that has influenced my life repeatedly. Having a cold makes it extremely difficult for me to breathe. It feels as though a giant is standing on my chest and just won't back off. As I lay in the hospital bed, gasping for my next breath, I realize how important breathing is. I wonder, *Why can't I just breathe like normal people? Why do I have to go through the pain, struggle, and fear I face each time I have an asthma attack?* As I hear the buzz of the nebulizer and feel the mask on my face, the pain of trying to breathe finally begins to ease and I realize that God is still in control. It can be hard for me to see how something good can come from my lack of breath. Then I remember all of the times God has given me breath again. He knows the pain I have been through, but he has never left me alone. Having asthma makes me see that there are times when I can't do anything but use my inhaler—which is when I need to rely on God most. I know He is in complete control and has great plans for my life. He does not waste anything.

Stacey Krieger, 16, Nebraska Christian High School, O'Neill, NE

God, I am so glad You are in control! I am thankful that nothing that happens is out of Your hands.

January 5

reckless words

Reckless words pierce like a sword,
but the tongue of the wise brings healing.

PROVERBS 12:18

Reading this passage brought back many memories of what I used to be like. To everybody else, my relationship with my mom was good. That is because no one knew of the real words I spoke to her. If I even disagreed with her, I would turn the situation into such a huge problem. My reckless words were piercing her like a sword, and it was affecting the dynamics of our entire family. The words I spoke towards my mom were so sharp, negative, and disrespectful that it was impossible for us to have a loving relationship. Of course, my mother was always quick to forgive and show her affection, yet I always pushed her away with my words and attitude. One day the tension between us got so bad that I ran out of the house to take a walk and think things through. I was so sick of living like that, and I was ready to admit that I was terribly wrong. As I walked I couldn't stop crying because I kept asking myself how I would feel if I had a daughter that treated me like that. The pain I felt was so real, and like Proverbs says, it pierced like a sword. I felt so ashamed and I wanted to change my ways so much. I knew that to make things better I would have to work really hard on watching the words that I said and the way I said them. It was difficult, but I found that if you try saying three good things every time you say a negative thing, your speech will improve remarkably. Today I have an amazing relationship with my mom.

Chloé Truehl, 18, Adelaide, Australia

Why do I hurt people so often with my words?
I want to show Your love, Lord, instead of hate.

a powerful story

Love your enemies and pray for those who persecute you, that you may be sons of your Father in heaven.

MATTHEW 5:44–45

I love to read, and I'd have to say the book that's impacted my life the most was a true story about a group of Anabaptist Christians in Austria in 1539. They were captured and put into a dungeon because they believed differently than the Catholic faith, Austria's national religion. Their faith amazed me because they were willing to do anything for the Savior. The book describes how they tried to witness their faith to the jailor and then how they were willing to become galley salves rather than renounce what they believed was the truth. On the long march to the sea in chains, they were amazingly able to share the gospel to many people. Then when they reached the sea, God delivered them from the galleys, the soldiers, and the chains and dungeons. They were able to really glorify God through this situation. After reading this book, I became really convicted. Am I willing to die for my faith and for Jesus, who died for me? How much do I love my enemies and even bless them? How much of my life have I given to Christ? Would I be willing to let Him lead me through whatever He wanted? I still have so much to learn, but that book still challenges me so much. My life has changed; I have a different goal now. The firm believers in that book are my role models as I try to live a life where I am willing to sit back and let God drive!

Hannah Reeves, 14, home school, Central, SC

Please, give me faith that can move a mountain.
I want to use it to do something great for You, Father!

January 7

my best friend

The LORD himself goes before you and will be with you; he will never leave you nor forsake you. Do not be afraid; do not be discouraged.

DEUTERONOMY 31:8

Reading the story of Robinson Crusoe, I could not believe it was based on a true story. He arrived on an island by accident. He was miserable in the beginning, but later embraced religion as a balm for his unhappiness, and he adapted to life on the island. I understood Crusoe's feelings. Arriving at the Memphis airport from Korea, I couldn't find anyone who had my yellow skin color. Fear attacked me. My mom was not there to wake me up in the morning, and I had no friends. The first day of school in America was the worst day of my life. In English class my teacher asked me, "Where are you from?" My answer was short and clear: "Bathroom." Everyone started to laugh at me. I didn't understand because I *had* actually just come from the restroom. Then, I couldn't find friends to sit with at lunch, so I left the cafeteria with a piece of bread. The school was huge, but it seamed like an uninhabited desert. Attending church with my host mom made all the difference because I was treated like a member of their community. I joined the choir and learned to speak English and to praise God. God was my friend, and He was there to help me through the hardships, and He helps me to not be afraid. Crusoe overcame loneliness, and I will endure all my afflictions with my best friend, God.

Grace Park, 17, Houghton Christian Academy, Houghton, NY

Help me to remember that I'm not alone. Too often life can make me feel like I'm on a deserted island by myself.

my grandpa

Whoever claims to live in him must walk as Jesus did.

1 JOHN 2:6

My grandpa was diagnosed with Parkinson's disease about three years ago and the struggles he endured with his health were painfully difficult for him and our whole family. After a fall out of his chair that resulted in a broken hip and a change in him...he was never the same. His medicine made him hallucinate and say crazy things, and he was in and out of the hospital for the next several months. Eventually pneumonia filled his lungs and his health continued to worsen. On his last hospital stay his doctors gave no encouragement that he could live very much longer. We all struggled with what was happening to this man we all loved so much. We knew that he was a very godly man. He knew much about the Bible, and he went to church every Sunday that he was able. He had such a positive influence on me. In April he passed away. He was at home at the time with family around him. His death was hard for me. I wanted to just curl up in a ball and hide from the world. I had lots of friends that were there for me during that time. My friends helped me get through it...some of them I hadn't treated too well before, but they were still there for me when I really needed them. I know that my grandpa is in heaven right now. That experience made me a lot stronger and helped me to not take my life for granted. It really made me ask myself, *What kind of legacy would I leave behind if I died now?*

Bethany Musgrove, 17, home school, Hermitage, TN

I want my life to mean something, Lord.
And the only way it will is if I live for You.
Help me to do that.

God, please challenge my faith

The testing of your faith develops perseverance.

JAMES 1:3

I was spending a week hiking in the high peaks of the Adirondack Mountains with five other girls and two counselors, and they had just announced that it was quiet time. I found a nice, secluded spot in the woods and prayed. *Dear God, please challenge me in my faith this week, challenge me to deepen my relationship with you.* When we started on our overland hike to the next campsite, it was just the right temperature and my pack felt light on my shoulders. But after a while I was sweating as I jumped from rock to rock with my huge pack to avoid the thick mud, but my pants got muddy anyway. A fly buzzed around my head, and I got all wet from the rain on the bushes. Then I hit my head on a log that hung across the path. When we finally got to our campsite, I discovered that we were sleeping in the lean-to with the spiders instead of our nice bug-proof tents. Tears came to my eyes, and I was thinking, *Okay, God! What's with this? Why am I having such a miserable day?* Then I remembered that I asked Him to challenge me in my faith. I realized He was challenging me to be cheerful in all circumstances, and I was failing miserably. I prayed that God would give me the strength to be cheerful, even though I was having a crummy day, and He gave me just the strength I needed to continue on through the next few days in the high peaks.

Allison Engel, 16, Wheaton North High School, Wheaton, IL

Dear God, please challenge me in my faith today. Challenge me to deepen my relationship with You.

walking away from the mirror

So whether you eat or drink or whatever you do, do it all for the glory of God.

1 CORINTHIANS 10:31

"I am beautiful. I am a worthwhile person. I am lovable." I honestly think that these are statements that every girl doubts. It is so much easier to believe that I am ugly, I am a worthless screwup, and no one cares about me, but these statements are completely untrue. I, like so many other girls, wanted to be thinner, more beautiful, and popular. My feelings of inadequacy started in kindergarten. I felt I wasn't good enough for anything. As I entered high school, I really started to struggle with my weight, and it became very hard for me to be healthy: physically, emotionally, and spiritually. One night a friend read me 1 Corinthians 10:31 and that changed my life. The phrase "do it all for the glory of God" amazed me. When I wake up, when I eat, when I speak, when I walk to class, when I talk to a friend, or do my homework, I am to glorify God. It was so easy to believe all the nasty things about myself because all I was focused on was *myself*. I had become so obsessed with who I saw in the mirror that I no longer saw someone made in the image of God. When I was able to begin walking away from the mirror and striving to know and glorify Him, things became much easier. By no means has my struggle ended; I am still learning how to glorify God with my life, but I begin every morning trying to see in the mirror what Christ sees when He looks at me.

Lisa A. Osler, 18, Nebraska Christian High School, Kenesaw, NE

Jesus, it's hard to glorify You when I'm so focused on what I don't like about myself. Help me see more than just what's in the mirror.

January 11

feeling frazzled?

Trust in the LORD with all your heart and lean not on your own understanding; in all your ways acknowledge him, and he will make your paths straight.

PROVERBS 3:5–8

Stress seems to fill my life. It's that physics test I have tomorrow and that massive zit on my forehead that just will not go away. Some days I feel like I'm under this shadow of commitments and responsibilities that I can't fulfill. Then I read this Proverb and wonder what it really means to "trust in the Lord with all [my] heart." Does it mean freaking out when I have a big paper due the next day? Does it mean staying up until 11:30 p.m. working on homework and then waking up at 6:30 a.m. to squeeze in some more? Does it mean taking that stress out on my family and friends? Is that trusting God? No. It means casting all my cares at the foot of the cross. It means that I have to give up those precious controls that I always try and hang on to. I constantly find myself thinking, *If I try a little bit harder, I can get this done!* Notice the key word: "I." Every day I try and rely on myself, my own strength, to get me through, and every time I fail and end up exhausted and frazzled. Over the years, I have come to realize that anxiety has everything to do with trust. Verse 6 tells us that if we place our trust in God, he will make our paths straight. He will be our strength. Try this: Every morning when you wake up, pray and commit your day to God. Give over to Him all your worries and concerns, and trust Him to take care of it all.

Grace Bricker, 16, Jonathan Edwards Academy, Greenfield, MA

Life is so stressful! That's why I'm so thankful I have a mighty God to turn to!

God values all life

He will rescue them from oppression and violence,
for precious is their blood in his sight.

PSALM 72:14

There was a time when I attempted suicide. I will never forget that night. Lots of thoughts ran through my head, and I started to believe the things that were popping up to be true. *I'm not good enough*, *I don't deserve to live*, and *Why am I here if I can never get anything right?* were the confusing messages being released into my mind at that moment. It seemed the more I tried to stop thinking the more thoughts scrambled through my mind to make me think the worst about myself. So that night I attempted to cut my throat. I believe the only things that stopped me were my younger sibling walking in on me and snatching the knife out of my hand and the prayers from the people who cared for me, because that next Sunday at church my youth minister approached me. She asked if everything was all right. When I explained it wasn't, she offered to talk with me. She let me know God had told her to lift my name up in prayer the very same day I wanted to kill myself. God loved me so much that he had someone pray for me that I would have never expected to without me asking. This showed me that He truly cares for all his creation, and He will do what it takes to make sure his creation knows it.

Jazma Parker, 16, Martin Luther King Magnet School, Nashville, TN

It's so amazing how You take care of me
in so many ways. Thank You for all the things
You do for me that I don't even ask for.

January 13

let's dance

When Jesus spoke again to the people, he said,
"I am the light of the world. Whoever follows me will never
walk in darkness, but will have the light of life."

JOHN 8:12

Earlier in the summer I had the opportunity to go contra dancing (which is a little like square dancing) with one of my friends at a nearby college. Once we arrived I was able to see people of all ages dashing through the parking lot, water bottles bouncing, towards an old barnlike structure. Inside, twirling skirts crowded the building, and lively music filled the air with excitement and anticipation. Being a former ballet dancer, it was difficult for me to catch on to dancing with a partner. Fortunately, my friend has been dancing for a while, and he was able to guide me through the succession of complicated steps that the announcer sang out to the crowd. As the summer has progressed, I have come to realize that dancing is a wonderful picture of my relationship with Christ. Jesus is the ultimate lead dancer, and in order to make the dance work, it is imperative for me to follow in his steps. While dancing, it is easy to become disoriented and confused about where to go and what to do. At those times, instead of trying to go the way I think is best, I must trust that my partner will guide me in the right direction. Even when life gets tough and I don't want to go on any further, I know that Jesus has his arms wrapped around me. He's whispering, "C'mon, let's dance..."

Meredith Koontz, 17, North Buncombe High School, Weaverville, NC

Lord, I want to learn lessons about You
from everything I do. I want to see You
in every activity, every day, so I can know You better.

thanks mom and dad...for everything

Hear, ye children, the instruction of a father,
and attend to know understanding.

PROVERBS 4:1 (KJV)

God has blessed me with a wonderful, loving, Christian boyfriend with whom I want to spend forever. The journey of falling in love has been the most beautiful experience of my life...*But I thought this was about our parents?* Well, to be honest, I don't know what I would do without them being a part of my love life. Every step of the way they have been by my side as I've fallen deeper in love. As weird as this sounds, this has made the experience even more wonderful. I can't tell you how special it is to experience love with your family, sharing every precious detail with them! Having my parents to talk to about anything from kissing, to God's will, to watching movies has been more help than I could have imagined. Not only that, but by staying accountable to my parents, it has been easier to control the physical intimacy of our relationship because we aren't fighting the temptation of sex alone. We have a God-given support team to back us up! Our parents have been in love before. They've had breakups. What they have to say about relationships is priceless. I have had times when I was lost and so full of emotions and hormones I couldn't even see straight, but my parents are always there for me. Decisions can be tough, and there is immeasurable value in the advice of our moms and dads. God gave us parents to love and guide us...even when it comes to guys! Don't throw that gift away! Sure, it may be awkward sometimes, but trust me, it's worth it!

Hannah Reed, 16, Jonathan Edwards Academy, Greenfield, MA

Father, it's hard to tell my parents some things.
Help me to open up to them even when I'm scared to.

a special man

Do to others as you would have them do to you.

Luke 6:31

My aunt is a home attendant who cares for senior citizens and mentally handicapped patients. For the past three years she has been caring for Freddy, a twenty-four-year-old man with the mental capacity of a seven-year-old. His case came with many challenges and a lot of extra work. This special man had not been taught to depend on himself for anything. With the help of my aunt he learned how to brush his teeth, eat, and speak without spitting all over the place. Of course, I don't dislike the mentally handicapped…but I don't reach out to them either. One day my aunt brought Freddy to church with her. Nobody said anything as they watched him drool, though there was whispering. I didn't even greet my aunt that morning. Church was full that day and the only available seat was next to this…very different man. I sat, resigned to endure the worst church service ever. During the service there is a chance to greet your neighbor. In my mind I had already decided that I would skip this part and run to the bathroom. The time came for greetings, and I could not get past the couple sitting beside me. I turned around and there he was, smiling at me. As I reached to shake his hand Freddy embraced me with a big bear hug. I was stunned. I sat down and listened to the pastor's message from Luke 6. I'm still a little hesitant when I see Freddy, but I always put myself in his shoes. I would certainly want to be loved no matter what my impediments.

Judelkiss Demostene, 17, Houghton Christian Academy, Houghton, NY

I don't want to be afraid of people who are different or judge them. I want to see You in them and love them.

January 16

faith

Without faith it is impossible to please God.

HEBREWS 11:6

Last night I was mad at God. Actually, I guess I've been unhappy with Him for a while. It feels like He has given me desires and talents, and then said, "No. That's not what I want you to do." God is not making much sense in my life right now. I am a freshman at a small Christian college that I did not plan to attend. I don't know what I am going to major in, and the only major that I am really interested in is not available at my school. I am here because I know that it is where God wants me—but I don't see why. I've battled with jealousy as I see people I know going to their dream school to study things that they are passionate about. I've told God that I would do whatever He wanted me to do if He would show me what it was. Either He hasn't shown me yet or I've completely missed something, so sometimes panic sets in. I think, *God, what are You doing? I'm so confused. Nothing makes sense!* In His incredible patience He lets me rant and rave. God never promises to make sense. Hebrews says that God "rewards those who earnestly seek him" (11:6). Noah spent years building an ark to prepare for a storm that was unbelievable, all because of his faith in God. For the same reason, Abraham left everything he knew to go...well, he didn't know where! This "great cloud of witnesses" (Hebrews 12:1) encourages me to keep going, earnestly seeking God, even if He doesn't make sense and I don't know where I am going.

Maryanna Jensen, 19, North Greenville College, Asheville, NC

Dear Jesus, sometimes I do get mad at You because I don't understand what's going on. Help me to see Your plan, and not get too impatient with You.

January 17

God, how do you stand us?

Then Peter came to Jesus and asked, "Lord, how many times shall I forgive my brother when he sins against me? Up to seven times?" Jesus answered, "I tell you, not seven times, but seventy-seven times."

MATTHEW 18:21–22

Lord, why do I have such a hard time being nice to my brother? I am always mean and bossy and grouchy. He just gets on my last nerve and I can't seem to control myself. It's like he can do whatever he wants and then afterwards just apologize and everything is okay. I don't know how to hold my tongue around him. I want to show him how much I love him, but it's so hard. Although, I guess that's kind of how we are with You. We hurt You and are mean to You, we curse You and ignore You, we tell lies about You and could care less about what it does to You, and then after all of it, we just apologize. Then we go and do something else and just come back and apologize to you afterwards, thinking that everything's okay. Well, we're lucky enough to have a God who does forgive us every time and who lovingly takes us back even when we don't deserve it (like how I think my brother doesn't deserve my forgiveness). Please help me to forgive him and love him the way that You forgive and love us. I really want to please You, and I really want You to be glorified in me.

Holly Scott, 18, North Buncombe High School, Weaverville, NC

Lord, help me to show others the grace and forgiveness that You give to me every day.

responsibility

We are therefore Christ's ambassadors,
as though God were making his appeal through us.
2 CORINTHIANS 5:20

We Christians have a great responsibility. There are many people in the world around us that are living in darkness. Jesus Christ has sent us into the world to be the lights to the dark souls. I pray that we may all realize that people watch how we act and we leave an impression on them, whether good or bad. My brother, Daniel, joined a military-like service organization last year. They are known by all who have met them as being very well-mannered and polite Christian young men. Daniel said that when he puts on the uniform he immediately becomes attentive to anyone who might need help, he does not act foolishly, and he is very careful to say "Yes, sir," "Yes, ma'am"...all the things to keep this high reputation that the program has. He pointed out to me that in the same way he is concerned about his actions when he is wearing the uniform, so we should be concerned about our actions as Christians. We are wearing Christ's "uniform." What are we going to do with His reputation? People are watching us. Shine your light and keep His reputation high!

Nina Lewis, 18, home school with tutorial, Clemson, SC

It's a little overwhelming to think I represent You, Lord.
You are perfect! I know I can't be perfect, but help me to do
the best I can to let Your light shine through me.

January 19

a way of escape (part 1)

When you are tempted, [God] will also provide a way out so that you can stand up under it.

1 CORINTHIANS 10:13

It was my first time in a public school, and I had no idea what to expect. I was shocked at how big it was, but I thought, *Great! Here's an opportunity to meet more people!* I felt welcomed and even had a group to hang out with at recess and lunch. This group of popular kids had expectations of each other to be cool and/or rebellious. I began to feel they wanted me to be like them, to act like them, talk like them, and do what they did. Some of them would go behind maintenance sheds at break and come back stoned, while others would come back from lunch tipsy. I started losing respect for them, and I found it hard to share with them *why* I didn't get into that kind of stuff…it was such natural behavior for them. I was up against a wall as the only Christian there. In my loneliness, I fell into the trap of underestimating God's power in the situation. But He would soon show me that I should never doubt Him.

Alexandra Truehl, 15, Adelaide, Australia

God, I forget how powerful You are too easily. I don't want to doubt You.

a way of escape (part 2)

When you are tempted, [God] will also provide a way out so that you can stand up under it.

1 CORINTHIANS 10:13

My heart broke for my former friends because they had no idea what it was like to know God, and I would cry over them almost every day. I asked God to bring me a Christian friend, and that's when Hailey came along. I realized I wasn't the only one feeling like I was alone in following Christ. We would share our thoughts and feelings and pray about the situation. Hailey helped me stop underestimating God and start asking Him more and more for help and guidance. I saw how much people were broken and how much they needed Him. I cried out to God daily to comfort and strengthen my heart. I asked God to break my heart for the lost and needy, and from that I have grown much stronger.

Alexandra Truehl, 15, Adelaide, Australia

I want to help those who are lost, not be led astray by them. Give me the strength and wisdom to do that, Father.

January 21

an unexpected blessing

We know that in all things God works
for the good of those who love him.

ROMANS 8:28

One night my house caught fire as I slept, and the smoke detector screeched. Our kitchen was burning. My mom woke me up. I was scared, so I ran to the kitchen and then went to my handicapped sister's room. I tried repeatedly to get her to come with me before the house was consumed, but she refused. I ran outside to the neighbors' house and pounded on the door. I told them to call 911 and that my mom and sister were stuck in the fire. They were trapped in my mom's room. Then I ran to my aunt's house and after I told her, she took me back to my house. There were firefighters, fire trucks, and ambulances. My mom was not as burned as my sister, who had been hypnotized by the fire. Once they rescued my mom, they took us by ambulance to the hospital. I was praying throughout this time. At 10 a.m. my sister was taken to a burn unit in another town, and she stayed there for eight days. She couldn't open her eyes or talk. Before that, we were not in contact with my dad. My relatives on his side came in and helped us with food, money, and clothes. The fire united my family. It was something I was praying for. Even though it was difficult, God put us through it for His glory and our good, and not for any bad. It is weird how the Lord answers our prayers, but it is awesome!

Amanda Liegl, 17, Nebraska Christian High School, Columbus, NE

A tragedy can be a blessing?! God, it amazes me how
You can take our imperfect world and make it
into something that glorifies You!

get to work!

Never be lacking in zeal, but keep
your spiritual fervor, serving the Lord.

ROMANS 12:11

Susan! I thought I told you to take out the trash an hour ago! Get up here and do it now!" Does this sound familiar? Unfortunately, this conversation is probably all too familiar. We often wait until the last minute to do what our parents tell us to do, then come up with great excuses for why we hadn't gotten around to it yet. Treating our parents this way is bad enough, but do we actually treat God this way as well? Do we wait until the last minute to do what God asks of us? God is our friend and a father, but He is also the creator of the world, and He deserves far more respect and honor than we give Him. When He says jump, we should be ready to fly. God doesn't need wishy-washy Sunday Christians who put off His work until the last minute. He needs true servants who are willing and ready to serve Him at a moment's notice. In fact, our whole lives should glorify our Lord. We should live as though someone were always watching, because guess what? He *is*!

Amy McKoy, 18, Bryan College, Dayton, TN

God, I want to be doing Your will all the time.
I want You in my life every single day.

January 23

for all eternity

In my Father's house are many rooms;
if it were not so, I would have told you. I am going
there to prepare a place for you. And if I go and prepare
a place for you, I will come back and take you to be
with me that you also may be where I am.

JOHN 14:2–3

Recently my family and I drove across town to meet my cousin and her parents at her new apartment. She is going to be a senior in college, and I know she is looking forward to having her own place rather than living in another dorm. We all busied ourselves with various tasks like arranging furniture or unpacking silverware. Before too long, I found myself in the kitchen removing labels from her dishes while marveling at all of the work they had put into preparing the items for her apartment. Cute pillows made by my aunt adorned her couch and chairs, and her lampshades followed the shabby chic trend by sporting the same material. Everything fit perfectly together to create a unique home for my cousin. Amid the cups and cabinets, I considered the fact that just as we were preparing a place for her to live, Jesus is preparing a home for us in heaven with even more tenderness and care. The great news is that Jesus loves us and He wants to be with us. In fact, His love for us is so great that He died in order to create a way for us to live with Him for all eternity. "Come to me," Jesus says. "Forever is waiting!"

Meredith Koontz, 17, North Buncombe High School, Weaverville, NC

I can't wait to come and live with You, Lord.
I am so looking forward to being in heaven with You.

mr. perfect

Marriage should be honored by all,
and the marriage bed kept pure.

HEBREWS 13:4

Of course I like boys—I'm a teenager. When I turned thirteen, my parents had a ceremony for me. They invited my close relatives over, and they presented me with a beautiful necklace. On it was a round circle that split in half and had a scripture imprinted on it. It is called a Mizpah coin. They gave one half to me and one half to my mom, who will give her part of the necklace to my husband when I get married, signifying that I saved myself for him. My parents gave that to me, and I promised them I would not sleep with anyone before my wedding night. I want my first kiss to be with the man I know I will marry. Some of my friends think I'm crazy, and some try to tell me that I should just try dating, but they know that I'm better off in the long run. I don't have any parts of my heart that belong to someone else. My heart has never been broken. The best part is they respect my commitment. How awesome will it be to say to my one and only boyfriend, "I saved myself for you. I have wasted nothing. My heart is unbroken; you can have all of it." Even though I've made this commitment, I'm still normal. Sometimes I wonder what it's like to have a boyfriend to love and hold me when I'm sad, what it would be like to kiss him. But I can get to know my Father in heaven and learn how to love Him first. When I meet Mr. Perfect, I will know how to love him like Jesus does.

Katie-Lee Kroeker, 16, home school, Medicine Hat, Alberta, CA

God, I am so impatient. Help me to
understand that Your timing is better than mine.

January 25

are you sure about this, God?

Therefore go and make disciples of all nations, baptizing them in the name of the Father and of the Son and of the Holy Spirit.

MATTHEW 28:19

One of the many things that I struggle with is sharing my faith and standing up for my beliefs. I go to a public school, so everyone there is very open about what they believe, and their beliefs are sometimes very different from mine. This summer I went to a two-week "camp" that teaches about all the different worldviews. My roommate for this camp had a lot of different beliefs than I did. We talked about anything and everything. So this gave me an opportunity to practice stating my beliefs and the reasons to back them up. I think witnessing is one area that a lot of people struggle with. I would always say, "Well, as soon as I know how" or, "Once I learn more of what to say and how to get it across." I will tell you from experience that you will never be perfect at witnessing and that each time you witness it is different. But the only way that you are going to be able to share your faith and beliefs at all is if you just start one day. As much as I wish there was a class on all the possible scenarios and things that could happen, there really isn't, and you just have to get out there and do it. This is one of the many things that God is still working with me on, and I know that He will forever be working to improve me in this area.

Holly Scott, 18, North Buncombe High School, Weaverville, NC

Telling other people about You is so important… and so hard. Please give me the words to say to them when I'm too scared to speak.

Jesus is our light on dark nights

The LORD is a jealous and avenging God; the LORD takes vengeance and is filled with wrath. The LORD takes vengeance on his foes and maintains his wrath against his enemies. The LORD is slow to anger and great in power; the LORD will not leave the guilty unpunished.

NAHUM 1:2–3

I used to fall asleep watching television. I would fall asleep like this every time my mom worked the graveyard shift, and I would wake up the next morning when she got home. However, on a night in March 2003, someone else woke me up in the middle of the night. As I slept, a guy came into the room and assaulted me. I woke up and started kicking him until he left. Later that night I was subjected to an assault kit at the hospital from 2 until 8 a.m. I got sick after that. I thought, *Why did this happen to me?* But then when I moved, the church I went to was the same one I had gone to when I was little, and the pastor's wife helped me out. She pointed out Nahum 1:2–3 and the verses helped me out A LOT!! I was able to forgive the guy that did that to me and move on. It also helped me become stronger in Christ, just like it can for you. I know it happened for a reason that I did NOT understand at the time. We don't always understand things, but what happened to me makes me feel stronger because I can help others who have been through what I went through. That brings a smile to my heart!

Amanda Liegl, 17, Nebraska Christian High School, Columbus, NE

People do such horrible things to each other sometimes. There are so many bad situations, so please, God, help me to make the best of them.

justify it!

A person is justified by what he does
and not by faith alone.
JAMES 2:24

As a 5'1" volleyball player, I have found that most people do not look at me and think, *She must be a spiker*. Even my friends need convincing that I can get my hands above the net. During a game last year, a set came to me, and I simply reacted, sending the ball over the net and into the floor. When the point was recorded, shouts of joy mingled with much surprised laughter as the team's "Chihuahua" finally justified herself. *Justify*, according to Webster's, means 1) to prove or show to be just, right, or reasonable; 2) to qualify (oneself) as a surety by taking oath to the ownership of sufficient property. The reminder "saved through faith in Jesus," is in every salvation message. After this good news, what often gets tuned out is what James addresses in chapter two. He states the importance of our deeds after we claim faith, clarifying that without actions to back it up, a confession of faith is useless. He is not saying works redeem, but that they justify. They are the tangible testimony of Jesus' work in our hearts, just as my successful spike was the evidence of many hours of hard work. St. Francis of Assisi challenged, "Preach the Gospel at all times and when necessary, use words." Just as believing I could spike never convinced anyone else, simply stating you are a Christian does not usually affect others. High school is one of the most difficult places to live out your faith, and we all make mistakes. But you must always try to live what you believe so that you will leave no doubt about your true faith.

Molly Jo Spateholts, 17, Houghton Christian Academy, Houghton, NY

I don't want to just talk about faith.
I want to live it so everyone I know will see it.

the least of these

"The King will reply, 'I tell you the truth,
whatever you did for one of the least of these
brothers of mine, you did for me.'"

MATTHEW 25:40

Last spring I went on a weekend trip to Boston with my Mom. We stayed at a fancy hotel, went to the Boston Opera House, and ate at Quincy Market. As we walked through the city, I was amazed at how many poor, homeless people there were. Disheveled men and women wearing old, torn clothes hovered around street corners, begging for even a few coins. My heart broke for them, and I realized that I had been selfish and ungrateful for what God had always provided. On the way back to our hotel, one particular man caught my attention. He was an older man sitting all alone on a bench, the picture of hopelessness. I knew God wanted me to do something for him. I felt it would not be enough to throw a few pennies at him as I strolled by without even glancing in his direction. I walked straight towards him, smiling, and gave him some money. I asked him if he was hungry, and his eyes lit up when I gave him a granola bar from my purse. I smiled again, looking into his eyes—the eyes of one of God's precious children—and I wished him a good day, truly meaning it. The entire weekend was memorable, but that might have been the most rewarding moment of the trip. I walked away knowing that I had listened to God's voice directing me.

Julia Postema, 16, Jonathan Edwards Academy, Erving, MA

Lord, You have given me so much.
Help me to give to others.

January 29

mystery

"The wind blows wherever it pleases. You hear its sound, but you cannot tell where it comes from or where it is going. So it is with everyone born of the Spirit."

JOHN 3:8

Sometimes I have no idea where I'm going. When I first learned to drive, I would get lost so easily. My mom would never let me go anywhere without an explanation as to how I would get there. One time my drama teacher invited us over to her house for cider and a movie. She tried to explain how to get there, but I thought I was following somebody, so I didn't really pay any attention. Somehow, however, I lost the girl that I was supposed to follow. It was dark and I literally drove around for an hour trying to find the drama teacher's house. I'm kind of stubborn, and I really wanted to find her house. I finally arrived and called my house so that they could stop worrying. It was such a HUGE relief to be sitting in that living room drinking hot cider and watching *Elf*. I feel that way in my Christian life sometimes too. I want to do God's will, but I have no idea what he specifically wants me to do. Like the wind, I know that God is working, but I'm not sure how I fit in. I now try to always have a map with me when I drive. And I try to use the Bible in my life like I use my map on the road. Following Him is the most important decision we will ever make. So make sure you read His roadmap for life before you go driving off on your own.

Calista Turner, 17, Donelson Christian Academy, Nashville, TN

Jesus, show me the way when I'm just wandering around. I'm lost and confused a lot, so I really need You.

no other God

You were shown these things so that you might know that the LORD is God; besides him there is no other.

DEUTERONOMY 4:35

Not very long ago my life was unraveling. You see, Brady, my boyfriend of three years, decided to go teach English in China for five months. When he told me, I was angry and afraid. For a long time I simply wondered how God could move the most important thing in my life so far away. I tried to look at it positively and be supportive of Brady's decision, but inside I didn't know how I would get through five months without him. It hurt so much to say good-bye. The first two days he was gone it was all I could do just to get through the school day without him there. I tried to write about what God was teaching me through Brady being away, but I couldn't get to the real issue. I didn't know why my heart was broken, and I didn't know how to fix it. My English teacher read what I had written and noticed how fragmented it was. God gave her a special insight, and she shared it with me. She encouraged me to place God at the center of my life and recognize that Brady could never fill the hole in my heart that God was supposed to fill. I cried as God showed me places where I had let my boyfriend become too important in my life. I had to ask God's forgiveness and for Him to teach me how to love Him first. It is a hard lesson to learn, but there is a peace in my heart when I really let God be my God.

Carmen Dockweiler, 18, Nebraska Christian High School, Central City, NE

Guys can really distract me from You, Father.
It's so easy to think that having a boyfriend is really important.
But I want to believe having You is more important.

January 31

i want to be more

Listen, my child, to what your father teaches you. Don't neglect your mother's teaching. What you learn from them will crown you with grace and clothe you with honor.

My child, if sinners entice you, turn your back on them! They may say, "Come and join us. Let's hide and kill someone! Let's ambush the innocent! Let's swallow them alive as the grave swallows its victims. Though they are in the prime of life, they will go down into the pit of death. And the loot we'll get! We'll fill our houses with all kinds of things! Come on, throw in your lot with us; we'll split our loot with you."

Don't go along with them, my child! Stay far away from their paths. They rush to commit crimes. They hurry to commit murder. When a bird sees a trap being set, it stays away. But not these people! They set an ambush for themselves; they booby-trap their own lives!
Such is the fate of all who are greedy for gain.
It ends up robbing them of life.

PROVERBS 1:8–19 (NLT)

my big brother

May he be enthroned in God's presence forever;
appoint your love and faithfulness to protect him.

PSALM 61:7

I am seventeen years old, and I have a brother who is nineteen. We are very close, even though we get in fights occasionally. (Hey, what are brothers and sisters for?) Last year my brother decided to join the Marines. It didn't shock me because he had always been fascinated by the military, but it still made me sad that he was going to leave. On May 15, 2005, we waved good-bye as he headed to Paris Island, S.C., for boot camp. For the next four months, life was a little boring without my brother. We heard about the grueling training he was going through in his weekly letters. He wrote to us how he could tell the difference between him and the others who didn't have someone praying for them. It was good to know that we made a difference in his life even when he was far away. Finally, in August, we drove to Paris Island to watch him graduate as a United States Marine. It was like Christmas, and the best part is that he got to come home with us. He hasn't changed much; he's still my same old brother. I think the differences are that I enjoy and respect him more, and I don't take for granted the time I get to spend with him. He recently informed us that he is switching from the Marine Reserves to active duty, which means he could be sent over to Iraq. It scares me, but I know the Lord loves my brother more than I do, so I will trust Him. Don't forget that big brothers (or any siblings for that matter) are precious.

Claire Englehart, 17, Cedar Hall School, Bell Buckle, TN

I want to thank You for my family, Lord.
They are one of the greatest blessings You have given me.

what is faith?

Now faith is being sure of what we hope for and certain of what we do not see.

HEBREWS 11:1

Before I was saved, I never knew what faith exactly was. No one ever really took the time to explain it to me. I think if you want someone to have faith about something, you should first tell them what faith is. Then explain what they need to have faith in. If you're witnessing and don't clarify what faith is, you're missing most of the testimony. It's kind of like giving someone the ingredients to make bread, but not the recipe. What do they do with it then? Sit and look at it? Anyway, as I started wanting to follow God more and more, I wanted to find out exactly what faith was. I asked friends and family, and they didn't know. Then I looked it up in the dictionary—the definitions were not very clear. I finally realized that I was looking in all the wrong places. If God wanted me to know Him, then He would help me see. So I looked though my Bible and came to Hebrews 11:1. God is so good—He does listen to us teens. He cares about us as much as He does adults. If we have faith that God listens to us, then we cannot lose because "faith is being sure of what we hope for and certain of what we do not see."

Anna White, 15, Walnut Grove Christian Preparatory School, Zionsville, IN

I want my faith in You to be so strong, Lord Jesus.
Sometimes it's hard to believe in what I can't see,
but I know You'll help me.

my "friend complex"

For anyone who does not love his brother, whom he has seen, cannot love God, whom he has not seen. And he has given us this command: Whoever loves God must also love his brother.

1 JOHN 4:20–21

I guess you could say that I have a friend complex. It probably came from hearing "Katie, you are my best friend" one day and being completely ignored the next just a few too many times. One time I got so frustrated, and I asked God why this always happened to me. He didn't directly answer me, but my questioning got me thinking about my "friends." They all went to church on Sunday, and would then do everything in their power to keep anyone at school from finding out how they spent their Sunday mornings. I began to realize that these friends were using people, not loving them, and gossiping about people, not encouraging them. Maybe you know what I am talking about. Maybe you've experienced a similar situation with people you call "friends. Or maybe you are on the other side, one of the ones using and gossiping, instead of being a good friend. Think about it. We all want true friends. I have found some friends who live out the meaning of friendship. They are passionately in love with Jesus and this love overflows to people all around them. They challenge me to be different for Christ. Are you willing to make some changes, to be challenged? Maybe for you that means learning to love like a true friend and apologizing for the ways you have failed. Or perhaps it is finding some different friends who want the love of Jesus to be obvious in their lives. Either way, let's be the kinds of friends that we want to have.

Katie-Lee Kroeker, 16, home school, Medicine Hat, Alberta, CA

God, please give me friends who love me, and help me to love them back.

"i'm fine"

Listen, my son, to your father's instruction,
and do not forsake your mother's teaching.

PROVERBS 1:8

I get mad at my mom a lot, even though I know that I shouldn't. Everyone knows how the drill goes. School just got out, there's a million things on your mind, and you really don't want to talk to your parents about it. So you tell them that your day was "fine," and you rarely expand beyond that single-word definition. At least that's what happens with me most of the time. I know it's not her fault that I get so annoyed by her. Usually she doesn't really do anything wrong, but I happen to be in a bad mood and take it out on her. And that's not really fair at all. Lately I have been trying to give my parents a chance, to talk to them, and even to listen to them. They're wiser than they let on! As I have begun to be more patient and to let my mom into my life, she has really helped me out in several tough situations with friends. Sometimes when my mom starts a story off with, "Well, I remember when I was your age..." I still want to loudly declare, "Well, it is different now!" But *some* of her stories *have* taught me to love and respect her even more. I am beginning to wish that I hadn't wasted so many years and conversations with my blunt, conversation stopper: "I'm fine." I can't change that, but I can change how I talk with my parents from here on out.

Kerstin Jones, 17, Stillwater Christian School, Kalispell, MT

Sometimes my parents really bug me. A lot.
But they love me, so please help
me to be more patient with them, Father.

am i good enough?

For you created my inmost being;
you knit me together in my mother's womb. I praise you
because I am fearfully and wonderfully made;
your works are wonderful, I know that full well.

PSALM 139:13–14

In the back of my mind lives this fear: What if I am not good enough? I know that when I look in the mirror, I usually don't love what I see. My grades are average, and my athletics are way less than average. My idea of style is a T-shirt and jeans. I am just not someone you would walk by and say, "Wow! She is special." I have struggled with this for a long time, always hating my imperfections and wondering what people were thinking of me. I found ways to lessen the fear, like skipping meals, wearing extra makeup and highlighting my hair, but it never went away. The more I tried, the more inferior I felt. I thought it would always be like that, but then one day I found myself discussing my feelings of inferiority with a group of my good friends. One of the guys looked at me and said, "I don't want you to struggle with that. God doesn't make mistakes." I was amazed by how freeing those words were. I may not command human attention, but God thinks I'm worth His time. How cool is that? I don't have to spend hours trying to look a certain way. I don't have to wonder if I'm good enough and worry over all my imperfections. I just have to do my best, knowing that God made me the way I am for a reason.

Carmen Dockweiler, 18, Nebraska Christian High School, Central City, NE

Is it true You made me, God?
Made me just the way I am? I'm just not sure I believe it.
Help me to believe today, and feel it in my heart.

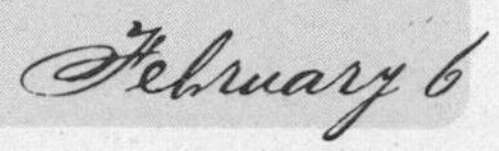

the truth about suicide

Be self-controlled and alert. Your enemy the devil prowls around like a roaring lion looking for someone to devour. Resist him, standing firm in the faith.

1 PETER 5:8–9

To me my life was horrible. My parents divorced when I was three. My dad moved to Oklahoma when I was five. I have two half sisters that hate me. I was always over weight, and therefore I was picked on. My father emotionally abused me, saying I was ugly. I remember being ten years old and wanting to die. I mean, can you imagine being ten and wanting to kill yourself? I was the perfect candidate for the devil. I hated myself. The devil knew that and used it to his advantage. When I was in seventh grade, things got bad. Instead of just *wanting* to die, I started thinking about ways to actually kill myself. One day I almost swallowed some pills, but I stopped. Something told me not to do it. I ran downstairs and told my mom I needed help. I was admitted to the hospital. When I got out, my family and I started going to church. The youth group there was great. I told them my problem and they said that the Lord was watching over me. That night I realized that I needed God to help save me from the devil. I asked Him to come into my heart and change me. Now instead of thinking about dying, I think about *living* for Christ.

Courtney Pinto, 15, Walnut Grove Christian Preparatory School, Fishers, IN

Sometimes things can get so hard I just want to give up. Lord, help me to keep going.

a great leader

Whoever wants to become great among you must be your servant, and whoever wants to be first must be slave of all. For even the Son of Man did not come to be served, but to serve, and to give his life as a ransom for many.

MARK 10:43–45

Have you ever been in a group where one person automatically rises to the top as the leader? I am not someone that automatically does that, even though I do enjoy leadership and the responsibility of it. What I've learned is that leadership isn't always about taking charge and telling people what to do. The best leaders I have seen, and the kind I want to be, are the ones who are servants to those around them. Service is a requirement of leadership. Being a leader is not only about control, but also about listening, helping, encouraging, and, of course, serving others. A good leader is willing to step back and give someone else the reins and the control. But you cannot become a great leader without first looking to Jesus. The best leader is one who follows the greatest leader of all, Jesus Christ.

Holly Scott, 18, North Buncombe High School, Weaverville, NC

I want to learn to lead by serving, but it's not easy, Lord. Today, please show me ways I can do this so that I can be more like You. Amen.

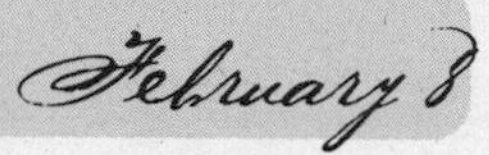

bruises on the inside (part 1)

I can do everything through him
who gives me strength.
PHILIPPIANS 4:13

From the time I was conceived, no one ever wanted me. My mom, who was a drug addict, tried to have a miscarriage while she was pregnant with me. After I was born, she didn't feed me, so I was placed in the hospital for not growing properly. She would leave me with people I didn't know for days at a time. After my brother was born, our mom continued to do drugs and leave both of us at home alone. I had to be my brother's mom, even though I was just a baby myself. Our neighbors would call the department of social services, and when the workers arrived, I would lie for my mom. I would say she didn't use drugs and that she didn't leave us alone. Then they would check us for bruises on our bodies—but they couldn't see the bruises on the inside. What I didn't know then was that God *could* see them and His plan to heal them was already in motion. He was with me and my brother giving us strength to make it through.

Kristin Abernathy, 16, New Covenant Christian School, Pageland, SC

Life can be so painful, God. Give me
strength to make it through whatever I face,
because I know I can't do it without You. Amen.

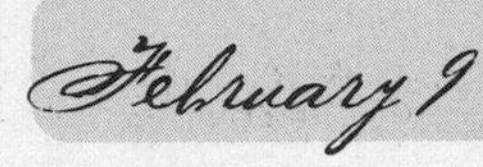

bruises on the inside
(part 2)

God has said, "Never will I leave you;
never will I forsake you."

HEBREWS 13:5

While my brother and I lived with my drug-addicted mother, life was really difficult. School was especially hard because I never cared about my work. I only cared that my brother was at home, alone. I was glad when he started school because then I knew he was safe during the day. Sometimes my mom wouldn't pay our bills, and we had no water to take baths. She used the little money she did have to buy drugs instead of food for us. My aunt came to get us, but my dad would not give up custody, so she took us to the department of social services. We were placed in a foster home. I hated my aunt for a long time after that because I couldn't see how what she had done was really best for us. I told my case worker that if she didn't move me, I would kill myself or run away. But I would soon learn that there was a much better way of escape...it was Jesus alone who rescued my brother and me.

Kristin Abernathy, 16, New Covenant Christian School, Pageland, SC

Sometimes I can't see Your plan, Lord, and I can't
understand why things are happening to me.
Help me to see things the way You do. Amen.

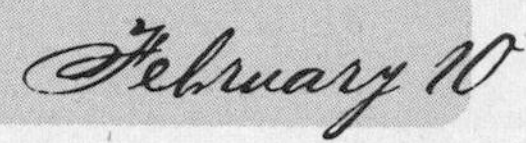

healed bruises (part 3)

So we say with confidence, "The Lord is my helper;
I will not be afraid. What can man do to me?"

HEBREWS 13:6

Eventually, my brother and I were taken to live with Mrs. Abernathy, my second-grade music teacher. I was disobedient and violent, but she loved me anyway. No one had loved me before. Mrs. Abernathy adopted us. She takes us to church and loves us. I know God kept me strong though it all. I thank God every day for changing my life and for giving my brother and me a home, a real home. I see now that God's plan was at work in my brother's life, and in mine, the whole time. God meant it all for good. God gave us a loving Christian home to live in where we are not lonely, we are loved, and we are taught about the love of God. God cared so much for us that He did not forsake us. He will not forsake you, either, no matter what the circumstances that you live in might be. He is there with you and for you, and He sees the pain on the inside when no one else can.

Kristin Abernathy, 16, New Covenant Christian School, Pageland, SC

Thanks for the people in my life
who love me no matter what.
They are amazing blessings to me, dear God.

grounded at eighteen?

Children, obey your parents in everything,
for this pleases the Lord.

COLOSSIANS 3:20

When I was a junior in high school, my family moved to Tennessee. This meant that my boyfriend and I had to have a long distance relationship. It was tough because my parents put a thirty minute per day limit on our phone calls, and my boyfriend lives about eight hours away, so I didn't see him very often. My parents really wanted me to break off the relationship completely because we were both being consumed by it. For a while, we continued to talk on the phone, but pretty soon it just got too hard to constantly be pushing the limits my parents had set. We stopped talking to each other for a while, and it surprisingly turned out to be a good thing! We both learned more about who we are, individually, as people and in Christ. Eventually, with my parent's permission, my boyfriend and I started talking again. We began e-mailing encouraging verses to each other and talked about how God had been working in our lives. We knew that making our relationship work was going to be hard, but we believed God had put us together for a reason. We began to put Christ first in our relationship and our relationship changed a bunch. This past summer we served as counselors together at a Christian camp, which was an amazing chance to work and serve together. Now that our parents support our relationship, it feels less like I am grounded in my own house and more like my parents are an incredible and wise part of my life.

Janelle Mitchell, 18, Siegel High School, Murfreesboro, TN

The older I get, Lord, the harder it is to listen
to my parents. Help me remember that they
know a lot and they want to help me.

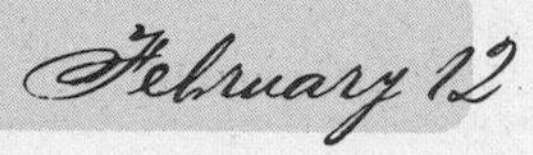

newer me

I can do everything through him who gives me strength.

PHILIPPIANS 4:13

When I arrived in the United States, I was filled with panic, fear, and confusion. People looked very strange and somewhat intimidating since they all appeared so different from what I had known in Korea, and they spoke a language that I could not understand. I felt like the people at the airport were staring at me like a monkey in a zoo. There was no one to protect me in this strange environment. I was alone. My parents were back in Korea, praying for me to have a safe trip to my new school. Loneliness overwhelmed me. Even after I started the new school year, I still felt scared. When nice American girls asked, "What is your name?" I looked away and pretended that I did not hear them, because I could not understand them. On my first day of science class, the teacher assigned homework, which was due next class. I did not understand what "due" meant and didn't comprehend the homework. I went to the next class with an empty binder and received an academic warning. I definitely needed someone to help my situation and comfort me. My mom shared a verse over the phone to encourage me. Because I was in such a foreign situation, the verse touched me more than ever. "I can do all things through Christ who strengthens me." As soon as I heard the verse, I realized that God had always been there for me, and I started to develop confidence. I still get nervous when talking with Americans, and I still struggle with my English. I still get homesick and cry, but I am not scared anymore. God is always with me.

Stephanie Ki-Yeon Yoon, 18, Houghton Christian Academy, Houghton, NY

Life can bring some really big,
really frightening changes. When it does,
I want to trust You to get me through, Father.

a tough choice

I also want women to dress modestly, with decency and propriety, not with braided hair or gold or pearls or expensive clothes.

1 TIMOTHY 2:9

I remember one day in particular when my friends and I went on a huge shopping spree. It seemed like all of our favorite stores were having sales, and the sales racks were actually full of cute clothes. We piled into the dressing room with our arms to start trying everything on. I squeezed into a shirt that was the hottest style at the moment. My friends *oohed* and *aahed*, saying how grown up it made me look. I asked if they thought it was too tight, and they said no. But when I bent over, we all realized it showed way too much skin. Later, we started talking about how hard it is to find clothes that we like that are also modest. Someone mentioned that her mom always said to imagine that she had a stamp on her forehead saying "Image bearer for Christ," and if she wouldn't be comfortable in the outfit with that on her forehead, then she probably shouldn't buy it. My friend had always thought it was a silly way to think about it, but it sort of made sense now. One of my friends announced that she was going to take back a skirt that she had just bought because it was too short for her. I don't think it is easy to make choices like that, to say no to something we really like, but when my friend did that, I was so proud of her. And it challenged me to strive to be a pure example of Christ in what I wear and what I do.

Danae Downs, 15, home school, Grand Junction, CO

It's hard to give up things I really like, even if I know I should. God, give me strength to make the right choices.

obsession

See, I have engraved you on the palms of my hands.

ISAIAH 49:16

Desire for a dating relationship consumed me because I never thought I was important unless I had that charming guy standing beside me. My desires for intimacy, affection, and love seemed to have no substitute that I was willing to accept. I finally realized there was no "substitute," but instead a God that fulfilled my heart's desire like no other. My Savior provides intimacy because He knows my heart. Intimacy with God comes from searching His heart and finding the unending knowledge He has for His child. Intimacy was only half of the struggle. I longed for affection, and I found that My God supplied it. In any situation I can call on His name and His arms are opened wide to receive me. Although I cannot feel His arms, they never let go. The day I accepted Him as my personal Lord and Savior, His arms embraced my heart. My God showed the greatest love of all by sending His only Son to die on a cross so that I might obtain a relationship with Him. As goofy teenagers, we often write the name of the one we love on everything, but in Isaiah 49:16, we find that Jesus has our names written on His nail-pierced hand. Jesus is more than anything we could ever want, and He desires a relationship with us. I pray that you may find a relationship with the one Ephesians 3:17–19 speaks of "so that Christ may dwell in your hearts through faith; that you, being rooted and grounded in love, may…know this love that surpasses knowledge, which passes knowledge—that you may be filled to the measure of all the fullness of God."

Joni Timmons, 16, New Covenant Christian School, Pageland, SC

I want to be loved, Lord. I want it so much. But I have such a hard time remembering that Your love is all I need. Please make Your love enough for me.

voices

You were bought at a price;
do not become slaves of men.

1 Corinthians 7:23

As teenagers, we search the most and find the least, but perhaps the measure of what we find lies in where we look. It is difficult to capture anything in this world of darkness, simply because we cannot get direction in our lives unless we can see. The world is blind and lost. Instead of guidance into a pathway of light, we are misdirected by the echoing voices that lead to destruction. These voices aren't always as obvious as those on MTV or in *Teen People* magazine. Some of the influences we are faced with are subliminal. The media plays an enormous role in what we Christian girls are thinking. I have learned the most damaging influence can sometimes come from those you consider good friends. God ordered us to come out from the world and be separate. Sadly, we are becoming more like the world instead of more like Christ, our Savior. God is not the god of this world, so what is esteemed by the world should not change our perspective of what this life is all about. The devil is the master at imitating God. God sends messages, and so does the devil. God influences, and so does the devil. Remember when God told Moses to throw the staff down, it turned into a serpent. Pharaoh's magicians were able to do the same thing through the power of Satan. The devil has some power, but Jesus Christ has all power. God's serpent ate the devil's because imitations are cheap. They don't last. Imitations have a lifespan, but our souls will last for eternity.

Marquita Massey, 17, Redemption Christian Academy, Guilderland, NY

A lot of people tell me who I should be.
But only want to hear what You have to say, Jesus.

February 16

why we should obey our parents

Children, obey your parents in the Lord, for this is right.

EPHESIANS 6:1

When I was younger, I felt there was no need to obey my parents. I argued with my mom. I've jumped out of the car and I've runaway from home all because I wanted to do my own thing. I refused to listen to my parents and rebelled instead. I didn't think of the consequences, such as being kidnapped or getting injured. Today I understand the blessing of having parents who love and care for me. I've come to this knowledge through establishing a close relationship with God. The importance of prayer and having a continual prayer life cannot be taken for granted. There are times when I reflect on my past actions with regret. We all have trials and struggles through life. However, with God involved I know I can make it through. Every day I awake and I thank God that I still have both of my parents. I thank Him because in spite of all my wrongs, they still love me. I want to encourage all young people, if you're doing what I did to my parents, stop. We are held accountable to God for our actions. Through disobedience to our parents, we will reap sorrow and regret. God is the answer to all of our problems. If it had not been for Him saving and keeping me, I don't know where I would be.

Sabrina Monosiet, 15, Redemption Christian Academy, Troy, NY

My parents are an awesome gift because they love me a lot like You love me, God—unconditionally!

the romance you never expected

Where has your lover gone,
most beautiful of women?

SONG OF SOLOMON 6:1

A love life? Sure, we all like to believe we have one, whether or not we really do. I always wanted a guy to write me a love song or letter. How romantic…to hear how you are adored, how beautiful you are, how the sun rises and sets in your eyes, and…well, you get the picture. When I'm reading the Bible, I normally skip over Song of Solomon. Personally, reading a book meant for married people never really did appeal to me. I never understood the whole "leaping gazelle" thing. So when I went to a Bible study and the leader announced we were studying that particular book, I glanced up to see if I was really in the youth devotional group or if I had accidentally found myself in the newly married couple's class. As we started the study, I began to discover what a gift the Song of Solomon is to us hopeless romantics. Christ is madly, head-over-heels obsessed with you—despite all your faults, mood swings, shortcomings, and not-so-great days. He wants to offer it to you, and, unlike a boy, He'll never break your heart. You can trust Him enough to love Him back *completely*. Fall in love over and over again with His beauty and His grace, and rejoice in your eternal bridegroom.

Mary Kaylin Staub, 16, Heritage Academy, Flowery Branch, GA

Lord, I want to believe that I can find all the love
I need in You. Please help me to do that.

set the bar high

Do not conform any longer to the pattern of this world, but be transformed by the renewing of your mind.

Romans 12:2

What are your standards? Are they set in stone, or do they change depending on who you are with? I personally tend to compromise a lot in the area of movies. I will make excuses such as: "Oh well, this movie only has ten swear words" (assuming taking the Lord's name in vain doesn't count). I often wonder, "How many swear words is too many? Where do I draw the line?" I find that after I have watched such a movie, I am very ashamed, and rightfully so. Then I have to come before God, knowing what I did was wrong. Besides movies, what about compromising in the area of relationships? You not only hurt yourself and God, but you end up hurting your parents and friends. I have a friend who compromised in her relationship with her boyfriend, and she ended up pregnant. I know she feels terrible, and I'm sure she is plagued with guilt because in her situation she has a constant reminder of her sin. However, she can be forgiven just like I can when I watch a compromising movie. Both are equally sinful in God's eyes. During a chapel at my school, the principal began speaking about telling the difference between nonbelievers and believers. He stated that our standards need to be higher than the world's. Then he said that he believes when he gets to heaven, he is going to wish his standards were higher. That thought has been festering in my mind. I keep asking myself, "Are my standards high enough or do I look like the world?"

Rebecca Brill, 18, Nebraska Christian High School, Aurora, NE

I want my standards to be Your standards, Jesus.
I want to have high expectations for myself.

hang in there!

Precious in the sight of the LORD
is the death of his saints.

PSALM 116:15

Yeah, I know, it's a pretty short verse, but it's so powerful. At least it is to me, and if you have problems with either depression or suicidal thoughts you'll know exactly what I'm talking about. I know this is all probably going to sound pretty corny, and you've probably heard it all before, but let me just try to say it. You are a precious and wonderful creation and even though it may not seem like it all the time, God loves you. Because there are quite a few people who are suicidal, it kind of gets to be cliché, and people underestimate how serious it is. You might be feeling just like this, like you're nobody important, just one of the billions who are living and who have lived, and nobody cares about whether or not you're suicidal. But you are different; you are a unique individual with your own incredible gift to give to humankind. No one could ever do for others and for God what you can. You were put on this earth for a specific purpose, and do you really want to disappoint God and fail that purpose? And always remember, everything—and I mean EVERYTHING—God does for you is totally for your own good! He loves you so much, and He has an incredible plan. So just hang in there. I promise you it will turn out all right if you keep on living how God wants you to. It might take a day, it might take until you die, but I promise you it will happen.

Stephanie Sherwood, 14, St. Ambrose Christian High School, Boise, ID

I am precious to You? Really?
It is so hard to believe that sometimes.
So please, God, remind me often.

what weirdos!

There is neither Jew nor Greek, slave nor free, male nor female, for you are all one in Christ.

GALATIANS 3:28

My dream of going to the jungle became a reality when my family and I went on a mission trip to Ecuador. One night, the cooks prepared all sorts of native foods for us. I told myself that I would try everything so I could get the full cultural experience. But when one of the missionaries took a monkey head out of a stew and took out the brain for us to eat, it really grossed me out. I thought, "What weirdos! Who would want to take out a monkey's brain and eat it?" It seemed to me a very barbaric and disgusting thing to do. But everybody was given a small piece to try and, not wanting to be rude, I gingerly put it in my mouth, bracing myself for the horrible taste. It was so small I could barely feel it, but I could taste it enough to know it was actually really good. I was so glad I had tried it because I realized that the missionaries were not crazy. They were eating monkey brains because that's what people eat in the jungles of Ecuador. They had been willing to give up a "normal" American life to go serve God in the jungles of Ecuador. I felt bad for judging them so quickly just because they did things differently from me. Because when it comes down to it, weird doesn't mean bad. It just means different.

Allison Engel, 16, Wheaton North High School, Wheaton, IL

I want to see everyone through Your eyes today, Lord, because You see the beauty in our differences.

make a joyful noise

Whatever your hand finds to do, do it with all your might, for in the grave, where you are going, there is neither working nor planning nor knowledge nor wisdom.

ECCLESIASTES 9:10

God gives us talents, and He wants us to use them. My talent is singing, but I used to hide it, and I would only sing in my mom's car or at home. Finally, I decided that I was going to use my talent at a banquet I was attending. I was overjoyed that God gave me the courage to do this. However, afterwards I began to hide my talent again. When another banquet came around, I decided to sing with a friend of mine, but after that I started hiding my talent again. By His grace, God gives us second and third chances to do His will. During the summer, one of the sisters in my church started a choir. When I found out, I was the first to sign my name because I was determined not to be afraid. I felt as though this was my opportunity to give God the glory with the talent He so graciously gave me. Because of this, I will forever make a joyful noise unto the Lord.

Larniqwa Merritt, 15, Redemption Christian Academy, Troy, NY

Whatever I do, I want to do it for Your glory.
I don't wanna waste a minute
of the time You've given me being afraid.

February 22

getting my focus

Let us fix our eyes on Jesus,
the author and perfecter of our faith.

HEBREWS 12:2

During ninth grade, my Aunt died of liver cancer, my grandmother died of lung cancer, and my mother was diagnosed with her second episode of breast cancer. As my mom and I talked about all that had happened, she reminded me that everyone has their season of tragedy and that this was ours. Even while going through chemotherapy, losing her hair, and with the recent death of her sister and her mother, my mom continued to love God with powerful confidence that we would be all right. Wow! I think that was the day that I decided that I should put my focus more on God. I still struggle like every other teenager. I mess up a lot, but I try to focus more on God every day. And when I'm wrong I ask for forgiveness. Honestly, my character is being built as I focus on God 24-7. I've discovered that He talks to me through His Word, His people, and His Holy Spirit all the time. I never knew that God would talk to *me*—until I got my focus!

Candace K. Croston, 16, King's Fork High School, Suffolk, VA

God, it's so amazing that I can actually talk
to You and hear You answer back, if I really listen.
I want to hear You! Amen.

i want to be in control!

Do not be anxious about anything, but in everything, by prayer and petition, with thanksgiving, present your requests to God. And the peace of God, which transcends all understanding, will guard your hearts and your minds in Christ Jesus.

PHILIPPIANS 4:6–7

I'm the type of person who likes control—not like the authoritarian, dictator kind of power, but simply control of my own life and my environment. If I don't feel comfortable in my surroundings, I leave because I can't control things. I really don't know why this is such a problem for me. I get super stressed about things that I have no say in. Like last year: My life was a wreck. My friends all seemed to be turning away from God, we were going through family problems, and I was contemplating switching schools. I tried to handle it on my own, but I couldn't. I was literally making myself sick worrying about all the things I couldn't control. After facing the harsh reality that I couldn't fix everything, I began little by little giving my worries and problems to the Lord. As soon as I did, that tremendous burden of worry was taken from me. I know that God's plan for my life is perfect, and I should trust Him and His plans for my life, but it is hard. Still, I urge you, next time you feel stressed and don't know what to do, to ask God to guide you.

Lauren Chrisman, 18, Walnut Grove Christian Preparatory School, Sheridan, IN

Today, Jesus, I'm presenting all my worries to You. Thank You for being the kind of God that cares about me and my problems.

the test of the real world

"Where you go I will go, and where you stay I will stay. Your people will be my people and your God my God."

RUTH 1:16

My whole life I have gone to a Christian school, and I know that I have been protected from some things because of that. But I also know that once I leave my school and enter the "real world," my faith will be tested, and it will be really hard to stay true to what I believe. I have been blessed with a wonderful family and wonderful friends that encourage me to walk with the Lord, and I know that makes it easier. No matter where I am or what I'm doing, I don't ever want to abandon my faith in God, but in our world it sometimes is hard not to. One of my favorite moments in the Bible is when Ruth chooses to go with her mother-in-law, Naomi, instead of returning to her home. This sort of loyalty is so beautiful. It is the kind that I want to develop in my life: loyalty to my family, to my friends, and, mostly, to my God.

Kelsie Nygren, 15, Covenant Christian Academy, El Paso, TX

I know I'm going to be tested—that's the only way to see how strong my faith is. So, please, God, help me to be ready when the test comes.

just a small request

"Ask and it will be given to you; seek and you will find;
knock and the door will be opened to you.
For everyone who asks receives; he who seeks finds;
and to him who knocks, the door will be opened."

MATTHEW 7:7–8

The fifth period bell rang. I let out one of my heaviest sighs. There was not a doubt that I was going to be late to class. This was absolutely a bad day. My alarm didn't go off, I got lipstick on my favorite pair of jeans, and my mom drank the last of the coffee. This was all before I even arrived at school. Once there, I found that my best friend was not speaking to me for reasons unknown, my English paper wouldn't print off the computer, and a softball hit me in P.E. As the bell continued to ring, I searched frantically for my government homework in my locker. Why couldn't God just find that paper for me? Does every miracle that He does have to be big, important, and spectacular? Couldn't He do just a small miracle for me to make my day a little better? I know it was selfish, but I just needed a little help, a small miracle. It only had to be a miracle as simple as finding a paper in a messy locker. "God please let me find that homework! Please?" I moaned. Hardly a second passed when, from the top shelf of my locker, my government assignment fell down. I simply smiled in wonder as I rushed off to class realizing that God does care about the little things.

Chanelle Davis, 17, Houghton Christian Academy, Cuba, NY

It is just amazing how You're involved in
the tiniest details of my life.
I just can't believe how much You care for me!

psych ward or Jesus?

Do not be anxious about anything,
but in everything, by prayer and petition,
with thanksgiving, present your requests to God.

PHILIPPIANS 4:6

Do you ever worry? Well, I used to worry a lot, and I still do some now. I used to worry about everything, my hair, my grades…*everything.* If I got a B in school, I felt like a failure. Life was pretty awful, and I was miserable. Stress was like a rain cloud hovering overhead. Even after being on medicine for depression and after a stint in the hospital psych ward, I still worried and found that circumstances worsened and I was still depressed. Becoming a Christian and learning to give God my problems is what got me on the right road. I am not prefect, and sometimes I still try to solve my problems all on my own, but when I do, I end up digging a bigger hole for myself. After being a Christian for three years, life has improved. I have learned to let go of just about every little worry. I feel like the Lord has given me strength to fight my battles, and I know I am not alone. I have learned that you cannot control everything and worrying never makes things better.

Courtney Pinto, 15, Walnut Grove Christian Preparatory School, Fishers, IN

I know I can't do it all on my own.
So why do I keep trying to?
God, I want to ask for Your help more often.

macaroni

I praise you because I am fearfully and wonderfully made.

PSALM 139:14

I leaned against the bathroom wall, disgusted with myself. After flushing the partially digested macaroni, I rinsed my mouth out again and again in an attempt to purge the bitter taste of vomit from my tongue. This wasn't the first time I had tossed my meals. It was just that, well, I ate too much. I wanted to take it back. I didn't think I was fat; I just wanted to be thinner than I was. I stared at my reflection in the mirror, scrutinizing my flaws and defects. The thought, *This isn't right!* came into my head. And my mind responded, *But I need to lose five pounds!* My life appeared to be normal, and only the few people I confided in knew I had a problem. But whenever I ate a lot, I had an overwhelming urge to rid myself of that food by throwing it up. Later I would feel so guilty, so ashamed of what I had done. Finally, I stopped. I can't pinpoint an exact moment when I realized how much I was hurting myself, but it came with prayer. God was the only one I could talk to about this issue, because for a while only He knew. He showed me that He loved me so much and that I wasn't just hurting myself, but Him as well. I am God's creation, and "all of his works are wonderful." God wants me to not only accept the work He did in creating me, but also to thank him for the remarkable job. Sometimes I'm still tempted to dispel the food I eat. Accepting my body and myself has been a process, but I look the most beautiful when I see myself through God's eyes.

Meredith Janke, 17, Houghton Christian Academy, Houghton, NY

Lord, why do I hate myself so much sometimes? It doesn't make sense! I want to love myself because You love me, but it's one of the hardest things to do. Help me, please.

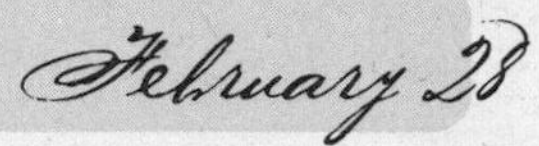

i want to be wise

The Lord grants wisdom! From his mouth come knowledge and understanding. He grants a treasure of good sense to the godly. He is their shield, protecting those who walk with integrity. He guards the paths of justice and protects those who are faithful to him.

PROVERBS 2:6–8 (NLT)

We worship and adore Thee, Bowing down before Thee,
Songs of praises singing, Hallelujahs ringing.
Hallelujahs! Hallelujahs! Hallelujahs!
Amen

no doubt

The Lord *is compassionate and gracious, slow to anger, abounding in love.... But from everlasting to everlasting the* Lord*'s love is with those who fear him.*

Psalm 103:8, 17

Am I really stupid or what?" After taking the SAT, I could not think of any other word except *stupid.* I studied for the test for over three months, but my score did not improve. I realized that it was not easy for international students, but all my classmates' scores were much higher than mine. Because I did not do well, I made my parents' financial sacrifice useless. I was so disappointed and frustrated. The journey I took from Korea to be an American high school and a college student seemed heading to a dead end. I started to have doubts about my future, even though I had a firm belief that God had prepared everything I needed. On Sunday, two days after taking the test, Pastor Joe preached on Psalm 103:8–17. If I see myself from a human view, there is nothing that I can brag about. However, I realized that there was no reason for me to feel inferior to others, because God created me and loves me. I had forgotten this simple truth. God does not criticize my weaknesses and shortcomings; rather, He sees my strengths, no matter how small they are. After this new awareness, I prayed, "Thank you, God, for loving me in spite of my shortcomings and imperfections." Having doubts about His mercy and grace was disrespectful to His ineffable love. The phrase "But from everlasting to everlasting the Lord's love is with those who fear him" is now hanging on my wall.

Sam Yun, 18, Houghton Christian Academy, Houghton, NY

Thank You, God, for loving me in spite of my shortcomings and imperfections. Amen.

perfect

As for God, his way is perfect; the word of the LORD is flawless. He is a shield for all who take refuge in him.... It is God who arms me with strength and makes my way perfect.

PSALM 18:30, 32

Being a teenager is so hard sometimes. There are so many pressures to be perfect, or at least close to perfect. Your parents sometimes seem like they expect way more than you can handle; your teachers expect you to get loads of homework done; your friends expect you to be cool and to fit in. It gets to be a heavy load, and sometimes you just feel like screaming. Not only this, but also your physical body is going through enormous changes. No wonder sometimes you feel like a big mangled mess inside! The best thing you can do for yourself is to set some reasonable goals, like: "By the end of this school quarter I would like to finish with at least Bs" or "By the end of this month I would like to put away at least $5 for savings." Just simple things that are doable and will encourage you. And always ask God to help you with these small goals. The more you ask for His help, even on small everyday things, the less stressful things will be. You can't be perfect, but He is. And with His help, you can get closer to perfect than you ever would on your own.

Stephanie Sherwood, 14, St. Ambrose Christian High School, Boise, ID

I know that I'm not perfect. But I still have a hard time letting You help me out, Lord. Help me to look to You for help all the time. Amen.

someone is watching!

Follow my example,
as I follow the example of Christ.

1 Corinthians 11:1

When I finally understood the gospel message at camp, I quickly accepted it as truth and asked Jesus Christ into my heart. I recall looking up to my counselors so much and thinking they were the greatest people on earth. Of course, they had their flaws, but I was a young girl and when I looked at them, all I saw was perfection. Well, as I've grown older, I see now that they aren't perfect, just like every other person on this planet. In the past few years, I've had the privilege of being a cabin leader at the same camp, and I love watching my campers enjoy their time there, having fun while learning more and growing closer to Christ. Because of my time volunteering at camp, I'm constantly reminded of what 1 Corinthians 11:1 teaches us. Now that I am a camp counselor of young girls, I recall how I looked up to my counselors, and I realize the importance of setting a good example and being a solid role model for them. A lot of the girls that I've had in my cabin see me in other places, not just at camp; and every time I see them, I'm reminded that they are always watching. It sort of keeps me in check so that I'll always try my best to set a Godly example, not only because it pleases the Lord, but also because I am setting a standard for those who look up to me.

Adrian Thistle, 17, Houston High School, Willow, AK

It scares me a little that kids might actually
look up to me. Lord, help me to take
that responsibility seriously.

March 4

guardian angels

They will lift you up in their hands,
so that you will not strike your foot against a stone.

MATTHEW 4:6

This verse from the book of Matthew has been with me ever since I returned from my mission trip to Auxier, Kentucky. While there, I'm sure I had at least twenty guardian angels all around me; I had one around me when I fell from the roof of the house we were demolishing, and another when I dropped a sledgehammer on my foot! I definitely had one watching over me when one of my colleagues dropped a twenty-pound sledgehammer that landed an inch from my shoulder! When I returned home, I realized just how many angels God had placed to guard me. Angels are God's messengers and our protectors. In everyday life, angels guard us. If you are driving down the road in a thunderstorm, you can know that the Lord Almighty has placed a pair of angels around your car to guide you home. Angels will surround us in our greatest hour of need and are our protection until God decides it is time for us to come home.

Pamela K. Locke, 15, Walnut Grove Christian Preparatory School, Noblesville, IN

It's amazing how You take care of me, Father!
I just want to thank You for all the times
You've protected me.

when parents say no

Children, obey your parents in everything,
for this pleases the Lord.

COLOSSIANS 3:20

One time a number of people from school were going to go see a movie in the theaters. I really wanted to go with them. I was so excited about it. So that afternoon after school, I asked my mom if I could go—and she said no. I was really disappointed because everyone else was going. I didn't think it was fair. And it seemed at the time that my life would be so much better if only I could do this one thing. (I'm sure you know the feeling.) But most of the time, if you think about it, your life wouldn't be that much better. Parents know best: Everyone hears this phrase all the time (I know I do). But it's actually true. We should remember that they were teens once too. They remember what it's like to be desperate to do something and then have someone tell them no. God has given us these parents, and we should obey them not only because it will make them happy but also because it will make God happy. So the next time you really want to do something but your parents say no, think, "Is this thing really that important?" You'll probably find that it's more important to listen to your parents, even if it doesn't seem like it at the moment. And by obeying them, you will have happier parents, and more importantly, God will be pleased with you.

Katie Davis, 15, Jonathan Edwards Academy, Millers Falls, MA

It seems like my parents say no all the time.
Lord, I need Your help in those times, so that I can
still honor them even when I think they're being unfair.

driver's ed

Peace be to you, fear not.

GENESIS 43:23 (KJV)

For three weeks, I had diligently studied during the classroom part of driver's education and passed with an A. The next week I was to begin the practical driving lessons. On the day of my driving lesson, my brother dropped me off and wished me good luck. I was so nervous I felt like I was going to puke. The instructor was very intimidating. He was big and tall. We jumped into the car, and he briefed me on the basics: gas on the right, brake on the left, and stuff like that. The first ten minutes went fine. Then we came to a stoplight, where I was supposed to make a right turn. Todd told me to dodge a puddle. Big mistake. When I tried to go around it, I almost hit a minivan! Todd slammed on the brakes, and we just missed it. Before my next driving lesson, I prayed that my drive would go smoother. It went off without any major problems, and I was even complimented on my driving. I am glad that God cares about the things that scare me. I just need to remember to ask for his help more often.

Heather Morris, 15, Walnut Grove Christian Preparatory School, Carmel, IN

Lord, there are so many new things
I have to learn. It can be scary, so thanks
for being with me through it all.

dealing with anger

For his anger lasts only a moment.

PSALM 30:5

Some say, "Never let the sun go down on your anger," but the truth is anger plays an active role in my life. Every day is a struggle to keep myself collected and to not explode. Several years ago my two sisters and I went to a school where my oldest sister was sexually harassed for two years by a member of the football team. She thought it was her fault, so she never told anybody until one day the boy shamed her in front of all her peers. She came home in tears. By the time my parents intervened, a lot of damage was done to her emotionally as well as physically: she had whittled away to a mere ninety pounds. When my parents went to the principal, the school gave the boy a one-day in-school suspension and allowed him to do chapel the next day, talking about holding each other accountable. When my parents told me what had happened, I remember feeling that my sister was weak and that I had to protect her against anyone who would try to hurt her. I remember telling my dad that if I ever saw the boy, I would kill him. However, I knew I couldn't live my life filled with anger, so I sought God's guidance. Eventually, I saw the boy and instead of sensing uncontrollable anger, I felt pity and prayed for him. It takes effort to not allow anger to control me, and if I can give that part of me to Christ, so can you.

Moriah Campton, 16, St. Ambrose Christian High School, Meridian, ID

The Bible says to be "slow to anger."
God, that's not easy advice to follow...please help me.

a little patience

Let us lay aside every weight, and the sin which doth so easily beset us, and let us run with patience the race that is set before us.

HEBREWS 12:1 (KJV)

I am the oldest out of five children. I have two sisters and two brothers, and there is a big age difference between us. I was eight when one brother was born, eleven when the other arrived, twelve when my first sister was born and then by the time the youngest sister came along I was fourteen. I've had to change a lot of dirty diapers in my life as well as put up with all their noise and their cranky behavior when they haven't had their naps. If there's something that I've learned from this, it has been *patience*. And I'm not a very patient person. I'm very short tempered and I need my space. I've never had to share my room (at least, not for very long). I'm constantly having to be careful about what I say and do in front of my siblings, but after all, I believe they have taught me a valuable lesson. It takes *patience* to teach your little sister to tie her shoelaces. It takes *patience* to try and decipher what your two-year-old sister is whining about. It takes patience to answer all their questions. It takes *patience* to help them clean up their messes and toys. And just like it takes patience for me to deal with my little siblings, Christ has to have a lot of *patience* to deal with us. Patience is an important trait to develop if we want to be more like Him.

Rebecca Wilson, 18, Maranatha Christian Academy, Oakwood, GA

Patience is something I'm very good at. So please, Lord, send people into my life who will help me learn to be more patient.

Him or me? (part 1)

I no longer live, but Christ lives in me.

GALATIANS 2:20

I remember the night I gave my heart to Jesus at summer camp. Even though I had been forgiven for my sins, the hardest part for me was yet to come. For the next few days we trained to go into the community and share the gospel. We had devotions every day, and we had time to talk to the Lord and just think about things. I love to spend time just talking with the Lord because He cares about everything—even the small things. Community outreach was just around the corner, and we had one more night to make everything right before we went out to share the gospel. We had a commitment service where we got to spend time alone to make a commitment to the Lord that we would continue to do His work in His way. This was the "no turning back" stage: It was either go hard or go home! I live on the big island of Hawaii, and it is bigger than all the other seven islands put together, so we had a lot of work ahead of us. Spending time with God and asking Him to give me strength helped me to face this big task. I knew that this would be a time when I had to give myself over completely to Him because I could not make a real difference in people's lives without Him.

Victoria T. Kaopua, 15, Kealakehe High School, Kailua-Kona, HI

Thank You, Jesus, for making me one of Your messengers! I pray that I will be brave enough to share Your love.

March 10

Him or me? (part 2)

I no longer live, but Christ lives in me.

GALATIANS 2:20

I think the first day that I realized the difference between living for myself and living for God was the day my youth group did community outreach. We went to churches all around the island and danced, performed skits, and talked about why we believed in God and how we each had gotten to know Him. Everywhere we went, we hoped that we would impact at least one person, but by the end we had seen *so many* lives change than we could have hoped for. Many of our new friends got excited about following God and living for Him, and it was an awesome thing to see. Before, I thought I was fine sort of going through life and not giving all of me to God. But when I saw Jesus working in people's lives for the first time, the idea that God only wanted part of me popped like a bubble and disappeared. For so long it was easy for me to make excuses to avoid doing what was right. But suddenly, I got tired of my many excuses. I have been finding out that change is not easy, but when I chose to let God really be my God, He made me alive for the first time. I made the choice to follow hard after God, and I hope that you do the same. It's just not worth it to live for ourselves.

Victoria T. Kaopua, 15, Kealakehe High School, Kailua-Kona, HI

When I tell someone about You, Father,
I feel so happy. I know I am doing Your work,
and I want to keep doing it!

pass the salt, please

Let your conversation be always full of grace, seasoned with salt, so that you may know how to answer everyone.

COLOSSIANS 4:6

I remember once taking a bite of a chicken and rice dish. It was most likely the blandest thing I had ever eaten. Needless to say, I didn't savor every bite. If you think about it, that is precisely how my conversations can be if I am not careful of what I say. Jesus said we are "the salt of the earth" (Matthew 5:13). Food should not be bland, and neither should our words. Salt is what makes bland food worth eating, and Christians can help to make a bland life worth living. As a teen girl, I have a tendency to gossip and to criticize. I can be quite sarcastic and opinionated. These things don't add flavor to life. If anything, they take away from it. Instead as a teen girl, and more importantly as a teen girl who is striving to be a godly woman, I should use my mouth to say things that are glorifying to God and edifying to those around me—things that put a little bit of heaven into life on earth. We should *say* more and chatter less. Jesus also said, "If the salt loses its saltiness, how can it be made salty again? It is no longer good for anything but to be thrown out and trampled by men." We should make sure to make our words count, to make them the "salt of the earth," because we only have a short time on this planet to make a difference for Christ.

Caroline J. Hornok, 15, Veritas Academy, Texarkana, TX

Help me to make the most of the time I have, Christ Jesus. I want to enhance people's lives, not bring them down.

March 12

stand firm in your faith

Do not be yoked together with unbelievers. For what do righteousness and wickedness have in common? Or what fellowship can light have with darkness?

2 CORINTHIANS 6:14

I am going to be completely honest about this, as I have not been honest with myself about this until today. I have done something that I truly regret: I have forsaken my first love that I found in Jesus. In the beginning, as a college freshman, I ignored the need to go to church every Sunday and attend on-campus Christian groups and became involved with a non-Christian boyfriend. In the beginning, I shouldn't have ignored my misgivings regarding my relationship, but I made inadequate justifications to soothe my wavering faith. I compromised my faith for my boyfriend, saying that because we had similar morals and standards that it was all acceptable. However, as I have been told by my friends and family, a small compromise will only lead to greater compromise later on, such as completely disregarding one's faith. But I chose to ignore my good Christian friends and the advice of my Christian parents. These people held me accountable for what I was doing and not doing. I wish I had listened to them earlier so I could have escaped the emotional baggage this has left me with. Yesterday my boyfriend broke up with me, leaving me with the need to reconcile myself to Jesus for abandoning Him and pursuing my own desires. I should never have compromised what I believe for what seemed convenient at the time. Now I really know the importance of standing firm in your beliefs and not being caught up in this world.

Kari Page, 19, Hanover College, Hanover, IN

Lord, when I start to wander away from You,
bring me back! Show me the way back,
because I never want to lose my relationship with You.

from the inside out

If you do what is right, will you not be accepted?

GENESIS 4:7

I am now a sophomore in high school, but I can clearly remember my junior-high years, and some of the things I went through then seem so ridiculous now. In junior high I was the odd girl in the crowd; I was the one everyone picked on. I was ridiculed, stepped on, never seen for who I really was; except by my friends. I tried everything to make people accept me for who I really was. I tried to wear the clothes, the shoes, the jewelry, talk the talk; do anything for them to just accept me. I got so tired of them picking on me and not accepting me that I transferred to a private Christian school. When I got there, I finally felt accepted. But in the eighth grade, I started feeling left out all over again. It took a few years for me to realize that some people will never accept me, but God has accepted me all along—from the inside out! God doesn't care about what's on the outside; he cares about your heart. It was hard to not be accepted by my classmates, but knowing that God accepted me even before I was born helps me know everything's going to be okay. It has been several years since my junior-high days, and I have never felt more accepted than I do now.

Hope Minor, 16, Veritas Academy, Texarkana, TX

Some things in my past still hurt me, even years later.
Help me to learn from those past experiences,
Father, instead of just letting them make me sad.

a big family

Be devoted to one another in brotherly love.

ROMANS 12:10

There are a lot of only children in the world who have no idea what it is like to have a brother or a sister. But God provides us with brothers and sisters even if we don't technically have siblings. I have two half-sisters, a stepbrother, and two guys that are as close as real brothers to me. We all have different parents, but we love each other as if we came from the same parents. We drive each other crazy, just like real sisters and brothers. God puts people in our lives to be our friends, and together we share back and forth the things that are important to us in life. We need to respect these friends and tell them we love them. When I think about it, I am pretty lucky to have people around me that I can just be real with, whether they are related or not. I try to remember to thank God for each one who is like family, and I hope that you will pray for those in your life that are friends "closer than a brother." Enjoy the people who love you and give back to them by praying for them and thanking God for them!

Courtney Pinto, 15, Walnut Grove Christian Preparatory School, Fishers, IN

God, thank You for making me part of Your family. I am blessed to be loved by so many people—especially You!

hello...where are You?

For the LORD searches every heart and understands every motive behind the thoughts. If you seek him, he will be found by you.

1 CHRONICLES 28:9

This verse holds a powerful promise. Do you really believe that if you seek God, you will find Him? Has anyone really found God? And what exactly are we looking for? These are the questions I was asking when I read this verse. But the more important question, I believe, is, "To *whom* does God reveal Himself?" He says it is the *pure in heart* that will *see* Him (Matthew 5:8), and that those who *seek Him with all their heart and soul* will *find* him. (Deuteronomy 4:29; Matthew 7:7–8) I was seeking Him with all my heart about six months ago when I was going through a course that included learning how to hear God's voice. I was praying, asking God to tell me where He wanted me to go next. All of the sudden, in my mind, the word *Saipan* clearly came up. I had never seen or heard this word before, so I thought I was just making up words. I decided to check out a map just in case, and I found a tiny island in the South Pacific called Saipan! Two months later I was there, fulfilling God's call! So be encouraged. God doesn't always speak that way, but neither is He always silent. I think sometimes He's just waiting for us to take a step closer, to get to know Him better. Perhaps there are a few things that He is just dying to share with us!

Sasha Truehl, 19, Concordia College, Adelaide, Australia

Lord, I want to come closer to You so that I can find out what You have to tell me. I know it will be something that will change my life!

the unruly rose

Cast all your anxiety on him
because he cares for you.

1 PETER 5:7

Help! Where did I put that rose? I know I stuck a safety pin on one of these roses before the play started. I've got to find it. Aaaggghhh! These frantic thoughts were racing through my head as I tried not to rip apart the rose bush up on stage. Earlier, I had put a safety pin on the back of a rose and placed it in a perfectly accessible spot on the rose bush so it was ready to pin onto my "sweetheart." My sweaty, clammy hands were shaking uncontrollably by the time I realized that I couldn't spend all of Act II searching for one specific rose. I started ad-libbing as fast as my paralyzed brain would go, saying something like, "But it has to be the perfect rose, darling..." After the play, I frantically questioned my sister about the glitch, and she didn't even know that something had gone wrong! This little experience made me think about the problems that we come up against in real life. 1 Peter 5:7 tells us to "cast all your anxiety on him because he cares for you." I realized that however big or small, significant or insignificant we think our problems are, God cares. So whether it's a misplaced rose in a play or a real-life hiccup, our God does not leave us. He wants to take care of us, and he wants us to trust Him. Because when we do, what we think is a huge disaster might not be after all.

Bethany Christensen, 18, Houghton Christian Academy, Houghton, NY

I worry too much about little things.
Help me to focus on what's important and
trust that You will take care of the little problems.

step by step

Your word is a lamp to my feet
and a light for my path.

PSALM 119:105

During our nightly prayer gathering, my dad prayed, "Dear Father, help Yunjoo to make the right decision. Give her Your wisdom and help her desire what You want. Lead her into the way that You have prepared." The most confusing time in my life was the summer of 2003. The previous winter, I had already made a radical choice to attend Dream School, an unaccredited Christian school in South Korea, giving up the chance to study in a prestigious school in the U.S. Although I pretended to be confident about my decision, I really felt insecure. At the end of the first semester, my entire class decided to study in Beijing for the next six months. When I heard about the dirty, crowded dorm, all my excitement and willingness to travel suddenly disappeared. Not going to China just because of the dorm sounded silly, but I felt strongly about not going. In the midst of chaos, Dad asked me if I wanted to study in the U.S. Within three days, I had enrolled in Houghton Academy in western New York. It was pretty chaotic, switching schools again and going to a different country. But as I look back, I realize that the places I stayed for even a short period were all necessary for shaping who I am right now. South Korea and New York were both places where I developed a true relationship with God. God is my lamp, and He continues to answer my father's prayer that He would lead me into the places that He has prepared for me.

Yunjoo Lim, 17, Houghton Christian Academy, Houghton, NY

Father, thank You for others who pray for me.
I want to pray for them, too, every day.

an unforgettable conversation

Above all else, guard your heart,
for it is the wellspring of life.

PROVERBS 4:23

I'm not going to lie. The subject of modesty isn't exactly the most popular one to discuss with friends after a Friday-night movie. For a long time I approached it with a sort of hands-off, deal-with-it-when-my-parents force-me-to attitude. One night I was headed to meet some friends in town. My dad asked me if I was going to hang out with boys. I told him that it was a girls' night out and no boys were invited. I will never forget the words he said then. My dad, gently and honestly, told me how much what women wear affects men, old and young. He described the unbelievable temptation a scantily dressed woman is to a guy, even one who is trying NOT to look. For the first time I realized that what I wear really does affect guys. When I was getting dressed that night, I had not been trying to flaunt my body or to make guys lust after me. I just wanted to look cute. My conversation with my dad showed me that even more important than "cuteness" is modesty, for my sake, as well as for guys' sakes. He told me that a modest girl with discretion is far more attractive than a girl who flaunts her body. So talk to your parents when trying on outfits. Don't be afraid to ask your dad what he thinks of a particular outfit. I know it sounds odd, but praying about what I am going to wear helps me decide if my outfit shows discretion. So, no, it's not particularly popular, but God cares about our modesty, and He loves it when our hearts are willing to obey Him in this.

Jessica Runk, 19, Patrick Henry College, Purcellville, VA

Jesus, You have given me a great gift in my parents.
Most of the time I don't recognize it, but they have so much
knowledge to share with me. Thank You!

full of metal

In this you greatly rejoice, though now for a little while you may have had to suffer grief in all kinds of trials.

1 PETER 1:6

Growing up, I was made fun of a lot. To put it bluntly, I didn't have a profile. My face went straight back below my nose. When I was born, I didn't have a roof in the top of my mouth and my jaw had stopped growing before I was born. On top of that, I was very short. After three surgeries on my mouth, I had a roof, but my jaw was still set back. I took growth hormone shots for two years and finally made it to five feet tall. During school, I'd walk through the halls and people would point and talk about my face. It devastated my self-esteem. The one bright spot was that I had a great orthodontist throughout this whole process. He tried to fix my mouth without doing surgery by putting two bars in my mouth that ran from the top back teeth to the bottom front teeth, plus braces. My mouth was *full* of metal. It helped but didn't fix my problem. Finally, when I was fifteen, I had the surgery, and it ended up taking nine and a half hours! I am now completely healed and people don't make fun of me anymore. But it hurts when I think about how I didn't have many friends because of how my face looked. I remember coming home after school and talking to God about everything. Sometimes He was the only real friend that I had. I still don't know why God put me in this situation, but I know that it has made me who I am today. I have definitely learned that God will give me nothing I can't handle with His help.

Sara York, 16, Antioch High School, Antioch, TN

Lord, I don't understand why I have to endure some of the things I do. But I want to learn to trust in Your wisdom, even when I can't understand it.

pray and pray and pray

"If you believe, you will receive whatever you ask for in prayer."

MATTHEW 21:22

Two years ago in my hometown of Yaoundé, Cameroon, I was living with my grandmother. From her I learned about God and the power of prayer. My dream was to study in a foreign country and speak a language other than my mother tongue, French. And my greatest dream was to play basketball, and this is what I prayed for. God answered my prayer. I now attend Redemption Christian Academy, a Christian boarding school. Here I attend church four times a week, where I am built up spiritually, and I'm on the varsity basketball team, fulfilling my biggest dream. I encourage you to not stop praying until you get His results. Many of us lose confidence in prayer because we don't recognize the answer. We ask for strength and God gives us difficulties, which makes us strong. We pray for wisdom and God sends us problems, which develop wisdom. We plead for prosperity and God gives us a brain and strength to work. We plead for courage and God gives us danger to overcome. We ask for favors and God gives us opportunities. I am a living testimony that God does answer prayers. Keep listening, keep praying, and get ready to be surprised.

Laure P. Mbiandja, 16, Redemption Christian Academy, Troy, NY

I love that I can talk to You, God,
and ask You for anything I need. Help me
to appreciate Your answers, whatever they are.

when i am weak, You are strong

"My grace is sufficient for you, for my power is made perfect in weakness...." For when I am weak, then I am strong.

2 CORINTHIANS 12:9–10

As I face new daily challenges, I am constantly amazed at how often God reminds me of His plan for my life. There are times when everything is going great and I'm SO thankful for all God has given me. Then there are those times when things aren't going so great and being thankful is much more difficult, and it seems as though it would be easier to give up and walk away from the Lord's plan rather than to *stand firm* in my faith and look at how I can grow from each individual experience. Anytime that I'm feeling frustrated with a situation in life and it seems as though I'm too weak to get through it, 2 Corinthians 12:9–10 reminds me that it's okay to show signs of weakness because I'm not supposed to go through life on my own. I need to lean on God for EVERYTHING. It's at these times that God steps in and really works in my life, showing His power and greatness. Thankfully we serve a loving God who knows each and every individual inside and out, and He will draw close to us at exactly the right moment so He can be a source of help and protection when we need Him the most.

Adrian Thistle, 17, Houston High School, Willow, AK

Thank You, Jesus, for finding ways to use my weaknesses for Your glory. Even when I make mistakes, You turn them into something good! Amen

island breeze

May the Lord make your love increase
and overflow for each other and for everyone else.

1 THESSALONIANS 3:12

I am Polynesian and have lived in the South Pacific most of my life. My family is part of Island Breeze, an International Luau Production Company headquartered in Hawaii and also a ministry of Youth With A Mission. At Island Breeze we are like one huge family, made up of all the different teams. I love it. Of course, like any family, we are not perfect, but we all love each other deeply. I know that when I get a boyfriend, he will face about two million questions before he can date me! Thousands of people from all over the world are a part of Island Breeze. If I am not related to someone, I will nonetheless call them "Auntie" or "Uncle" if they are older than me. It reminds me of the other family that I am a part of—the family of God. Many Island Breeze members are a part of this family, too, but it extends way beyond that. With Island Breeze, God has given me a little taste of what the gathering of many peoples and nations in heaven will be like. Wow! I can only begin to picture it!

Victoria T. Kaopua, 15, Kealakehe High School, Kailua-Kona, HI

Father, heaven is going to be so wonderful!
Thank You for sending Jesus to die for
my sins so that I can be there with You one day!

true worship

Worship the L*ORD with gladness;*
come before him with joyful songs.

Psalm 100:2

I was finally there! It seemed like I had been waiting to go on the mission trip to Kenya for so long, and now the people living in the slums of Dandora were right in front of me. I was shocked by their poverty. There was hardly any electricity, and most people lived in tiny shacks made with sheets of metal. The children's only hope for a good education in the area was at Kinyago-Dandora School, where they not only got a good education, but also were fed lunch and were introduced to God. Soon after we arrived, some of the older girls at the school sang for us. I recognized some of the songs from my church at home, and I was surprised that these girls who lived in a slum in Kenya knew them too. But there was something different about the way they were singing. They were dancing and clapping. Some were closing their eyes, while others raised their eyes to heaven. It was obvious that their thoughts weren't on pleasing *us* with their music. They were thinking about worshiping God. Sometimes when I sing worship songs, I'm not really worshiping. I sing the words with my lips but don't worship God with my heart. Even though it seems like I have much more reason to worship God because of my material possessions, the Kenyan girls were *truly* thankful for what little they had. Now, when I start to mindlessly sing the words, I remember those girls and how deeply they felt every word they were singing. That is something I hope I never forget.

Allison Engel, 16, Wheaton North High School, Wheaton, IL

I take so much for granted in my life, Lord.
I want to be more thankful for every
single thing You give me.

the best gift ever

I am not ashamed of the gospel,
because it is the power of God for the
salvation of everyone who believes.

ROMANS 1:16

What would you do if someone gave you the biggest, most beautiful diamond in the entire world? How about that one gift that you have wanted for so long but know you will never get? What would you do if you actually got it? Of course, you would say thanks, but what would you *do* with the gift? Would you even consider sticking it in your closet, between mounds of shoes you never wear and the pile of too-short pants you keep forgetting to give away? Probably not. You would display it, show it off, and invite your friends to come and see it. God has given us the best gift ever, the gift of eternal life, and He wants us to share it with people around us. Yet so often we try to hide it, ashamed of what people might think of us and say about us. But truthfully, the gift is not about us and it is not ours to conceal. This gift is all about God reaching out to people. So let's forget ourselves and our insecurities and let God's gift be what He intended it to be: the best gift ever.

Danica Woods, 17, Nebraska Christian High School, Central City, NE

I don't want to hide how amazing
You are, Christ Jesus. I want to tell everyone!!

the answer was yes

For I can do all things
through Christ who strengthens me.

PHILIPPIANS 4:13 (KJV)

One day my Mom and I were sitting in our living room talking when she boldly asked me if I had been having sex. I could not lie to her. The answer was yes. I will never forget the disappointment on her face. The next day, a home pregnancy test was positive and soon afterwards a doctor confirmed it. I was officially going to have a baby. I still thought of myself as a kid, but I was going to have a baby! My senior year of high school was upon me, and I had thought I was ready, but it ended up going a whole lot different than I imagined it would. I refused to allow my sin to stop me from finishing high school, and I decided not to abort or give away my baby. So I moved to a Christian ministry that helped me out. Months later, with God's strength, I graduated from high school with honors, while I was still pregnant. I had my son and am now attending the University of Tennessee at Chattanooga and raising my son with the help of my mom and the ministry. What I did was sinful, but my son is not. He will be one year old soon, and we are both doing well because people chose to care. They did not give up on us during any of it because they believed in a God who doesn't give up on us either.

Rachel Eggensperger, 19, Bethel Bible Village, Hixson, TN

I know I'm going to make mistakes, Father, because I'm not even close to perfect. But I am so thankful that You will never give up on me and will always forgive me.

same clothes every day

For I have learned to be content whatever the circumstances.

PHILIPPIANS 4:11

Last summer I went on a mission trip to Matamoros, Mexico, with a group of thirty youth and adults. We slept in Brownsville, Texas, and drove over the border each day to do Bible school with children in the village. They all lived in shacks made with pieces of scrap materials that had dirt floors. We went to help and teach them, but they ended up teaching us. The people in the village owned very little, so the children had few toys and clothes. Some of them came to VBS barefoot, and many wore the same clothes every day. Even though they certainly could use more things, they seemed content with what they did have: their friends and family. When we did crafts with them, they usually wanted to give what they had constructed or colored to us because they found joy in people more than in material things. God used this to show me that material things are not what make people happy. Since then, I have tried to appreciate what I already have and to not be anxious to buy more clothes, CDs, shoes, and other stuff. Although I often want more, I am slowly learning to be more like the kids in the village, content and thankful with what I do have.

Christina Jensen, 15, Dogwood Christian School, Asheville, NC

I want, I want, I want...
What I really want, Lord, is to stop wanting
so much and just praise You for what I have.

where's daddy?

Trust in the L*ORD with all your heart*
and lean not on your own understanding

PROVERBS 3:5

When I was about seven and a half, my parents separated. I remember asking lots of questions like, "Where's Daddy?" and "When's Daddy coming home?" The gentler term "separation" became "divorce" a few days before my eighth birthday. I still was too young to really understand what was going on, but it didn't take long for me to see that Mom and Dad didn't love each other like they used to. It made me angry. I was asking God so many questions, trying to figure out why this had happened and what was going on. One day I realized that if God made me and knows every thought I have, then He can control all the situations in my life. I needed to let God take over. When I was finally able to let God have it, the divorce my parents went through got a little easier. It still hurt really badly and I would not wish it on anyone, but I know that am still loved by both my parents and by God. In God's love I have been learning to be strong even though life for me and my family is really tough right now.

Lindsay Oliver, 15, Cedar Hall School, Nashville, TN

Some things are just out of my control, Father.
Give me strength to endure them.

why worry?

Therefore do not worry about tomorrow,
for tomorrow will worry about itself.
Each day has enough trouble of its own.

MATTHEW 6:34

Every day, when I have a couple of minutes, my mind wanders and I begin to think of everything I have to do that day or the next. Really what I should worry about is the here and now. I once heard a quote that read, "Worry does not empty tomorrow of its troubles, it empties today of its strength." I should worry about how many more people we can win for God's kingdom, not whether a certain boy likes me or not. Why worry about the things we cannot change the outcome of or things that are trivial? You cannot control everything, and sometimes you are not even in control of your own life. "What ifs" only cause worry, and do not change the outcome. Our problems and worries are minor compared to leading others to Christ and eternal salvation. Satan ultimately is the one who puts that worry in our heart. He enjoys seeing us rely on other things to resolve our worry instead of coming to God when He calls us back. So bring your troubles to God, who does not think of our problems as trivial; they are of utmost importance to Him. He loves you, and is waiting for you to hand Him your worries and problems.

Jessica Morel, 17, Riverdale High School, Rockvale, TN

Lord, what concerns me concerns You,
so help me to learn to not lean on my own understanding,
but to cast all my cares upon You. Amen.

but i'm a teenager!

Children, obey your parents in the Lord,
for this is right.

EPHESIANS 6:1

I love my parents! They are the most amazing people in the world. I hang out with them like they are my friends and tell them everything. But I still treat them horribly at times, yelling at them, slamming my bedroom door, or refusing to clean my room. Deep down, I know that everything they tell me or make me do is probably for my benefit, but somehow, since I'm a teenager, I feel like I'm allowed to be messy or rude or irresponsible. Our society has engrained into us that being a teenager has to mean we don't like to talk to older people, we sleep in until 4 p.m. on Saturdays, and we never have to make our beds. I have been realizing that saying I am a teenager shouldn't give me an excuse to do or not do anything. It struck me the other day that I am disrespecting the people who pretty much pay for me to live, and, on top of that, I am disobeying God. Maybe instead of telling our friends how annoying our parents are, we can talk about how thankful we are for the things they do.

Katie-Lee Kroeker, 16, home school, Medicine Hat, Alberta, CA

Dear Jesus, help me to be better
than the world, to live the way You want
me to rather than the way society expects.
I know I will be happier if I do.

a tough choice

If anything is excellent or praiseworthy,
think about such things.

PHILIPPIANS 4:8

Music is a gift from God—but Satan can also use it against us. Several months ago, I began listening to a secular radio station that played many songs with awful lyrics, but I loved the style and sound of the music. I convinced myself that I was a strong enough Christian and that the suggestive lyrics wouldn't affect me. Honestly, though, I knew they were changing me. One day I turned on a Christian station and listened to it for a while. I heard a song based on Philippians 4:8, and I realized that my music habits were hurting my relationship with God. That night while listening to the secular station, I clearly heard God speaking to me. He said, "You know that you are sinning, yet you are still listening to this music. Kimberlee, you are disobeying me." I decided that night that I would stop listening to that particular station. It was a hard decision to live out; I often flipped through the stations and found myself stopping on that old secular station, listening to the familiar songs. But throughout the whole struggle, God was guiding me away from the temptation and teaching me to worship Him with my entire mind.

Kimberlee DeGroot, 14, Petra Academy, Bozeman MT

Sometimes I don't realize how much the things I do take me away from You, Lord. Guide me to things that will help me worship You more, rather than keeping us apart. Amen.

i want to trust

Trust in the L*ORD with all your heart*
and lean not on your own understanding;
in all your ways acknowledge him,
and he will make your paths straight.
Do not be wise in your own eyes;
fear the L*ORD and shun evil.*

PROVERBS 3:5–7

What a might God we serve!
What a mighty God we serve!
Angels bow before Him,
Heaven and earth adore Him,
What a mighty God we serve.

Composer Unknown

from the inside out

O LORD, *you have searched me*
and you know me.

PSALM 139:1

I don't think I've ever met a girl who has told me she thinks she's gorgeous. Personally, I'm very critical of the way I look. I think my nose and head are too big, my hair is fuzzy, and I wish I had longer eyelashes. Sometimes I think I'm just plain old...plain! People always tell me that true beauty isn't on the outside, and I always nod and think, *Yeah, yeah, I know, I know.* Then, about two months ago, the pastor at my church gave a very moving sermon on Psalm 139. Now, we all know that God made us in His image. That alone makes us beautiful. But on top of that, He has known us forever and has made us "fearfully and wonderfully." When I think about the God of the universe making me unique and special, it really does touch me. I don't know how else to put it except that you, too, are made in His image and you are an awesome wonder. It doesn't matter what your face looks like or how skinny you are. God cares about the condition of your heart. And once Jesus inhabits yours, you are a "new creation," and the beauty of your changed heart is free to shine from the inside out.

Grace Bricker, 16, Jonathan Edwards Academy, Greenfield, MA

I like the idea, Lord, that accepting You
as my savior makes me beautiful. Thank You for
giving me the kind of beauty that will last forever.

life in a bubble (part 1)

Keep your head in all situations,
endure hardship, do the work of an evangelist.

2 TIMOTHY 4:5

When I was thirteen, I went to Fiji on a mission trip. It was a big thing for me, since I had never been away from home for very long. As excited as I was to be going with all my friends to a foreign land, I was also scared to be away from my parents. I had lived on the Big Island of Hawaii my whole life, and anything outside of that was a different world to me. My parents and the leaders of the team going to Fiji tried to prepare me, but I had no idea what to expect. When we got to Fiji, we drove for four hours to get to Suva and as soon as we got settled, some of us we went out into the city. We met so many people on the sidewalks begging for money. By the end of the trip, I had almost given away everything I had in an effort to give something to each person. My introduction to life outside of the bubble that I had always lived in was scary. There I was, wanting to be used by God, but shaking in my sandals and wondering what it really meant to be a light in a dark world and if I could even do it?

Victoria T. Kaopua, 15, Kealakehe High School, Kailua-Kona, HI

God, give me the chance to go
somewhere new, to be taken out of my
comfort zone, so that I can learn more about You.

getting outside the bubble (part 2)

But you, keep your head in all situations,
endure hardship, do the work of an evangelist.

2 TIMOTHY 4:5

While we were there, we helped out with and performed at the South Pacific Games. It was great to be with all the national athletes and their supporters, and the best part was every performance I got to see people give their hearts to Jesus. But even though I was so happy about what we were doing, I was also sad because I missed my parents and brother so much. I would cry myself to sleep just thinking about them and wishing I could be with them. I knew I was in Fiji for a purpose, so I asked God to give me comfort and strength to get to the end. Every day when we didn't perform, we worked on our routine to keep ourselves sharp. We knew we needed God's strength, so we spent a lot of time keeping our hearts clean and our attitudes right, praying and reading the Word. Of course, the enemy of God's message of hope did try to make us fail. We had several minor injuries, relationships were tested, and attitudes were challenged. At one point, we even came close to splitting into two groups. But by the end of the outreach, we had mended all those things and God had even healed us of our physical pains.

Victoria T. Kaopua, 15, Kealakehe High School, Kailua-Kona, HI

Lord God, sometimes even when I know
I'm doing Your will, it's still hard. Give me
peace and strength so that I can do great things for You.

bursting the bubble (part 3)

Keep your head in all situations,
endure hardship, do the work of an evangelist.

2 TIMOTHY 4:5

At the final performance for the closing ceremonies of the South Pacific Games, in front of the entire nation of Fiji and all the spectators watching by television, I could feel God's awesome presence. Dancing made me feel so complete, and it was so good to worship God in that way. We were touching these people in ways we will never know. I knew that we were showing people that it's okay to use parts of your culture, like dance, to worship God. I had learned a lot from the people of Fiji. I learned that just because God is on my side, doesn't mean that I will never feel sad or go through hard things. I learned to work hard to be at peace with my friends. I learned to do what God tells me, even if my friends aren't doing it. These lessons I learned during that trip expanded my little world. I realize that I have been to some places some people only dream of going to, and I've had some pretty amazing experiences along the way. Despite this, I still have a lot to learn about life. In fact, so far, life has not really been what I expected. I thought it was all about adventure, freedom, and fun, but I am finding out there is more to it than that. But I am also finding out that God is a lot bigger than I thought, and He is still able to take care of me as the world gets bigger.

Victoria T. Kaopua, 15, Kealakehe High School, Kailua-Kona, HI

I don't want to be afraid of new experiences, Jesus.
I want to see more of You as I see more of the world.

God's beauty pageant

"The LORD *does not look at the things man looks at.*
Man looks at the outward appearance,
but the LORD *looks at the heart."*

1 Samuel 16:7

Whenever I look at a fashion magazine, I start to notice my every flaw and wonder why I can't be as perfect as the models are. I'm sure that some of you are as beautiful as those models in the magazines, but the truth is, if you aren't beautiful on the inside, then the outside really doesn't matter. God made us just the way that we are physically, and when He made us, he didn't go, "Oops, my bad!" No, he said "There, that's exactly what I want. Look how incredibly beautiful she is!" It may be hard to believe, but God is madly in love with you, and He thinks that you are amazingly beautiful. The hard part is forgetting the culture's definition of beauty and getting it into your mind just how beautiful *God* thinks you are. As Christian girls, a lot of times we're told (or feel like) enhancing our outer beauty is sinful or vain. It totally can be, but God *does* want us to take care of ourselves. He created beauty and our bodies and our smiles and our eyes, and he wants us to take care of and enjoy them. God doesn't mind us using makeup or fixing our hair, but I think He wants us to care more about what we look like on the inside, rather than the outside. Our creator is the only one who can really judge a person's beauty, not the world. He is the only One who sees deeply and truly.

Holly Scott, 18, North Buncombe High School, Weaverville, NC

I am so glad You judge me by a
different standard than people in this world.
Yes, I want people to think I'm beautifull,
but most of all, I want You to think I'm beautiful.

is flirting bad? (part 1)

Daughters of Jerusalem, I charge you:
Do not arouse or awaken love until it so desires.

Song of Songs 8:4

Your heart rushes when he walks by. The blood pumps swiftly through your body as you watch him cross the room. He's the guy you've been eyeing for a week, or has it been two weeks now? Oh, but then, who knows or really cares? What matters is getting this guy's attention. You slip across the room, slyly easing your way towards the group of people he's with. You pretend to notice him for the first time, raising your voice to a sultry level, as you say his name. He turns and smiles. You giggle, tease, and coyly compliment him as your banter proceeds. You know you've got him wrapped neatly around your finger by the end of the conversation, and that is exactly what you wanted. You feel good about yourself because he responded so wonderfully to your advances. Yes, it's true: You have a lot of power over guys. With a few choice words, one deft touch, and a sexy outfit, you can send his mind racing through the cosmos. You have the power to make him feel like a man with something as seemingly insignificant as the look in your eyes. If he thinks you're interested, he might pursue you. He might even ask you out. Then, a month later, when your affections shift, you have the power to break his heart. Few of us are quite this powerful, but most of us like to flirt (or at least want to). But is flirting bad? Or maybe the better question would be: What good does flirting do?

Amy McKoy, 18, Bryan College, Dayton, TN

God, I want to be liked by guys.
I need Your help to know how to keep
my feelings from leading me to do things I shouldn't.

is flirting bad? (part 2)

Daughters of Jerusalem, I charge you:
Do not arouse or awaken love until it so desires.

SONG OF SONGS 8:4

Maybe it's a silly question, but when you flirt with a guy, is he someone you would consider marrying? Are you flirting with him because he's good-looking or because he's a great person? Flirting can be so much fun and seems so harmless that it's easy to get caught up in it. But stop and remember what it feels like to be on the receiving end of no-commitment flirting, or think about your friend who was convinced that some guy loved her, only to find out he was dating someone else. Guys get hurt in the same way when we lead them on. They feel deceived and angry, just like we do. So, let's be careful and aware of what message our actions are communicating to the opposite sex. Please don't think I'm saying to cut off all ties with guys, to never talk to guys, or to stop laughing at their jokes. I think we know the difference between being a friend and being a flirt. Let's cherish our friendships with our guy friends, learn to guard their hearts (as well as our own) when we are hanging out, and love them like real friends do.

Amy McKoy, 18, Bryan College, Dayton, TN

What I do affects other people and their feelings.
I don't think about that a lot, Lord, but I should.
Help me to think of others and not just myself.

had to tell

Let us not become weary in doing good,
for at the proper time we will reap a harvest.

GALATIANS 6:9

The gravel on the road beneath the truck was the only sound that could be heard. Although I was thankful that my brother's music wasn't blaring in my ears, the silence was making me uncomfortable. I glanced over to my brother, in the driver's seat. I had been praying for a moment to really talk to him about God ever since he had told me he was an atheist. Every time I brought up Christianity, he made fun of me or just wouldn't listen. But I couldn't just let it go. If I didn't tell him, I honestly didn't know who would. So for the first time, I told my brother I loved him and that God loved him too. I told him everything I could think of. The words just floated off my tongue, and all I did was let them pass. Unlike all the other times I had talked to him about God, he didn't groan or roll his eyes. He didn't make fun of me or shake his head. He just looked at me, a half smile on his face, and went back to driving. I don't know if he really heard anything I said or just pitied me for how hard I was trying. Either way, I was happy that he didn't laugh and that he listened. All I can do is keep telling him the truth, and maybe someday I'll get to hear my brother say that he too is a believer. It is not easy, but I am commanded to share this truth, and that day in the car with my brother, I just had to tell him.

Chanelle Davis, 17, Houghton Christian Academy, Cuba, NY

Jesus, I don't want to ever give up on
telling people about You no matter how
many times they laugh at me.

since we were born

Greater love has no one than this,
that he lay down his life for his friends.

JOHN 15:13

When my mom was pregnant with me, she and my dad befriended another couple that was also going to have a baby. Our families became really good friends, and I was born about a month before their baby, Calista. So Calista and I have literally been friends since we were born, and as we grew up, we played together much of the time. When we were around five years old, Calista and her parents went to Cameroon to be missionaries. I was young, so I didn't really understand why my best friend in the entire world was leaving. Calista's family visited us every summer, allowing Calista and me time hang out and become best friends all over again. Her family moved to Guatemala and then to Oaxaca, Mexico, as missionaries over the next twelve years. Recently I found out that they were moving back to Tennessee, and I was ecstatic. We've been through a whole lot of life together, and I am thankful for such a precious friend. I know that our friendship is one to hold on to because it has already endured so much change. I want to keep learning what it means to be a real friend, the kind that Christ is to us.

Bethany Musgrove, 17, home school, Hermitage, TN

Father, thank You for my friends.
They are such an amazing gift,
and I don't know what I would do without them.

a trip i will not forget

Delight yourself in the LORD, and he will give you the desires of your heart.

PSALM 37:4

I recently had the opportunity to visit New York, New York. Before the trip, I did not know how I was going to pay for it because my parents were struggling financially at the time, and although I had a job, I had not saved enough to cover the whole trip. If I did not find a way to get enough money, I knew I would have to be okay with not going. The man in charge of the trip asked me if I was still interested in going. I told him I was, but that I did not have the required money. He told me he would talk with my parents to work something out. I knew my parents would not be able to contribute much, so I did not really get my hopes up. To my surprise, the next day, my mama told me the trip was paid for. The only thing I had to pay for was spending money! The experience in New York was truly a blessing for me, and it just reminded me of how good God is.

Jazma Parker, 16, Martin Luther King Magnet School, Nashville, TN

Even when I think something is impossible,
You always find a way. Thank You,
Jesus, for proving me wrong sometimes.

mirrors of Jesus

Let your gentleness be evident to all.

PHILIPPIANS 4:5

We are called to be gentle, compassionate, and tender people. As we interact with our friends and family, this must be at the forefront of our minds. It's easy for me to say harsh words when my friend gets on my nerves or to lash out at my brother who is being annoying, but I can't get rid of the feeling that this callousness and anger is not what God has called us to. As Christians, we are watched closely by the world, and everything we do is a reflection of Christ. Sometimes my actions and attitudes surely do not represent a true picture of God to others. I have seen in the Bible that God is compassionate, merciful, and gentle, and Jesus embodied these traits while on earth. Hundreds of people came just to hear Him speak; He had compassion on them and healed many. Christ wasn't obligated to show gentleness, but He did. As an ambassador for Christ, am I presenting the Gospel as Jesus lived it? Do my words convey God's love or are they harsh, biting, and sarcastic? These are important questions to ask because the only Jesus some people know is the Jesus that they see in me and you.

Jessica Runk, 19, Patrick Henry College, Purcellville, VA

Jesus, I must remember that people get to know You through me. That's a big responsibility for me to have, and I want to make You proud. Amen.

defined by whom?

Your beauty should not come from outward adornment....
Instead is should be that of your inner self...
which is of great worth in God's sight.

1 Peter 3:3–4

Who really came up with the definition of "beauty" anyway? Was it in some magazine? Was it in a book? Was it just established by culture, over time? If it's from a magazine, it would be constantly changing with the latest fad and style. If it's from a book, it would differ depending on the author's opinion, background, and experience. If it's established by culture, then you have to pick which culture has it right because in some cultures it is beautiful to be plump and in others it is beautiful to be slender. There are so many ideas floating around of what true beauty is. Some people think that a well-rounded woman is the most beautiful of all. Some think that women that have almost no body fat are the true knockouts. Some like women with flat heads or women with feet that are threes inches long. The worldly definition of beauty has many angles and perspectives. But God's definition of beauty is completely different. It really has nothing to do with appearance, and everything to do with the heart. So many of us compare ourselves to super models or actresses that we see all around us, but we forget the alternate standard set by our God. When Christ becomes the center of our lives, His kind of beauty, true beauty, will shine through us with a radiance that is undeniable. So the next time you catch yourself looking at your "disgusting hair" or your "humongous thighs," STOP. Turn away from the mirror and look to God to find what true beauty is.

Annie Nickel, 17, Nebraska Christian High School, Cairo, NE

Lord, I want You to be my mirror. Because when
I see myself in You, I'll see a person I like.

closer still

"My grace is sufficient for you,
for my power is made perfect in weakness."

2 CORINTHIANS 12:9

Many nights I come home and I cry myself to sleep. I am so confused and frustrated! God has been silent in my life for a long time now, and I am longing to meet with Him again. I don't understand. Doesn't God want me to grow closer to Him? Why do I feel so far away from Him? I struggle with motivation to actually spend time in His Word, and I wonder if he does not want to listen. I struggle with depression every day because it seems like His truth applies to everyone but me. Recently I read a verse in Isaiah that says God will quench the dry ground. Right now I am the dry ground. I am that dry ground that will one day be given water. I believe God has put this time in my life to draw me closer to Him. I believe this because Christ has said so, and so I must hold on to that truth! Perhaps God is whispering so quietly because He wants me to come closer to hear what He is saying. And when I finally hear Him, I will be much closer to Him than I ever was before. And so I will continue to come closer to God, until I hear his whisperings of Truth and of Love.

Hailey Howerton, 16, home school, Greenville, SC

Thank You, dear Lord, for taking away
my emptiness and filling me up with Your love!

dare to be disciplined

For God is not a God of disorder but of peace.

1 CORINTHIANS 14:33

Do you ever have the feeling there is so much to do that you don't know where to start—and to make matters worse, you are totally disorganized? Is your room so messy you don't even want to enter it? I know the feeling. You may not be one of those people that goes around cleaning and organizing, (I know I'm not!), but we all desire the peace that comes with organization. We have been taught to be disciplined. *Discipline*—yes, that is a nasty word that involves so many things we hate to do, like exercising, doing our school work, keeping a room clean, or getting our laundry in order. But have you ever watched the Olympics? It is absolutely incredible to see how the swimmers, gymnasts, and sprinters perform. And their performance is all a result of disciplined practice and day-by-day work. We as Christians can be like those athletes in the spiritual sense. By reading the Bible daily and being fed spiritually by other means (like this book), we can become spiritual studs. This sort of spiritual discipline is obvious, but if we want to please God, we must also try to be disciplined in other areas of our lives. Our rooms and time management are a reflection of our spiritual lives. Being responsible and disciplined shows care and respect for the life God has given us. Our God is not a God of disorder and chaos, but of order, reason, and discipline. If we are to be imitators of God, we must follow Him. And following Him will lead to pleasant results, for who doesn't want a more peaceful and less stressful life?

Caroline J. Hornok, 15, Veritas Academy, Texarkana, TX

So often I think I don't have time for You, Lord,
because I'm so stressed. Help me to remember that
making time for You gets rid of my stress.

chocolate and jelly beans

"He is not here; he has risen, just as he said. Come and see the place where he lay."

MATTHEW 28:5–6

When I was a little girl I received chocolate and jelly beans for Easter. I remember bubbling with excitement as I ran into the kitchen on Easter Sunday to see what the Easter bunny had left on the counter. When I got a little older, I wondered why I didn't get that excited about the true gift of Easter. Jesus' Resurrection is the most amazing story in the Bible. Our risen Savior triumphed over sin and death in order to bring us broken and hurting people to life, hope, purpose, and joy. *That is something to celebrate!* Had Christ not risen from the grave, His sacrifice would have been meaningless and we would still be caught in the entangling grip of sin. That makes the Resurrection story the best, most incredible story ever. My question is, *Do we allow this story to shape and affect our lives?*

Jessica Runk, 19, Patrick Henry College, Purcellville, VA

Jesus, I want to get excited about what
You've done for me, more excited than
I've ever been about anything else!

Easter every day

But because of his great love for us, God,
who is rich in mercy, made us alive with
Christ even when we were dead in transgressions—
it is by grace you have been saved.

EPHESIANS 2:4–5

We have all heard the Easter story, how Jesus laid his life down for us on Good Friday and rose on Easter Sunday. But do we really take time to think about it? For me, Easter is the day we dress up especially nice. We go to church. We see people we haven't seen. We usually have a big lunch afterwards. And sometimes we even have an Easter egg hunt. I usually think about what I am going to wear and who I will see, and I end up missing the whole point. And the point that I am missing is *Jesus Christ.* Without Jesus, we would not be celebrating. Without His humanity, His life, His death, there would be no such thing as Easter. Without Him there would be no opportunity to be forgiven. Without Him there would be no hope of Heaven. Without Him there would be no such thing as a Christian. We celebrate Easter because Jesus' resurrection gives us power to live, to change, to love, to be forgiven, to be hopeful, and to be fulfilled. Wow! When I think about it, I realize that Easter is not something to be celebrated once a year. I want to remember *who* and what this day stands for every day of my life!

Candace K. Croston, 16, King's Fork High School, Suffolk, VA

You died for me! What an amazing gift!
I never want to take it for granted.

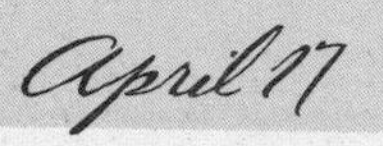

who's your mama?

This is what the LORD says—he who made you, who formed you in the womb.

ISAIAH 44:2

Who's your mama?" is one question I cannot biologically answer. I have never even seen my mother. When she was fourteen, my mother went to her doctor for a physical and found out she was pregnant. The time for legal abortions had passed, so her only options were to keep me or give me up for adoption. She chose adoption. The same doctor had another patient who had always wanted a girl, and this man soon became my father. The papers were drawn up, and everything was ready for me to be born. Finally that day came, and as soon as I left the womb, I was taken from my mother. She never saw or held me. I was washed up, made presentable, and brought to the room where my new adopted family was waiting for me. I have lived with them for all my life, and this is my favorite story. I love it because it is one of the biggest things that make me unique and because it shows me how in control my God is. Not only did He create me, just as I am, he also made every detail work out between a fourteen-year-old girl and the people who would become my family. I am a part of the family that is perfect for me, in so many ways. The last reason I love this story so much is because through my new family, I learned what it means to be a part of God's family.

Wendi Ferguson, 17, Metro Christian Academy, Madison, TN

It is awesome how You have my life perfectly planned out. I am so thankful I know the God who knows everything.

gaining an identity (part 1)

For God so loved the world
that He gave His one and only Son.

JOHN 3:16

At my father's house, I had to deal with a lot of verbal abuse throughout my childhood. I vividly recall both my father and my stepmother telling me that I was stupid, lazy, worthless, ugly, fat, and so on. After a while I began to listen to their insults and believe that they were true. My thought life consisted of self-abuse. I hated me and everything about me. When I was fourteen, my mom became very concerned because I kept getting more and more depressed. She took me to a Christian counselor who talked with me about my identity in Christ. During one session, the counselor said, "I'm selling you my car, and you offer to pay me $15,000 for it. How much is the car worth to you?" I responded, "$15,000." He said, "No one pays more for something than it's worth. What did God pay for you?" I said, "Christ." Then he said the words that have completely changed how I view myself. He said, "Then in God's eyes, you are worth Christ." I am worth Christ because God paid His Son for me (Romans 5:8). God also paid the same price for you. "For God so loved the world that He gave His one and only Son." My dear sisters, we are worth Christ to God!

Wendy McCain, 17, Grace Academy, Asheville, NC

Jesus, You were willing to give Your life for mine.
It's hard to believe I'm worth that much to You...
but I am so thankful that I am.

freedom (part 2)

It is for freedom that Christ has set us free.
Stand firm, then, and do not let yourselves be
burdened again by a yoke of slavery.

GALATIANS 5:1

My counselor helped me to find my identity in Christ, and this brought incredible freedom in my life. For me, freedom in Christ means letting go of the negative memories and harmful experiences of the past and refocusing my thoughts on Jesus and His truths. I used to struggle with bulimia because, if you remember, I hated everything about myself, including how I looked. One night when I was having a particularly difficult time, God reminded me that I am His child, that He is the King. It hit me that a princess does not spend her evenings with her head over a toilet, making herself throw up her dinner. For so long I had thought so poorly of myself that I had to relearn who I was to God. I had to "take every thought captive to the obedience of Christ" (2 Corinthians 10:5). Look in the Bible and discover the truths about who you are to God for yourself (John 1:12; John 15:15; Romans 8:1–2; Romans 8:35–39; 1 Corinthians 3:16; Ephesians 3:12). By reaffirming these truths in our minds, our lives begin to change and the power of Christ becomes more evident in our lives. Seek out who you are in Christ and you will soon know freedom and show your true identity.

Wendy McCain, 17, Grace Academy, Asheville, NC

Father, I want to know who I am in You.
Only when I know that will I be the best person I can be.

why?

"For I know the plans I have for you," declares the L*ORD*, *"plans to prosper you and not to harm you, plans to give you hope and a future."*

JEREMIAH 29:11

One day changed my entire life. It was the day my mom passed away. She was thirty-six years old and had cancer. It hurt to watch her suffer for all those years, and it still hurts today. My mom and I were best friends. When she took that final breath, I knew it was her time to go. But after she died, I was mad at the world because I didn't know WHY God had done this. I still don't really understand it all, but I now believe that God needed her in heaven. He is taking care of her, and she doesn't have to suffer any more. More than anything, this experience has made me realize that God IS in control and that with Him, I really can get through anything. Those are not just cliché words to me anymore. I believe them because I have lived them.

Erika Blackmon, 16, Nebraska Christian High School, Central City, NE

God, help me to accept the things I can't understand and to trust that You know what You're doing.

heroes of the faith

"Have faith in the LORD your God and you will be upheld; have faith in his prophets and you will be successful."

2 CHRONICLES 20:20

Do you ever wonder where the modern-day Pauls, Ruths and Martin Luthers are? When you accepted Christ, did you want to face the persecutions that Paul did or have faith like Esther? When I became a Christian, I never intended to be a "hero of the faith." I think most of us want to live a Christian life that is safe and predictable. We don't really ask for a faith that throws us out of our comfort zones or gives us an opportunity to risk our lives to obey God. I wonder why we don't ask if we could be the Ruth of our generation, who gave up all she knew and loved and traveled to a foreign land. Perhaps we don't even think in these terms because we don't have a wide enough scope for God. If God is merely the guy who gets us to heaven, but is pretty confining and grumpy along the way, then He's not worth risking comfort and security for. But what if we came to know God as unpredictable, wild, and untamable? Would we be willing to surrender our entire lives, to take risks, and to struggle through many obstacles for this kind of God? I think our God is a bit more ferocious than we think, and that He is waiting for us to trust Him, to want to experience some of His power. Maybe when we begin to understand that He is far greater, bigger, more powerful, and more worthy than we ever knew, we will find ourselves becoming the heroes of the faith in our generation.

Mary Kaylin Staub, 16, Heritage Academy, Flowery Branch, GA

Give me the faith that will be remembered throughout history, Lord, not for my own glory but for Yours.

an insane schedule

Remember how short my time is.

PSALM 89:47 (KJV)

I am seventeen years old. I have a full school schedule, I work forty or more hours a week, and I try to keep a normal, healthy social life. I definitely know what it means to be busy. Sleep is something that I barely do. Typically, I wake up around seven, get dressed, and rush to school by seven forty-five. I sometimes sleep through a lot of my classes, probably out of a mix of tiredness and boredom. School ends at two forty-five, and then I rush to get to Chick-fil-A so I can be ready to clock in at three-thirty. My shift lasts until ten thirty at night, and I get a thirty-minute break for dinner. After work, I get home as soon as possible so that I can start on my homework. The biggest challenge now is to stay awake while reading my physics or American government book. Finally, I will shower and go to sleep at about two or three in the morning. The next day, the process repeats. The only way I have found to survive this somewhat insane schedule is to be laid back and cheery in the midst of it. Life is short, and it is a waste to stress over the little stuff. When you start getting overwhelmed, relax and remember that Someone bigger and wiser than you is the one who is in control!

Wendi Ferguson, 17, Metro Christian Academy, Madison, TN

Life is just too much sometimes.
Thank goodness I have You, Lord, to carry
me through when I'm too tired to keep going.

run to win

Do you not know that in a race all the runners run, but only one gets the prize? Run in such a way as to get the prize.

1 CORINTHIANS 9:24

I knew I would regret it if I didn't play basketball this year, because it's my senior year of high school. It feels like this is my last year to really enjoy life without a lot of the responsibilities of adulthood. So I decided to play. I came to basketball practice excited and ready to start the season, only practice was not very pleasant. Basketball means running and sprinting, and I was out of shape! In the middle of running wind sprints, I had to rush out the gym door to...well...puke. To play a sport well you have to be determined and dedicated to practice. To play basketball, you must be able to run, and run hard. You have to push your body, and when you feel your legs cannot take another stride, your mind has to tell them they must. Following Christ is a lot like this. Paul writes of running a race and of striving to reach the goal. And our race is not a one-hundred-yard dash. It is a marathon. We must keep our eyes on the prize as we run. And like basketball practice, it will be hard. We are running towards the hope of heaven, and that is an incredible race to be in. So let's train hard and run to win!

Rebecca Wilson, 18, Maranatha Christian Academy, Oakwood, GA

I want to win this race, Lord. I want to be in heaven with You. Please keep me on track to cross the finish line.

stuck in the middle

Blessed are the peacemakers,
for they will be called sons of God.
MATTHEW 5:9

Have you ever been caught in the middle of friends or family members who are fighting? I have. So many times one friend will be mad at another and I will get caught in the middle, trying to make peace, trying to comfort, or even trying to separate. It is not easy being the one everyone goes to with their problems. I've finally learned that I don't have to solve everyone's problems. It is impossible, and I start feeling bad about myself because I am not perfect and I can't solve everything. But no one is perfect, except God. And God is the only who can change hearts and situations. "Blessed are the peacemakers" doesn't mean we have to make peace all the time. It means we need to not create chaos and strife. We need to give our problems to God for Him to solve, because He is greater than every problem we have. So, if you are caught between your friends, step back, give them to God, and be at peace.

Stephanie Warner, 14, Walnut Grove Christian Preparatory School, Carmel, IN

God, thank You for the peace You can give me.
Help me to seek it for myself and share it with others.

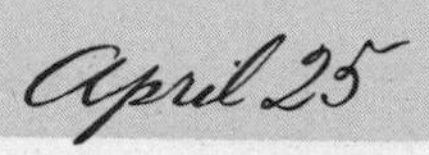

roller coasters, funnel cakes...and God

They ate and drank with great joy
in the presence of the LORD that day.

1 CHRONICLES 29:22

So many days I feel like I'm putting on a show, just going through the motions. So I'm thankful for days when I can really just enjoy life and be myself—like the day I went to the fair with my friend. It was a school day, so I wasn't sure if my mom would let me go. And my friend's family was staying out late, so they suggested that I ask to spend the night at their house. So I'm thinking that it is a school night and there's NO WAY my parents will let me spend the night at a friend's house. I really didn't want to call and ask, but I did and THEY SAID YES!! The fair was so much fun. We screamed on pretty much every ride. After that we came up with cheesy, funny pickup lines with the good-looking guy serving funnel cake. It was pretty late by then, so we thought everything anyone said was funny. I think that laughing and enjoying friends is part of what life is really about. In life, I so often feel like I'm acting on a stage. It is days like this one that remind me what matters in life is loving God and loving other people in a real and sincere way.

Calista Turner, 17, Donelson Christian Academy, Nashville, TN

Father, I want to thank You for those days
when everything just seems to go right,
when I'm happy and relaxed and I can just enjoy
all You have given me. Amen.

out of control? (Part 1)

Israel, return unto the LORD *thy God;*
for thou hast fallen by thine iniquity.

HOSEA 14:1 (KJV)

Lots of teenage girls have been in the same places I've been, and the only difference is, I got out of the situation. My grandmother raised my four siblings and me in Queens, New York. I was the middle child, and everyone said I was spoiled. Whenever I saw my siblings with something, I had to have it, and most of the time, I got it. For instance, both my older siblings joined the track team at our school, and I wanted to join. When I got on the team, I was better than my sibings, so they eventually quit. I excelled in track, indoor, outdoor, and cross-country. I traveled the country, went as far north as Toronto, Canada, as far west as Portland, Oregon, and as far south as Miami, Florida, and many stops between. This period of time lasted from elementary school until high school. Pretty soon after junior high school, I started hanging out with the wrong crowd. My older sister and brother were sent away to live with my father, so now I really had no guidance. It started small and simple. I was hanging out late. It didn't seem like a big deal because everyone else was doing it too. But very quickly, it got out of control. Have you ever been there? That place where you know you need help, but you can't stop the foolishness to get it? Thankfully, God was there all the time, and He didn't let me spin totally out of control. He got my attention, and He wants yours too.

Lissete Russell, 19, Redemption Christian Academy, Troy, NY

Father, sometimes it takes a whole lot to get my attention.
Thank You for trying so hard to reach me,
even when I just refuse to listen.

just one unruly teenager (part 2)

For they that are after the flesh do
mind the things of the flesh, but they
that are after the Spirit the things of the Spirit.

ROMANS 8:5 (KJV)

After a while, I spent more time on the streets. I stayed out really late; I was belligerent, involved with gangs, and just didn't care much about anything. By this time, I had quit the track team. I was really good at it, but I just dropped it one day because I felt like it was in the way. The people that I considered to be my friends at the time seemed to feel that I was doing the right thing. I guess I just wanted to fit in anywhere, as long as someone liked me. The kids I was hanging out with were from the neighborhood, most lived on my block. Whenever we hung out, we would try to be around the older kids. At this time, the older kids were selling drugs and were always involved with the law. My grandmother was getting sick, so it was real hard to keep up with all of us. I was the oldest in the house, and I remember hating having to do things with my younger brothers. Instead, I stayed out all the time. I often didn't come home from school until very late at night. My grandmother began to not trust me. When she started going in and out of the hospital, she would always call a family member to come over and watch us. While all of this was going on, God was working on me in ways I didn't see at the time. He had a plan for my life to benefit my future. He does not waste anything...not even one unruly teenager, if we allow Him room to work His perfect will in us.

Lissete Russell, 19, Redemption Christian Academy, Troy, NY

God, I'm so thankful that You can make
my mistakes into blessings. I don't want to mess up,
but I'm glad that when I do, You can make it right.

blessings and tragedies (part 3)

And we know that all things work together for good to them that love God, to them who are the called according to his purpose.

ROMANS 8:28 (KJV)

I ended up moving in with my mother, and I gave her a really tough time. By then, I was smoking, selling drugs, drinking, sexually active, and involved with gangs. Nothing could really harness me at this point. It seemed like I was allergic to school. I just stopped attending. I had gotten arrested at the age of sixteen for assault. A few months later, I was arrested twice within the same week. During all this commotion, the only thing that kept me focused was playing basketball. I started playing basketball in junior high but only for recreation. When I moved to Manhattan with my mom, I joined a team in Harlem. Even though it was a thirty minute commute to practice and games, I loved it! Ironically I was actually playing with a Christian team. The coach of the team became a true inspiration to me. Him and his wife were the people I talked to about any and everything. They knew all about the problems I was going through, and they also knew that the only resolution to my problems was Jesus Christ. I was introduced to Jesus in early February 2005. I was saved in March and baptized by April. I don't regret my past. It took a plethora of blessings and tragedies to get me to where I am now. Sometimes I just wonder where I would be if I had continued with track. And I wonder if I would even have met the Lord?

Lissete Russell, 19, Redemption Christian Academy, Troy, NY

Everything that happens, everything that I do can bring me closer to You, Father. That is so incredible! Nothing is out of Your control!

the outsider

A man of many companions may come to ruin,
but there is a friend who sticks closer than a brother.

PROVERBS 18:24

When I was seven, my brother and I went to live with my aunt and uncle. It was emotional leaving my dad, but living with my aunt and uncle didn't feel odd because they happily took us in. My aunt was a teacher in a small private Christian school when I came, so instead of going to public school like I was used to doing, I went to the private school she taught at. I became friends with four girls in particular during this time, but I found it hard to fit in because they had known each other for a long time. By the time I was a teenager, I felt even more like an outsider, even though I was told repeatedly that I was nowhere near that. But I'm the only one who hasn't grown up with my parents, and I probably had the hardest background as a kid, so it can be easy for me to feel left out. But I don't let that depress me. I have realized recently that the differences between my friends and me do not have to be a problem. With God's help, what makes me different from my friends doesn't have to hold me back.

Virginia MacKinnon, 15, Jonathan Edwards Academy, Turners Falls, MA

Sometimes I think no one understands me...
that I'm all alone. But thanks to You, Jesus, I never am.

i want to be free

Pay attention to my wisdom; listen carefully to my wise counsel. Then you will learn to be discreet and will store up knowledge. For the L*ORD* *sees clearly what a man does, examining every path he takes. An evil man is held captive by his own sins; they are ropes that catch and hold him.*

PROVERBS 5:1, 21–22 (NLT)

Be still and know that I am God.
Be still and know that I am God.
Be still and know that I am God.
In Thee, O Lord, I put my trust.
In Thee, O Lord, I put my trust.
In Thee, O Lord, I put my trust.

Composer Unknown

a new definition of purity

For man looketh on the outward appearance,
but the LORD looketh on the heart.

1 SAMUEL 16:7 (KJV)

When I hear the word *purity*, I think of sexual purity. In the Christian world that is the kind of purity that is most often talked about. In the general culture, the word *purity* seems sort of old-fashioned and not relevant. But both in church and in secular society, there is not much emphasis on spiritual or mental purity. I think that this sort of purity, the kind that you cannot necessarily see or label outright, is really important. This kind of purity might mean not looking at, listening to, or reading things that would draw us away from God or take our emotions and minds to places that are not healthy. At times, I choose to avoid reading books or magazines that are probably fascinating, but that I know contain impure things. I try to remember that God sees my heart and that I want my thoughts and emotions to be worthy of Him.

Rebecca White, 16, Walnut Grove Christian Preparatory School, Zionsville, IN

Sometimes my thoughts wander
so far from You. Lord, I pray that what
I think and feel will pleasing to You.

time for everything?

There is a time for everything,
and a season for every activity under heaven.
ECCLESIASTES 3:1

This is my first year of high school, and I want to do everything—all of the after-school activities such as basketball and even watching football and volleyball. My problem, however, is that I still want to do all of the activities that I did before school started, such as Irish Dance. When I joined the basketball team for the school, the schedule worked so I could keep doing all the activities I wanted. Then the schedule for dance changed, and I ended up having to drop piano to give more time for homework, sleep, and my family. But that still left the dance and basketball issue. Dance has been my life for eleven years. I couldn't drop that from my busy schedule too. And what about basketball? It's the first time I've really participated with a team. The feeling of knowing that someone will always try to be there if I need them is wonderful. I'm having fun with a lot of my friends. I really didn't want to drop basketball either. So I started praying: God, thank you for the ability to do dance and basketball, but what am I going to do about next year? Then it came to me: *nothing*. If I am suppose to do both basketball and dance next year, then God will make a way for me to do that. I just have to wait until God's plan unfolds.

Keegan Nitz, 15, St. Ambrose Christian High School, Meridian, ID

God, thank You for giving me so many opportunities,
so many things to enjoy. Just, please,
help me juggle them all! Amen.

completely satisfied

What I have said, that I will bring about;
what I have planned, that I will do.

ISAIAH 46:11

A couple years ago, I got a letter about how God wants us to be completely satisfied with Him before we are satisfied with anyone here on earth. The letter really spoke to me, and I have treasured it for a long time. God, to me, says He doesn't want me to even think about dating until I am satisfied and content with being loved by Him alone, knowing that only in Him can I be satisfied. Then God will give me the perfect human relationship that He has planned for me. When I'm ready, I know God will give me Mr. Right, who he is preparing for me at this very moment. Until we are both satisfied exclusively with God and the life He has prepared for us, we will not be ready to love each other the way we should. God wants us to stop wishing, stop looking for love in different areas. Just trust in Him and be satisfied. It can be incredibly hard at times when it seems everyone has a boyfriend except you. But I know if you focus on Christ and are completely satisfied with Him, it will be worth the wait. He is God. Believe in it and be *satisfied.*

Danae Downs, 15, home school, Grand Junction, CO

Lord, You are the One, the only One,
who can bring real satisfaction to my life.
Thank You that You teach me how to trust You completely.
Amen.

what God sees

The king's daughter is all glorious within.

PSALM 45:13 (KJV)

We all want to be beautiful, and I think that we were born with that desire. We all want to excel and to be the best, prettiest, and most wanted. And it is so easy to let those desires take over our lives. When we look in the mirror, we look to see if we look good enough, and if we don't, we'll pretty much change or do whatever is necessary until we reach our supposed state of perfection. However, I have been realizing that living simply to please my mirror is such an empty way to spend all my life! The world esteems beauty as the most important thing, but that kind of perfect beauty can never be reached. Even popular, rich actresses and supermodels are not happy with their lives and bodies. The Bible offers an alternative because God sees beauty in the good things we do. Through the Creator's eyes, what we call "beauty" is worthless because God looks through a different set of lenses than we do. When we are willing to look through His lenses, we'll find beauty in ourselves in a different way.

Hannah Reeves, 14, home school, Central, SC

Perfection isn't possible except in You, Jesus.
Help me to remember that today…and every day.

is pride okay?

But, "Let him who boasts boast in the LORD."

2 CORINTHIANS 10:17

One summer I had the pleasure of hitting the winning runs in the Junior Olympic Class C Softball State Tournament, helping my team advance to the championship game. I celebrated my hit and the victory with the rest of my team. We knew that we had accomplished a huge goal, but also that we still needed to focus on the next game. I realized that it was natural and good to be overjoyed that we won the game and that I had helped us do it. For the first time, I comprehended the difference between being cocky and arrogant and having a healthy, godly attitude about our achievements. If I had claimed to be the best player on the team or said I deserved all of the credit, then I would have been bragging. But as it was, I knew that there was no way I could have done it without the help of God and my teammates. We definitely wouldn't have made it to the championship game if we hadn't played together. I saw that it is possible be humble, while at the same time enjoying what you are good at and celebrating what you have done well. For me it has been a lesson in humility and gratitude triumphing over my arrogance and pride.

Ashley Stone, 18, Nebraska Christian High School, Central City, NE

Lord, I can't help wanting to win.
But I want to remember that when I win,
the glory is Yours, not mine.

for eternity

"Enter through the narrow gate. For wide is the gate and broad is the road that leads to destruction, and many enter through it. But small is the gate and narrow the road that leads to life, and only a few find it."

MATTHEW 7:13–14

As Christians, we are told to follow the "narrow way," but I don't think that's as easy as it sounds. It requires living differently than most of the world around us, and that isn't always comfortable. Along the narrow way, we have the promise of abundant, neverending life, but that still doesn't make it easier when faced with a decision to choose what is right but not popular. If we think about the narrow road as the same way that Jesus walked when he chose to die, so that we could be alive, it is a bit easier. Jesus walked this same road for years, and we are following Him. Yes, it is harder, but it is also so very worth it.

Hannah Reeves, 14, home school, Central, SC

Being a Christian isn't easy. I know You know that, Jesus. Please make me proud that I've chosen the harder road because it leads me to a better place.

journey into the unknown

You will keep in perfect peace him whose mind
is steadfast, because he trusts in you.

ISAIAH 26:3

Dreaming of adventure,
Venturing into the unknown where many do not survive.
Strength and wisdom are essential,
Friendship is a must,
And without bravery you are lost.
Stand strong,
For you are not alone in your journey into the unknown.
Struggling, fighting, going forward,
The explorers of the world must stick together.
The differences that enable our power are unseen,
 but lived.
Be strong my fellow travelers,
You are not alone.

Rachel Crane, 14, home school, Lewisburg, TN

You are with me, Lord. Every minute. Every day.
That's pretty amazing when I think about it.
Thanks to You I am never, ever alone.

sibling rivalry

Love is patient, love is kind.
It does not envy.

1 CORINTHIANS 13:4

That verse is easier said than done. My sister and I are very close, and I would hate for anything to separate us. I know that my sister is more popular at school than I am, and it's hard not to get jealous of that. I sometimes think of the story in the Bible where Joseph's brother's were so jealous of him that they sold him into slavery. I don't want to ever let my jealousy get that out of hand, but I know that if I ignore this feeling, it will only get worse, so instead of avoiding it, I am trying to solve it. My sister is my family, a part of me, and I do NOT want jealousy to come in between us. So, I have been talking to my sister about it, and she has been really kind. I have also been talking to God, which helps a lot!

Kristen Isaac, 14, Covenant Christian Academy, La Union, NM

I don't want to let my problems grow, Lord.
I want You to help me solve them. Please teach me
to go to You first when I'm having trouble with something.

living with your best friends

How good and pleasant it is
when brothers live together in unity!

PSALM 133:1

Do you ever wish you lived with your best friends? Why not make those you live with your best friends? It is possible to love your siblings, but it will take effort. One way to think of relationships is like a bank account. If you are constantly giving to another person, you will have a relatively "full" account. Likewise, the account of someone always criticizing would come up quite overdrawn. Can you see how this could cause a problem? Do special things for your family. If their coat is on the floor, don't yell at them. Pick it up for them. It's a pretty amazing thing to try, because after investing in their lives, we treasure and love them more. Criticism creates withdrawal. So resist the temptation to tear others apart and instead praise them. Praise them when they're diligent. Set out to invest in your siblings! This isn't natural or automatic and will not be easy, but through our Lord, we are more than conquerors and can harmonize with our siblings!

Carrie Lewis, 14, home school with tutorial, Clemson, SC

God, today I want to work hard
to show my family members I love them.
Please show me ways I can do this.

real beauty

Your beauty should not come
from outward adornment, such as braided hair
and the wearing of gold jewelry and fine clothes.

1 PETER 3:3

Society has lied to you! They've successfully convinced you that beauty lies in your outward appearance. According to their standards, your worth doesn't lie in a sweet personality, a giving spirit, or a loving heart. Instead, they tell girls having perfect bodies, makeup, jewelry, and clothes is the only way to become popular and fulfilled. They tell you looking good is all that matters, which is a flat-out lie! You are truly beautiful, no matter what you see in the mirror. I know, I know, you've probably heard the phrase, "It's what's on the inside that counts" a million times, and figure that's where I'm headed. Okay, so you caught me. It really *is* what's on the inside that counts. But what that phrase *doesn't* tell you is *what* makes you so beautiful inside. If you are a child of God, He has washed you clean inside, making you a new creation. If the creator of the universe thinks you're beautiful, what else can you ask for? So the next time you look in the mirror and decide you don't look enough like the model you saw in *Seventeen*, pick up your Bible, and see what God has to say about you!

Amy McKoy, 18, Bryan College, Dayton, TN

When I'm getting dressed or putting on my makeup, remind me that You are what makes me beautiful, Lord. Thank You for being my God and erasing my flaws.

pop off the page

"If you hold to my teaching,
you are really my disciples."

JOHN 8:31

When I was younger, I never really had a desire to read the Bible and I didn't see the point. After I decided to give my life to Christ, I tried to read the whole Bible in one year. As I read I began to enjoy it and would even forget how long I had been reading! If you read about three chapters each day, you should be able to read the whole thing in a year. When I read, if a verse seems to "pop off the page," I write it down. This is a good way to bring Scripture more into your everyday life. After you write it down, look for why God showed that specific verse to you. Often, it will be something that you have been wondering about for a long time. I've always had a problem with arguing with adults and saying things that are out of place, before I am asked. I also have wanted to learn to sit up strait, walk gracefully, and other "proper" things. For a long time, no matter how hard I tried I just couldn't succeed. Then the other day, I got the answer from Proverbs 4:9. It says that when you listen to the instructions of your authorities, wisdom "will place on your head a garland of grace; She will present you with a crown of beauty."

Bethany Pearl Reeves, 15, home school, Central, SC

I want to know that Your Word
is so important, Lord. I want to desire
to read it, rather than feeling like it is a chore.

spiritual warfare

He gave them power and authority
to drive out all demons.

LUKE 9:1

My father is a pastor. But I see him as more than that. He is also a warrior, fighting for people who are under spiritual attack from Satan. My father teaches me that to be a Christian is to be a warrior for Christ. There is a constant battle between good and evil. The evil spirits, the demons, are under the authority of Satan, the deceiver. They are our opponents in this war, but we have a big advantage over them. We are all warriors of Christ, who gives us the power over demons, through Him. If we trust and obey Christ, we have victory over them. Christ is so much more powerful than the demons, so they fear Him. And when we speak with the authority of Christ, they fear us. One day my father had to meet with a woman who was under spiritual attack. He wondered how would he confront this situation. A sudden wave of fear washed over him. But a thought other than fear also occurred to him: Could the spirits be more intimidated by him than he was by them? Then he knew he didn't have to fear. He remembered that Christ was with him, and he confidently confronted his opponents in Jesus' name.

Stephanie Warner, 14, Walnut Grove Christian Preparatory School, Carmel, IN

Lord, I need You to help me
put on the full armor of God so I will
be able to fight for You. Amen.

May 13

the next step

The steps of the godly are directed by the LORD. He delights in every detail of their lives.

PSALM 37:23 (NLT)

For me, figuring out the steps after high school seemed like camping in an unknown forest alone—and I am *not* an out-of-doors kind of girl, and the idea of "roughing it" does *not* appeal to me. In other words I felt really lonely, lost, and unsure of any decision I quickly needed to make. All the rest of my friends knew they were going to *this* school and studying *that* subject to obtain a career in this or that. I tried to think of all those things too, while also praying to God to direct my steps, but He remained silent! I had no idea what the next steps were, although all the pressure seemed to continue to pile up. Finally I gave up thinking about the answers to all the questions and began to listen to my heart. Although I am passionate about many things, there are a few particular things that I especially like. These things make me feel alive and enthusiastic about loving God more and living life more fully. My heart feels as if it were about to burst at any moment! Thinking about my passions in life gave me guidance to make my choice. God didn't send a huge sign. Instead, He whispered to me that I should follow my heart—and thankfully I was listening.

Audrey Foster, 19, Hanover College, Fishers, IN

God, I want to be able to hear Your voice.
Teach me to really listen, so that Your words can guide me.

love conquers all

Hatred stirs up dissension,
but love covers over all wrongs.

PROVERBS 10:12

For years I have had problems with my mother. I used to write terrible things about her in my journals, things that now I severely regret and have a hard time forgiving myself for. Then one day she read those things and confronted me about them with rivers of tears flowing down her face. I had broken her heart. I had done the one thing that no child should do to a parent who loves her as much as mine does: I had kept horrific accusations and lies about her to myself and had grown to dislike her, but I had never asked her about those things or confronted her. These have been three of the most heartbreaking and painful years of my life; but one thing has not changed between her and me, even though we've had some pretty harsh words with each other: We never stopped loving each other—and with God's blessing we never will. I know for a fact that my mother loves me more than her own life; she's said that more than a hundred times. But until now, I've never actually taken those few words to heart. Ever since she read my journals we've had a better connection. Love covers all our sins. And I am very thankful that my mother's love for me—and my love for her—is more powerful than the terrible things I wrote about her.

Pamela K. Locke, 15, Walnut Grove Christian Preparatory School, Noblesville, IN

Your love is amazing, Lord!
It is so strong, so unstoppable that nothing
I can do will drive You away!

May 15

anger

For man's anger does not bring
about the righteous life that God desires.

JAMES 1:20

Of all the emotions, not one could be more useless
than anger.
Fighting,
bickering,
arguing pointlessly.
Fear breeds Anger, and what a senseless emotion is fear.
With fear comes greed, and what a worthless emotion
is greed.
Trailing to the source of these emotions,
We cannot say any different.
What a useless emotion is anger.
I stand here fighting the anger, battling the fear, conquering the greed.
Anger,
what an empty emotion.

Rachel Crane, 14, home school, Lewisburg, TN

Help me, Father, to fight my bad attitude.
I should be rejoicing in You rather than being disagreeable.

peer pressure

Do not conform any longer to the pattern of this world, but be transformed by the renewing of your mind.

Romans 12:2

Peer pressure: It's all around us. People trying to telling us how to look, act, dress, what to be good at. They are continually telling us to fit in, be like the world. However, the apostle Paul tells us the complete opposite: Don't conform to the world, or in other words, don't let the world put you in a "mold." But how do we stop ourselves from becoming like the world we live in every day? Paul says we must be changed by the renewing of our minds, and this can only happen when we are continually *in the Bible*. When we are reading and studying the Bible, we will stop focusing on ourselves and the world, and start focusing on God. We are no longer thinking only of our will but of God's will for us. When we are focused on God, being popular and cool in the world's eyes won't matter quite so much. We are called to be lights in our world, to stand out from the world for all to see. And the only way we can shine is to know God's word and live it.

Tiffany Heetderks, 15, Petra Academy, Bozeman, MT

Father, help me know Your Word so that I become more like You and less like the world.

my mission

The Spirit of the LORD God is upon me; because the LORD hath anointed me to preach good tidings unto the meek; he hath sent me to bind up the brokenhearted, to proclaim liberty to the captives, and the opening of the prison to them that are bound; to proclaim the acceptable year of the LORD, and the day of vengeance of our God; to comfort all that mourn; to appoint unto them that mourn in Zion, to give unto them beauty for ashes, the oil of joy for mourning, the garment of praise for the spirit of heaviness; that they might be called trees of righteousness, the planting of the LORD, that he might be glorified.

ISAIAH 61:1–3 (KJV)

Have you ever questioned what God would have you do in your life? I ask often: "God, show me Your way so that I can walk in it." Isaiah 61:1–3 really stuck out one day as I read my devotional. Christ has called me to preach His Word to the humble and the broken, and He has anointed me to do it. God has commanded me to show sinners that they can be freed from their internal prison and tell them that Jesus is the only key that will unlock the chains. Many times Christ has allowed me to do this, but it is only by His grace and strength that I can speak about Him. It is truly His anointing. At the end of these verses, the Lord makes it clear who we should do this for...HIM! All the glory belongs to God. Today, pray for your friends, family, and others that you will be able to speak to them about your mission in life—Jesus.

Danica Woods, 17, Nebraska Christian High School, Central City, NE

Lord, give me a desire for Your will.
Show me Your Way so that I can walk in it.

youthful thinking

Don't let anyone look down on you because you are young, but set an example for the believers in speech, in life, in love, in faith and in purity.

1 TIMOTHY 4:12

So who really cares what you do? You're still just a kid right? Sorry, but that's not a good enough excuse when it comes to doing God's will. You don't have to be an "adult" to start living for Christ. Sure, you might not know what He wants you to do right now, but that's where prayer and Bible reading come in. It isn't likely you'll hear the voice of God if you aren't spending time with Him daily. And once you do find the will of God for your life, you need to get out there and do it! Your age shouldn't hold you back, no matter what people will think of you. In Daniel 3 we find the story of Shadrach, Meshach, and Abednego. Most people assume these guys were full-grown men when they were faced with the fiery furnace. The truth is they were probably no more than teenagers when they were given the choice to kneel before the golden statue of King Nebuchadnezzar or be thrown into the furnace. They knew it would be wrong to worship the statue instead of the one true God, so they chose to be burned alive in the blazing heat of the furnace. But because of their obedience, God saved Shadrach, Meshach, and Abednego. These three young men were a testimony to the King, and a Christlike example to all of those around them. They didn't let a little thing like being young stop them.

Amy McKoy, 18, Bryan College, Dayton, TN

Father, my age can keep me from doing so many things I want to do. But it doesn't have to keep me from doing Your will. And that is what I want to do most!

May 19

get ready. get set. go!

I, being in the way, the L*ORD led me.*

GENESIS 24:27 (KJV)

I am constantly on *the go*. I jog the wayward path of ambition and personal expectations along with so many others. In this constantly moving world, I get tangled up in all the rush and start sprinting to what I think is the ultimate target. But while I'm sprinting, I'm zipping by all those people who aren't doing quite as well, or are just plain tired of it all. If I stopped and took a look at the people jogging around me, I might see more than just the blur of a passerby. Those people may look just fine from my perspective, but underneath that tailored smile or the spiffy suit, they could be falling apart. We are called by Christ to spread the good news. So we need to stop running the wrong path and start walking with the Lord at our side. The world is ready and waiting for us to bring it hope. Now, this may seem impossible, but it's not. It doesn't have to be something huge. The possibilities are endless: babysitting for the newlyweds down the street, tossing someone's paper up to their door instead of leaving it on the sidewalk, baking cookies for the widow in your church, or talking to that boy or girl that has no friends to sit by at lunch. With the Lord at your side, you are invincible! So, start today. Pray that God will give *you* the courage to get off *your* own track, and open *your* eyes to the hurting world around *you*. Get Ready. Get set. Go!

Annie Nickel, 17, Nebraska Christian High School, Cairo, NE

Jesus, I want to start walking
with You now. Show me what I can do
today to get on Your path and stay there.

jump or die!

The Lord is not slow in keeping his promise, as some understand slowness. He is patient with you, not wanting anyone to perish, but everyone to come to repentance.

2 PETER 3:9

Smoke billowed from his daughter's second-story window. The once-beautiful white house was now swallowed up in flames. "Honey, you just have to trust me. I am here! Now, please, jump!" Her father frantically yelled. "Daddy, I can't see you. I can't let go!" The strangest images began to flash through his mind. She loved that room so much. Her perfectly patterned window seat, trimmed in white lace, was now surely blackened from the soot. "Please, have faith," he whispered as a sob caught in his throat. He was starting to realize that his precious daughter had to make a life-changing decision. Trust her dad, or die. This is a decision that we all must face at one point in our lives. We are all just like that daughter, scared because of the wrong things we have done. We hear our heavenly Father, God, whisper our name. He is saying, "Jump my child, and I will rescue you!" However, we fire back our excuses: "I can't see you" and "You can't handle this, God!" God is faithful and He continues to plead with us. God is above any issue we struggle with and He wants to rescue us. The father's daughter finally trusted him, and he saved her from certain death. Christ has already paid our debt and is waiting for us to trust Him and jump into His waiting arms.

Danica Woods, 17, Nebraska Christian High School, Central City, NE

God, You are my loving, protecting Father. I want to trust You enough to jump into whatever You call me to do.

i am somebody!

God created man in his own image, in the image of God he created him; male and female he created them.

GENESIS 1:27

All of us have pictures in our minds based on how we view ourselves, and others. Often we don't like how we view ourselves and tend to think that if we could be just like so-and-so, or do this or that, we would really be somebody special. What we don't realize is that when we imagine ourselves looking like someone else, we are questioning how God made us. God wants us to respect ourselves because we were created in His image. We are members of His family living in His household, built on the foundation of His word. God values all of his children, no matter if they are rich or poor, black or white, short or tall, athletic or nonathletic. He made each one of us very carefully, so every one of us is Somebody, even if we don't believe it. In a message Jesse Jackson was giving to a graduating class, he had them repeat these words: "I am somebody! My mind is a pearl! I can learn anything in the world and be anything I want to be! I am somebody no matter what anyone says to me! I AM SOMEBODY!" You are somebody no matter how many times you may fail. Repeat these words: "I AM SOMEBODY!"

Ashley Stone, 18, Nebraska Christian High School, Central City, NE

I am somebody in Your eyes, God!
That is an amazing truth. But I forget it so often.
Help me see myself as Your child.

when grace is enough

For it is by grace you have been saved, through faith—and this not from yourselves, it is the gift of God—not by works so that no one could boast.

Ephesians 2:8–9

I think a lesson in life that is harder to learn than respecting your elders or holding your temper is the lesson of grace. We all know of grace as Jesus dying for *our* sins, but do we ever think of Jesus dying for *other people's* sins? So often I have been terribly hypocritical when it comes to extending grace to someone else, especially if they've hurt me in some way, yet I expect grace for myself every time. I can remember being young and having one of my five siblings tease me and get in trouble for it. I always felt so justified. "It serves them right!" I'd say—but I always wanted grace, rather than punishment, whenever I annoyed them. I was always so loathe to give the very thing that they needed most. Now it's not just my siblings I need to share grace with, but also my friends. When one of them hurts or wrongs me, it's so hard to show forgiveness and grace. I just want to see them punished. The fact is, I realize, that Someone already has been punished. Every time someone sins, it is covered by the blood of Jesus. He showed me how to forgive others by forgiving me. If we show grace to others we show them Jesus himself, for His grace is sufficient.

Danae Toman, 17, Stillwater Christian School, Kalispell, MT

Jesus, I have so much to learn from You.
Please teach me forgiveness, because
no one knows more about that than You.

May 23

life verses

Because of the LORD*'s great love we are not consumed, for his compassions never fail.*

LAMENTATIONS 3:22

I first heard about someone having a life verse through a friend of the family. Her son is named John, and his birthday is March 16, therefore, his life verse is John 3:16. When John told me about his special birthday verse, that made me want to grab the Bible and find out which verse I could use to guide my life. To get a life verse, take the month of your birth and put it as the chapter. Then, use the day you were born as the verse. If your name happens to be a book of the Bible, a character, or an author, I would start looking in that book first. Sometimes it depends on the certain point you are in in your life that decides which one you choose as your life verse. I once found all the best applicable verses for my youth group members and gave a copy of the verses to each of them for their birthdays. For me, it was a gift that kept on giving. My verse gives me faith and reassurance. I have often found myself concerned over the fact that I can't see where my life is heading. I suppose that is when you realize that you have got to have faith. Faith is just that, not knowing what lies ahead but trusting God to see you through it anyway.

Haley Cheek, 16, Oconee County Christian Academy, Seneca, SC

Father, I want Your Word to be a big part of my life, the place where I find guidance and comfort.

too proud

Pride goes before destruction.

PROVERBS 16:18

I used to have a *huge* ego because I was one of the strongest kids in my school. I would arm wrestle with some of the older boys and would win. I got pretty caught up in winning. Whenever I lost at something, I would get very upset because things didn't go my way, and I would blame others for it. My pride was making itself right at home inside of my heart, and I had no more control of it. It would be years before I would have the discipline to control my temper and my ego. Proverbs 16:18 tells us that "Pride cometh before the fall" and that is totally and absolutely correct. I look back at the previous years of my short life and realize that I fell many times but never realized it. Only in the past two years have I been able to let go of my pride and let God take over. This verse has stuck to my memory and other people have helped me with my uncontrolled ego as well. Now, whenever my pride starts to get me in a bad mood, I just ask God for his grace and strength, and I remember that verse.

Pamela K. Locke, 15, Walnut Grove Christian Preparatory School, Noblesville, IN

God, thank You for blessing me with things that I'm good at. Help me to remember that they are gifts from You, and I'm not succeeding all on my own.

burning flame

Neither do people light a lamp and put it under a bowl. Instead they put it on its stand, and it gives light to everyone in the house. In the same way, let your light shine before men, that they may see your good deeds and praise your Father in heaven.

MATTHEW 5:15–16

Every day teenagers go through life conforming to the ways of the world. As Christians we are supposed to step above the things of this world and live differently. Matthew 5:15–16 states that we as Christians are supposed to be a burning candle to light up this dark world. When I go to school each day, it is sometimes hard for me to remember that I am supposed to be a light and act differently from the people of this world. I have a testimony, and I need to live it every day so that people can see Jesus through me. So just remember when you are somewhere surrounded by evil, take out your flame and let it shine for Jesus. We have been given what we need by Jesus to be mighty in this world. We simply need to let Jesus work through our lives to be a bright shining light in a dark world.

Jessica Bayly, 17, Donelson Christian Academy, Donelson, TN

Father, You've done so much for me. I should want to show Your greatness to other people. Please help me be Your light.

God's guidance

I will instruct you and teach you
in the way you should go;
I will counsel you and watch over you.

PSALM 32:8

Around my freshman year, I started wondering if God was going to use me for His work. In church I would hear the pastors saying that God had an individual plan for everyone's life. At first I didn't believe this was true because I am just a simple person, so what could He use me for. Then I decided to start praying that God would use me and lead me to what He wanted me to do. A couple of months later I heard that my friend's youth group was going on a mission trip to Costa Rica, and I was asked to go. I knew this was what God wanted me to do. The trip was a life-changing experience, and I could feel God's presence in an unbelievable way the whole time. I am thankful to God that He chose me. I needed to learn to trust Him because His guidance always leads down the right path. Are you patiently waiting for God to show you the plans He has for your life?

Katelyn Westfall, 15, Dover High School, Dover, OH

God, lead me to what You want me to do.
I can't find out what it is without Your help.
And I desperately want to know.

May 27

in perfect peace

I will lie down and sleep in peace, for You alone,
O LORD, make me dwell in safety.

PSALM 4:8

My parents used to be missionary teachers. One of the places we lived was called Oaxaca, Mexico. Some of the houses there are built so that they are very open and airy and there is no air conditioning. Because of this, we often had the doors open. At another one of our houses, the roof was flat, and we would sometimes sleep on it out under the stars. The neat thing about was that the heat caused us to open up our house to the world around us, the world that God made. And the neat wasn't so bad while looking up at the night sky and seeing the stars and the beautiful moon. I slept peacefully knowing that my heavenly Dad was watching over me.

Calista Turner, 17, Donelson Christian Academy, Nashville, TN

When I see the stars, I want to see You in them, Father. You have made such a beautiful world for me to live in, and I want to praise You for it.

just pray

Then hear from heaven their prayer and their plea,
and uphold their cause.

1 Kings 8:45

Have you ever felt like you were not good enough, pretty enough, or skinny enough? A better question might be, Who *hasn't* felt that way? So many people have negative feelings about themselves, and sometimes they'll do really drastic things, like have sex or try drugs, to feel better about themselves. I talked to one of my friends recently about this, and he opened my eyes to a very good point. He asked me if I really wanted help or if I wanted to stay feeling bad about myself forever. I told him I wanted help, and he said two simple words: "Just pray." I'm all the time trying to take on my entire load of problems and all the burdens and guilt that come along with it. He told me to just ask for help. Wow, it is just as simple as that. Because isn't that what God's there for?

Kim Scott, 17, Oconee County Christian Academy, Seneca, SC

All I have to do is ask for Your help.
Thank You for making trusting You so simple.
Help me to stop making it so hard.

summertime

But may the righteous be glad and rejoice before God; may they be happy and joyful.

Psalm 68:3

When school lets out for the summer, I am so happy. For three months I do not have to worry about turning in homework or waking up on time in the morning. It's funny, though, because after a couple of weeks I start to feel lonely and to miss my friends that I am used to seeing every day. Usually about this time I make up an excuse to have a party and invite all my friends over. I think God wants us to enjoy and encourage each other consistently. He made us to be together, to be in families, to get married, and to have friends. He did not make us to be alone. So as great as summer is, being with my friends every day during school makes the homework a little easier to bear (although I think I will always love those first few weeks of summer, before I start to miss everyone).

Ali VanMinos, 15, Oconee County Christian Academy, Seneca, SC

God, You did not make me to be alone.
You gave me friends and family and even
Your own Spirit to keep me company. Thank You!

God took my boyfriend

You will keep in perfect peace him whose mind is steadfast, because he trusts in you. Trust in the LORD forever, for the LORD, the LORD, is the Rock eternal.

ISAIAH 26:3–4

Last summer my boyfriend of two years broke up with me. Everything I knew or found comfort in disappeared. When I was with my boyfriend, I felt like my future was set and that I knew exactly what was going on. But without him, I suddenly had no idea what I was going to do with my life. Because I placed all my trust in him, I felt I didn't have to trust God for anything. During the first two weeks after the breakup, all of my other friends were gone on mission trips or vacations, so I felt very lonely and desperate. Seriously, the only person I had to rely on was God, and I think that's exactly what He wanted. God took my boyfriend away so that I would learn to trust Him. Through those weeks, my love and trust in God grew tremendously. I realized that God is a jealous God, and He has the power to quickly take away anything in my life that is holding back my relationship with Him. Now *God* is who I trust in and where I find comfort. I have grown to love Him more than ever before. Even though it's been tough for me these last months, it was all worth it because of the relationship I now have with my Lord. It's through the hard times in my life that I grow closest to God—and for that I am grateful!

Charice Schweitzer, 18, Nebraska Christian High School, Cairo, NE

Father, make my relationship with You strong and help me to never let anyone take Your place.

May 31

i want to be like an ant

Take a lesson from the ants, you lazybones.
Learn from their ways and be wise! Even though they have
no prince, governor, or ruler to make them work, they
labor hard all summer, gathering food for the winter. But
you, lazybones, how long will you sleep?
When will you wake up?

PROVERBS 6:6–9 (NLT)

Create in me a clean heart, O God,
And renew a right spirit within me.
Create in me a clean heart, O God,
And renew a right spirit within me.
Cast me not away from Thy presence, O Lord,
And take not Thy Holy Spirit from me.
Restore unto me the joy of Thy salvation,
And renew a right spirit within me.

Composer Unknown

mail hugs

A cheerful heart is good medicine.

PROVERBS 17:22

Five years ago my friend Kaitlyn moved away, so I made her a card to let her know I missed her. I was thrilled when she wrote me back, and at the time I had no idea we would grow into pen pals and would still be writing today. Kaitlyn's sunny letters encourage me so much; they are like a snug hug. She is always upbeat and enthusiastic about her basketball team, her family, her trips, and her life! Often she decorates her notes with stickers or bright markers. Sometimes she sends photos, Bible verses, or posters she's drawn of my name. She makes me feel loved and cared for. She's shown me a whole lot about Jesus' love by the way she considers my interests and shares in my joys and my daily life. So many activities and things in life keep changing, but not our pen-pal notes. Even though we only get to see each other a couple of times a year, we still stay close. When I go to the mailbox, drained after a long day of school, Kaitlyn's faithfulness to write gives me an instant internal high-five. Kaitlyn lets God use her to bless me. I hope God will use me to encourage Kaitlyn and all my family and friends by being cheerful, really caring, and faithful over time.

Christina Jensen, 15, Dogwood Christian School, Asheville, NC

Jesus, help me to be joyful and caring
all the time so that even the small things
I do will show Your love to others.

June 2

beloved zits

Your beauty should not come from outward adornment....
Instead, it should be that of your inner self,
the unfading beauty of a gentle and quiet spirit,
which is of great worth in God's sight.

1 PETER 3:3–4

We all have days when we feel that zits are taking over our face, that we're too fat to ever be attractive, or that we have absolutely zero cute clothes to wear. But in a week, it's just not going to matter which pair of jeans you wore to the football game or if your zit peeks out from under the cover-up. It's hard to not be super concerned about what we look like and how popular we are, and it's easy to forget what's really suppose to be our number-one priority: inner beauty. God created every one of us uniquely and He loves everything about us. The verse above reminds us just how important inner beauty is. It amazes me that God loves us for what's on the inside of us. He never looks at you or me and says, "Well, today you're having a bad hair day, so I love you just a little bit less." No! He loves every detail about us. He loves every quirky flaw and funny characteristic because that's how He created us! When he looks at us He says, "It is good." So next time you look in the mirror and start criticizing yourself, remember that you are God's beloved.

Danae Downs, 15, home school, Grand Junction, CO

Father, I can't believe I'm saying this but...
thank You for my zits—and all my flaws—
because they should remind me that what
You care about is not how I look but who I am inside.

dreams

Surely you desire truth in the inner parts;
you teach me wisdom in the inmost place.

Psalm 51:6

Some have dreams, others nightmares.
One moment's pain expanded upon the mind,
Or one happy thought of peace.
It seems so real, yet you think you know it's not.
You think it's all a lie.
Dreams aren't just pictures of happiness or sorrow,
They are images of the world around you.
They show the things you want,
Or the things you refuse to accept.
My dreams are cloudy and too often forgotten,
But when they're remembered,
Dreams can set you free.

Rachel Crane, 14, home school, Lewisburg, TN

Father, thank You for giving me dreams.
And thank You for teaching me
Your wisdom so that I'm able to accomplish them.

June 4

happily ever after

And we know that in all things God
works for the good of those who love him,
who have been called according to his purpose.

ROMANS 8:28

This past year, my youth pastor announced that he and his family would be leaving us. This was right before our heavily anticipated mission trip together. He announced it during the church service one Sunday morning, and it came as a shock to the youth group, which hadn't suspected a thing. We all were crying. While talking to a friend I realized that she and I both felt confused and deserted in a way. Although he was only going about two hours away from where we lived, he was a major part of our lives, and it was hard to imagine him being gone. He joined us on the mission trip as planned, and those students who went got to spend some cherished quality time with him. He left a week or so after we got back. At first I thought youth group would never be the same. We all missed him so much. Then I realized how selfish we were being. He was going to go help lots more people at his new home. The youth group banded together and grew stronger and closer. We have all been forced to assume some leadership roles, and as the verse says, it has all worked out for good. I know that our youth pastor would be proud of us. He helped us through one stage of our lives when we needed him most, and now he can do that for other students as well.

Erica Freeman, 17, Nebraska Christian High School, Central City, NE

All things work together for good. I wish I could remember that when I'm really upset about something. God, help me to do remember it—and believe it.

whitewater rafting

Let us fix our eyes on Jesus.

HEBREWS 12:2

The first time I went whitewater rafting I was really scared. The guide gave us some simple hand signals so that we would know what to do. When we came to the heavy rapids, another guide was supposed to be on a rock giving hand signals and trying to get us through safely. The key to staying afloat was to keep your eyes on the guides and follow their directions. If you tried to navigate by yourself, your boat would flip over and you would be in trouble. Just like I had to rely on the guide and trust him so my boat wouldn't flip, last summer I had to rely on Jesus to survive while away from home, alone on a mission trip to the Czech Republic. I was extremely homesick because my friends, were home and about to start soccer camp without me. I wanted to hop on a plane and be home in time for camp, but I couldn't. I was there for a purpose and I had to stay and finish it. I didn't just wake up one morning and feel better...it took time. With encouragement from my dad, daily devotions, and prayer, I overcame my homesickness. I was challenged just like whitewater rafting is challenging, but by keeping focused on Jesus, I got through the rapids and had a spectacular experience. When you're going through hard times, focus on Jesus, and you will have Him as your personal guide through the rapids that challenge you daily.

Jessica Lord, 17, Houghton Christian Academy, Houghton, NY

Keep my eyes on You, dear Jesus,
so that You can guide me through.

God hears!

I love the LORD, for he heard my voice;
he heard my cry for mercy. Because he turned
his ear to me, I will call on him as long as I live.

PSALM 116:1–2

Last September I heard that a local Christian conference center was looking for teen girls to provide one-day child care for a family conference. In order to be eligible you had to take a Red Cross babysitting class they provided free of charge. I had been wanting to take the Red Cross class, so I eagerly signed up. I was happy to take the course and get babysitting experience during the conference, but I really wanted families to babysit for regularly. I asked God to send me families I could babysit. Shortly after that, my cousin called and asked me to watch their six-month-old. Later, other friends asked me to sit with their children. Both of those families gave my name and number to their friends. Now I have a weekly sitting job with my cousin's friends to take care of their two-year-old girl. Also, three families call me sporadically. Each family is a joy! God clearly answered my prayers. This taught me how God cares about the details and desires of my life and makes me want to give every situation to Him. "I love the Lord, for He heard my voice."

Christina Jensen, 15, Dogwood Christian School, Asheville, NC

God, it is so awesome that You take time
to listen to me. You are the God of everything,
but my worries and wants matter to You. Thank You.

out of place

Consider it pure joy, my brothers,
whenever you face trials of many kinds.

James 1:2

This year I decided, after much debating, to leave my comfort zone and my friends at public school and attend a private Christian school my senior year. I had talked about doing this for a long time, but when the opportunity arose, I realized that I hadn't thought about everything that I would have to give up. I really wanted to graduate with my class and spend my senior year with my friends, but I knew that going to Nebraska Christian would benefit me spiritually. At NC I could obtain a firmer base in my faith before going off to college next year. After lots of prayer and consulting with close friends and family, I decided to leave the public school. Leaving was a lot harder than I thought it would be. NC doesn't have as many class choices as the public school, air conditioning, or roomy lockers. The school has a campus layout, so I have to go to different buildings for classes. These are small things that don't mean much, but they really make me realize the choice I made. My transition is especially difficult because my extremely close friends are not with me, and I am not quite familiar with the students, teachers, or classes yet. To be honest, some nights I cry because I miss my friends so much. I think this may be God's way of teaching me to rely on him. I know, though, that this will all turn out for good because I am doing it for the Lord.

Erica Freeman, 17, Nebraska Christian High School, Central City, NE

There are a lot of hard choices I have to
make in my life, Lord. I pray that I
will learn more about You as I make them.

rescue the perishing

Salvation is found in no one else,
for there is no other name under heaven
given to men by which we must be saved.

ACTS 4:12

People need God! Plain and simple! I pray that my heart is never hardened to the needs of the lost and hurting, and even saved people for that matter. I know in my own experience that the love and grace of God can heal every broken and wounded part of our hearts if we grab a hold of God and ask Him to heal us. Psalm 103: 3–4 says, God "who forgives all your sins and heals all your diseases, who redeems your life from the pit and crowns you with love and compassion" (I love that bit!). My prayer for others like me is that you will not forget to cry out to God in any hard situation you are going through. As we draw near to Him, we can know that He will bring us through any painful or difficult time. Turn to Him and experience His love and grace that is free for all!

Alexandra Truehl, 15, Adelaide, Australia

Father, I need You so much. I pray that
I will turn to You with every problem I face so
that I can experience Your love and compassion.

God knows best

For I know the plans I have for you,"
declares the LORD, *"plans to prosper you and*
not to harm you, plans to give you hope and a future."

JEREMIAH 29:11

WHAT?" I said when my parents told me we were going to be moving to Austria for a year to be missionaries. "I'm not going!" But about a year later I found myself crying on a plane as I was flying away from my country, my home, my friends, my family, my whole life. It was really scary going to a new school and a German-speaking church where I couldn't understand anything. It was especially hard to know that we couldn't do all the traditions we usually do with our extended family. I cried and asked God why He was doing this. But after a while, things started to change. I found three really close friends that I had as much fun with as I did with my friends back in the States. I was learning more and more German and was excited to go to our church to look up words I didn't understand. We got to experience Viennese culture: the Austrian foods, cathedrals, museums, palaces, and a more slow and relaxed pace of life. When it was time to fly back home, I cried all over again, not wanting to leave my home in Baden, Austria but wanting to go back to my home in America too. God knew all along that I would love the year I spent in Austria and that it would change me for the better. Because now I know that if something happens that I really don't want to happen, God has a plan to change it into good.

Allison Engel, 16, Wheaton North High School, Wheaton, IL

God, so often I fight and cry and say I don't want
to do something. But then I do it, and it turns out so great.
Thank You!

friends

I trust in God's unfailing love for ever and ever.

Psalm 52:8

I have met and made many friends from all over. I even have a best friend I have been friends with for ten years. I also have a friend I'm just getting to know. I feel like I can tell him anything. He's the type of person I can tell anything to and he won't tell a soul and he'll always be there for me. I believe God gives us friends so we don't feel alone or have to carry life's burdens all the time. A friend helps you when you are sad, makes you laugh, helps you get through the good and the bad times life brings you. In the same sense God is our friend. We can talk to him and tell him things we want nobody to know about, and He will love us and support us. For me, I know that I can trust God to keep my secrets and not tell a soul. God is my *best* friend.

Hope Minor, 16, Veritas Academy, Texarkana, TX

God, teach me to trust You like I trust my closest friend. Teach me to tell You all my secretes and to know that You will never stop loving me.

scared to death

The LORD himself goes before you and will be with you; he will never leave you nor forsake you. Do not be afraid; do not be discouraged.

DEUTERONOMY 31:8

As I walked into the audition for *Cinderella*, I was absolutely terrified. I had practiced all weekend and knew everything perfectly, but I was still scared to death. As a result, the audition did not go as well as I had hoped. Being a sophomore at the time, I was at a disadvantage because seniors were also trying out for the part of Cinderella. But I thought I would fit the role so perfectly because I feel like a Cinderella at heart. I am a hopeless romantic who dreams of being swept off my feet by a charming prince. I wanted to portray that feeling on stage, and I knew I could do it. All I had to do was convince everyone else that I could. The audition process was long and drawn out. Another girl was called in numerous times to read for the part that I wanted. I was becoming more and more discouraged. I did not get the part. I was so upset that day that I ran home and cried because I wanted that part so badly. I cried to my heavenly Father, asking Him why I didn't get the part. I've learned something since then. Even if things don't turn out the way I want them, God still has a plan, and He sticks with me, even when I don't feel like trusting Him.

Calista Turner, 17, Donelson Christian Academy, Nashville, TN

Lord, help me to know that when I don't get what I want, You have a very good reason for it.

how healthy is your thought life?

Take captive every thought to make it obedient to Christ.

2 CORINTHIANS 10:5

What is your thought life like? Do you indulge in daydreams and fantasies? Be careful what you think! Secret desires and inner dreams contrary to God's principles need to be rooted out and cast away. We enter into dangerous territory when we let our minds wander. In a world of R-rated movies, porn, and offensive music, we must shield our eyes and ears from unhealthy media. This may mean not attending a movie with your friends or turning off the radio in order to guard the purity of your mind. I have often wished that I could return to the innocence and naiveté of my childhood; it would be so much easier that way. But as we grow older, the world grows a lot less innocent. Prayerfully consider the things you think on. If you have trouble guarding your thought life or cannot maintain a steady devotion time, you should find an older, wiser woman to be your accountability partner. If you pursue Christ, Satan has no room in your heart. Ask God to fill your mind with Him, and focus on "whatever is true, whatever is noble, whatever is right, whatever is pure, whatever is lovely, whatever is admirable" (Philippians 4:8).

Jessica Runk, 19, Patrick Henry College, Purcellville, VA

Father, I'm glad I'm growing older,
but I pray that I will also get wiser so that
I will make choices that You will be proud of.

bye-bye boogie man

For I am the LORD, your God…
Do not fear; I will help you.

ISAIAH 41:13

I babysit for a family in my church. They have a three-year-old boy and a seven-year-old girl. Once, I just had the little boy. We made chicken and stars and grilled cheese sandwiches, played Pick-Up Sticks, watched a movie, and played with his motorcycles. He was all smiles until it was time to go to bed. After reading four books, saying a prayer, and tucking him in, I went to turn off the light. When I looked at him to ask if he was all set, I saw his eyes filling with tears, and his little lip began to quiver. The age of three is a very tender age. It's when kids are on the verge of understanding a lot of things, like why sticking every object smaller than their pinky in their mouth is not a good idea or how to climb the counter to the cookie jar without mom noticing. It is also close to the age that most children come to realize that they need a savior. They may not completely understand the true significance of the decision, but they know enough to be afraid and need someone to make them feel better. I didn't leave the little boy alone in the dark, and God won't leave us either. When we have the Lord as our Savior, we don't need to be afraid of silly things. He is at our side holding our hand, and we can count on Him always.

Annie Nickel, 17, Nebraska Christian High School, Cairo, NE

Lord, when I am afraid, please hold my hand.
Life is too scary without You.

simple faith (part 1)

"If you have faith as small as a mustard seed, you can say to this mountain, 'Move from here to there' and it will move. Nothing will be impossible for you."

MATTHEW 17:20

For my age, I have done more traveling than most. Recently while in Nepal for two and a half months, with a group of eight people, we served in churches, hung out with orphans, worked in fields, and with construction. We taught English to Nepalis and ABCs to kids, and we were involved in evangelization everywhere we went. Nepal is the only official Hindu nation in the world, yet it has the fastest growing church in the world! While there I could see how desperate the people were for truth. The younger generation is so focused on study because they want to grow in knowledge and have a better life. So when you meet Nepali Christians, they are faith filled and they have a strong desire to grow in their faith and knowledge of Christ. One day I was sharing a message with a group of women and at the end, one lady asked for prayer. She wanted prayer for her sore throat and that she would be able to sleep peacefully. I was taken aback that she put so much faith in me to believe with her! I prayed with her that God would bring healing to her body and give her the rest she needed. What a joy to know that because she believed she knew immediately that God was at work in her life to answer our prayer prayed in faith.

Chloé Truehl, 18, Adelaide, Australia

God, please give me the faith to completely believe that when I pray for help, You will give it to me. I don't want to doubt You.

simple faith
(part 2)

Now faith is being sure of what we hope for and certain of what we do not see.

HEBREWS 11:1

When Jesus' disciples asked Him why they had not been able to drive out a demon, Jesus' answer was so straightforward: All you need is faith. There is no formula or remedy; all you need is faith as small as a mustard seed and nothing will be impossible for you! That is an amazing promise! So faith is believing in the possibility of what seems impossible. Just focus on the promise instead of worrying how it will come to pass. It was so easy for the Nepali lady to believe in Christ's healing power because she also had experienced and known the power of darkness. When she became a Christian, she was given a storybook of the power of God in one man. That book is the Bible, and she has every reason to believe it is true. Sometimes I am so realistic that I forget there are other realms working for and against us. The power of the Kingdom of God is available to you today. Just make sure your heart is right towards God and ask Him for the miracle you are waiting for. Look beyond the problem. Can you see the fulfilled promise that is there for you to grab hold of? It wouldn't be called simple faith if it wasn't that simple.

Chloé Truehl, 18, Adelaide, Australia

Lord, I want to have great faith.
I want to look impossible in the face and say,
"It is possible." Teach me to trust You more.

standing strong

My flesh and my heart may fail, but God is the strength of my heart, and my portion forever.

PSALM 73:26

As I grow older, I'm faced with difficult decisions. Its just part of growing up, and I know that I'm not the only one thinking about college or marriage. But the most important decision is whether or not I'm going to follow the Lord wholeheartedly and give Him every part of me to do His will. A few years ago I had a close group of friends and the thing that held us together was that we were all striving to live our lives fully for Christ. We were in junior high and the Christian walk seemed easier then. As we've matured over the last few years, we've taken different paths that led us to completely different places. At first I didn't want to accept that we weren't really friends anymore. But I realized that God has a plan for my life, and this must be part of it or else it wouldn't be happening. Throughout the whole ordeal, I realized that I placed a lot of importance on my friends, not necessarily more than I did on Christ, but He should be my true strength, and I need to turn EVERYTHING over to Him. Psalm 73:28 helped me when I felt like I was alone in the world. When it felt like I'd lost the closest friendships in my life, it reminded me that God is my strength to get through anything, and I don't have to worry because He's in control of my life. There are still times when I miss the way things used to be, but I can't dwell on the past, or I'll miss what God has planned for me in the future.

Adrian Thistle, 17, Houston High School, Willow, AK

Father, even if my best friends leave me,
I know You'll still be there. Thank You
for being the one constant in my hectic life.

knowing your beauty

Charm is deceptive, and beauty is fleeting,
but a woman who fears the LORD is to be praised.

PROVERBS 31:30

In the lives of many girls today, feeling beautiful and accepted is a major problem. We need to measure up to the world's standards of being pretty. Having the most popular clothes, wearing the right makeup, being slender, and even having a tan complexion seem so important. If we aren't fitting in with the world, we can easily lose our confidence and feelings of worth. Through breakups and tough friendship problems we can feel as though we are no longer good enough or worth anything. It can seem that nobody deeply cares about us and how we feel. Through these tough times God wants us to lean on Him and know that He truly cares about each one of us. He thinks we are all beautiful and what he notices is our inner beauty and our relationship with him. We are worth more than any amount of money or prize in His eyes. Being accepted by God is the best that it can get and that is what we should truly strive for.

Stacey Krieger, 16, Nebraska Christian High School, O'Neill, NE

It seems like so many things that happen
just bring me down and make me not like myself.
Thank You, God, for being the one thing that
always makes me feel better.

dadless

I call on you, O God, for you will answer me;
give ear to me and hear my prayer.

PSALM 17:6

My dad died right before I was born, so it's tough at my house. Sometimes the only thing I can do to keep going is to pray. And sometimes I wish I had a dad like a lot of other kids, because my life would be so much easier. Many things are different since I don't have a dad. First, it changes the way I am with all men, because I'm not used to having guys around, so I always feel awkward and uncomfortable around men. Another thing is if my mom and I have an argument, I have no parent to talk to or get along with. I know it's silly, but sometimes I just want to be "Daddy's little girl." It's hard to watch other kids with their dads. No one from my family can participate in father-daughter or father-son events. We also do nothing for Father's Day. Sometimes it's hard to live without a dad because my siblings and I have to watch out for my mom since my dad isn't there to do it. We have to try to not make her stressed. It's a lot of work and responsibility. There's also the fact that my Mom is a stay-at-home mom, so there is not really much income. But somehow God always keeps providing. I may not have a dad here on earth, but I do have a heavenly Father who helps us out all time.

Sarah Lewis, 14, Walnut Grove Christian Preparatory School, Sheridan, IN

God, thank You for being my Father, for being the one who
watches over me and provides for me like no one else.
I am proud to have You as my eternal Dad.

the purity problem

For women who claim to be devoted to God should make themselves attractive by the good things they do.

1 Timothy 2:10 (NLT)

It's hard to not have sex until marriage. There are so many reasons NOT to wait. If you think you really love someone and he really loves you, then you might feel like having sex is okay. And you might think since you're using protection, you won't have to deal with pregnancy or diseases. But safe sex isn't always safe...and the "love" you two feel might not be as strong as you thought. The only real way to stay safe is to wait until marriage. The Bible tells us many times to remain pure. But maybe you've already had sex, so you figure you might as well continue. That is not true. You can stop, and it might mean breaking up with a boyfriend, which definitely is not easy. But God wants us to obey Him first and foremost. Purity is a great gift that we have received and that we can give to someone someday. But when it comes down to it, none of us is pure in every aspect or to every degree. We are always making excuses about doing things we shouldn't. Despite all our mistakes, the most amazing part of all this is that, if we let Him, God makes us truly pure, in mind, body, and soul.

Jessica Morel, 17, Riverdale High School, Rockvale, TN

Jesus, thank You for dying on the cross. Thank You for shedding the blood that washes away my mistakes.

June 20

they need our help

Paul had a vision of a man of
Macedonia standing and begging him,
"Come over to Macedonia and help us."

ACTS 16:9

There are always people struggling through difficult times. Consider traumatic and devastating events like the Asian Tsunami in 2004, 9/11 in New York; and the 2005 hurricane in New Orleans where victims were forced to evacuate and often separated from friends or family members. We watch the news and hear the stories and ask, "What can we do? Are we too young? Can we really make a difference?" We can do something...we can pray. People need to know there is always power available. Christians have power in prayer. We also have power in giving. I know we don't have much, but in times of crisis every little bit helps. Give toward helping others through your church. When you walk in or out of some stores, there may be a box from reputable organizations like the American Red Cross or the Salvation Army. Give up a movie or a value meal one week and drop a dollar in. We also have power through volunteering. For the past few summers I have been able to volunteer to help rebuild poor or elderly people's houses destroyed in hurricanes. Let's take time out and not be SELFISH but be SELFLESS, and you will feel like you have made a difference in someone's life. The ways that you help don't have to be big. Just do the most you can whenever you can.

Candace K. Croston, 16, King's Fork High School, Suffolk, VA

Lord, help me to give of myself to help others.
Today, guide me to give up just a little something so that
I can give it to someone else who needs it much more.

gone, but still in my heart

Though he slay me, yet will I hope in him;
I will surely defend my ways to his face.

Job 13:15

When I was about nine years old, my dad was diagnosed with this blood disorder that I can't even pronounce. He knew he wasn't going to live very long. I guess he lived longer than he expected. When I was eleven, going on twelve, my dad passed away at age fifty-one. Thankfully, he had a personal relationship with Jesus. I can still remember what happened on that day. His death didn't really get to me as much then as it does now. I get sad when I think about my wedding day and how I'm not going to have my father walk me down the aisle or have a father/daughter dance like many other girls I know. But you know what? He *will* walk me down the aisle because he will always be with me in spirit. But now, five years later, my mom is still single, and I think she's starting to date. Since I still feel like my dad is with us, it's hard to imagine my mom being with someone new. I wasn't very happy with her dating at first, but now I think I am okay with it. I know it makes my mom happy and that makes me happy. If it wasn't for God, I don't think I would be okay with her meeting someone new. God reminded me that mom can't be alone forever and that it's normal for a teenage girl to not want her mom to date someone other than her father. My dad will always be with us, even if mom does marry someone new.

Megan Bordenkircher, 16, Nebraska Christian High School, Central City, NE

Father, I don't want to let go of the people I love.
But I know sometimes I have to. Help me to be strong
and trust that You will take care of them.

June 22

coming home

Better is one day in your courts
than a thousand elsewhere.

PSALM 84:10

Stepping inside our seventh house within ten years, I exhale submissively. Moving has become a routine part of my life. However, it is annoying when I always have to ask my mom where we keep the Tupperware. Dragging my suitcase up the stairs, I flop down on my new bed in my bare room, the white walls silently screaming unfamiliarity. I cannot help but wonder how long we'll be staying. My family has lived everywhere from Chicago to Romania, where my parents were missionaries. I used to hate moving, tearing up my roots and attachments every few years, replacing friendships like a pair of shoes. I have spent a night in a thousand different beds: some new and exciting, some familiar, some lonely, some comforting, some scary, some encouraging, some I've revisited, and some I will never see again. The one location that I can constantly return to is the house of the Lord. Sometimes I find it while I'm curled quietly on a living room couch, sometimes in the majestic cathedrals of Eastern Europe, but it is always there. I can invariably call out to God, wherever I am. The verse above taught me to value my *alone* time with Christ in the consistent home of my heart. Though my family's roaming has been stressful and unstable, I wouldn't trade it for an unsellable house or an immovable bed; my permanent home is in heaven. Moving so often has exposed me to innumerable facets of life. It has trained me to find my stability and my home in the presence of God, a place that surpasses any residence.

Meredith Janke, 17, Houghton Christian Academy, Houghton, NY

God, I want my home to be in You. When I'm feeling lost and homeless, remind me that You are always there.

speaking for Jesus

They overcame him by the blood of the Lamb and by the word of their testimony.

Revelation 12:11

The first time I gave my testimony in front of people was at a small mother/daughter banquet that my youth group hosted on one of our mission trips. After refreshments the whole group gathered into a church sanctuary and as I stood at the small podium, I could feel my heart beating fast within my chest. I began to talk, explaining how I had grown up with just my mom. When I was seven, she married a wonderful man, and it was the first time I had ever had a father. My throat closed as I explained how I accepted Jesus as my savior not just through those years of being fatherless, but how He would always be my heavenly Father. I began to cry, and I saw two teenage girls sitting beside each other bawling. I didn't speak for long, but I was amazed how light my spirit felt as I realized that I had obeyed God's request of me. It was surreal, full, satisfying. The fear and burden was gone. All because I had trusted my God and not only listened to Him but obeyed Him and spoke when He asked me to. Later that night, I went on a long walk with the two girls I had seen crying. One of the girls had grown up without her father, just like me. I was able to hug her, understand what she felt, and reach out to her. My testimony opened the door to befriend the girls of the town we were visiting. Obedience to Jesus brings with it great joy and reward.

Rebecca Wilson, 18, Maranatha Christian Academy, Oakwood, GA

God, I want to share how You have changed me so that my experience can help change others. Salvation is the most amazing gift!

June 24

isn't it crazy

His divine power has given us everything we need for life and godliness through our knowledge of him who called us by his own glory and goodness.

2 PETER 1:3

Every day we are surrounded by temptations from the world, trying to fit in and living up to the world's expectations. We try to find things that will make us feel loved, happy, and complete. God has given us everything we could possibly need spiritually through the knowledge of Him. We would be crazy to choose the world over having eternity in heaven with God, because He has given us the desires of our hearts and everything we could possibly need. As we live each day of our lives, we should be trusting in God for everything instead of trusting what the world says we should believe in. The world can't give us hope, peace, and joy. The only place these things can be found is in the presence of our God. Even if the world tempts us we have the power to say no. We need to raise our voices like thunder and leave the world in wonder of this change that God has made in each and every one of us.

Ashley Stone, 18, Nebraska Christian High School, Central City, NE

I choose You, dear Jesus.
I choose You now, tomorrow, and forever.
And I want everyone to know.

to eat or not to eat?

Now the serpent was more crafty.

GENESIS 3:1

All humans have a sinful nature because of one important event in the history of mankindæAdam and Eve eating the fruit of the tree of knowledge of good and evil. Before they sinned and disobeyed God, everything was perfect, and they were naive to everything other than good. I am reading a book that is second in a trilogy called The Circle, *Red* by Ted Dekker. The book talks about how the serpent twisted God's words to make it sound all right to disobey what God had said. The serpent was very crafty, and he made it sound okay to eat the fruit. The woman said that God had told them to not eat it or they would surely die. Then the serpent said that they would not die but that they would be smart like God. Adam and Eve wanted to be smart, but what happened was far from imaginable for them. We should remember what happened to them when we are questioning God's words. When we trust Him, good things will happen. But disobeying Him will never turn out well.

Ali VanMinos, 15, Oconee County Christian Academy, Seneca, SC

Lord, teach me to trust in Your Word no matter what the temptation. I don't want to be led astray.

jumping in

Be strong and courageous. Do not be terrified;
do not be discouraged, for the L*ORD*
your God will be with you wherever you go.

JOSHUA 1:9

There we were, my friends and I, on senior retreat. Every fall, the seniors spend a weekend at a camp in the woods. I glanced at each of the girls as we marched down the hill in our swimsuits, the greatest friends I had ever had. I was closer to them then I was to anybody else. A small pain stung me inside for, in a couple months, I would have to say good-bye. But right now we were just a bunch of school girls going for a midnight swim. The night air was brisk, and the water was black. I was terrified to jump, I can't remember my heart ever beating that fast. We stood side by side, holding hands at the edge of the dock. "One…" somebody started to count. My heart pounded in my ears. *Lord, I'm scared, please be with me, right now. The water is dark and cold and mysterious*, I silently prayed to myself. "Two…" I prepared to jump. If my friends were going to do it, I could do it too. This was the first jump my friends and I had to take together this year. At the end of the year we'd have to jump into the cold, dark, unknown of college. But right now, I was prepared to take this jump. "Three!" We all jumped. The water was freezing, but as I surfaced, I could hear my friends laughing close by. We had done it. I smiled to myself and floated on my back. I looked up at the sky and was rewarded by God's beautiful stars. God was still there.

Chenelle Davis, 17, Houghton Academy, Cuba, NY

Father, give me the courage to jump into
whatever You want me to do. Help me to
remember that You will be jumping with me.

fear

For God did not give us a spirit of timidity,
but a spirit of power, of love and of self-discipline.

2 TIMOTHY 1:7

Differences in the world large and small,
Dark and light,
Mysterious and questionable.
People fear the differences; they fear change.
I don't fear the change, why do you?
My differences let me live, let me soar.
Why do you fear me?
Freedom is nowhere as long as you fear.
Allow yourself to change and become the truth.
Fear me no longer.
Embrace your differences and change.

Rachel Crane, 14, home school, Lewisburg, TN

I know You made everyone unique,
God, so there are many differences in this world.
Help me to see them as part of Your awesome creation
instead of fearing things that are different.

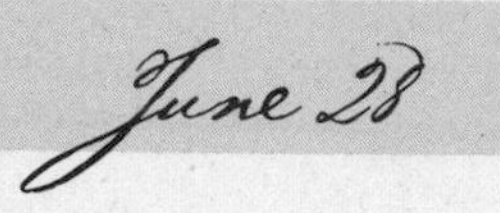

lifetime mission trip

I hope that I will in no way be ashamed,
but have sufficient courage so that now as always,
Christ will be exalted, whether by life or by death.

PHILIPPIANS 1:20

Mission trips. Going on them is definitely a great experience. But every time when I come home, I ask the same question: "Why can't I stand up for my faith at home just like on the trip?" After pondering this, I think I finally figured it out. My pride is so big that I don't want to be laughed at. No one knows us far from home, so it doesn't matter if we're "Jesus Freaks," but at school we are ridiculed, causing us to shut up. Paul, one of my favorite Biblical role models, stood tall and unashamedly proclaimed Jesus to everyone, everywhere. He didn't "zip the lip" when ordered to stop. He took the beatings, imprisonment, and stoning, yet still didn't give up speaking. We fight a battle within ourselves over whether or not we obey God's command to "go and tell all the world" or not. He never said only some places or only when you're away from home. If my friends and family die and go to hell, what am I going to say? That I didn't want to be called a 'Jesus Freak' or 'intolerant'? Jesus Freak? Who cares! It's my responsibility to show and tell those in my life about Jesus. I hope, like Paul, I won't be ashamed to be identified with Christ, but will have enough courage to speak out. Mission trips? I'm on one every time I jump out of bed in the morning!

Laura Reimer, 17, Nebraska Christian High School, Central City, NE

Father, I want to treat my entire life
as a mission to bring more people to You.
I do not want to be ashamed of You.

"why am i so different?"

And even the very hairs of your head
are all numbered. So do not be afraid;
you are worth more than many sparrows.

MATTHEW 10:30–31

How many times have you asked yourself, "Why am I so different from *everyone* else?" Sometimes your friends even inform you that you're weird. Don't you wish you could just blow them off and say, "Well, forget you, I never liked you anyway," or "Yeah, I am different! I have my own talents that make me special." Ideally, this is what we all would like: to have the confidence to take criticism and still be standing. I don't know about you, but I haven't got to that point yet. The fact is, sometimes truth *does* hurt. So what do we do when others treat us like being different is a bad thing, even though we know it's really not? God says we are of great worth. Not *greater* than other people, but valuable in our own way. Sometimes people point out our differences in order to hurt us, and sometimes they just say things without thinking. But no matter what their reason, we must try to remember that the things that make us different were chosen by God to be a part of us—and He knew what He was doing.

Laura Campbell, 17, Stillwater Christian School, Kalispell, MT

Lord, I pray that I will be proud to be
just as You made me. This may be the hardest
thing I will ever try to do. Please help me!

June 30

i want God's words to be a part of me

Follow my advice;...always treasure my commands. Obey them and live! Guard my teachings as your most precious possession. Tie them on your fingers as a reminder. Write them deep within your heart.

Love wisdom like a sister; make insight a beloved member of your family.

PROVERBS 7:1–4 (NLT)

This is My commandment that you love one another,
That your joy may be full.
This is My commandment that you love one another,
That your joy may be full.
That your joy may be full,
That your joy may be full.
This is My commandment that you love one another,
That your joy may be full.

Composer Unknown

transcending peace

And the peace of God, which transcends all understanding, will guard your hearts and your minds in Christ Jesus.

PHILIPPIANS 4:7

This past summer I broke up with my boyfriend after dating him for three years. He was both my boyfriend and my best friend. God had been impressing upon my heart for about six months that He did not want us to be together. I did not like hearing that, so at first I tried to ignore it. That did not work, so I began to pray that my boyfriend would break up with me so that I would not have to break up with him. This didn't work either. I went to work at camp and got away from the usual distractions and expectations of my life, and during that week God chose to speak clearly to me. By the time I went home, I knew I had to do it. God gave me a peace about it, and I truly felt His will and comfort. Ever since the breakup I have continued to feel that peace. It has been extremely lonely sometimes, but I know that it was the right decision. Sometimes it takes a quiet moment for us to hear God speak and to believe Him enough to do the hard thing. For me, it was SO worth it.

Rachel Thurman, 17, Cedar Hall School, Rockvale, TN

God, I want to really hear You.
Give me the silence I need to hear Your voice
and the strength I need to do what You say.

it's hard to let go

*Praise be to the God and Father of our Lord Jesus Christ,
the Father of compassion and the God of all comfort,
who comforts us in all our troubles.*

2 CORINTHIANS 1:3–4

God will comfort you in your sadness. It's hard to let go of someone you love when they die. About two years ago, my aunt, who was like my second mom, passed away. Her death was unexpected. A blood clot traveled from her leg to her heart, killing her instantly. My aunt was very close to my family; she always lived near us so she was at our home much of the time. When we would go out to eat, we would call and invite her to join us, and she usually would. We would ask her where she wanted to go because she meant so much to us, and we wanted to make her happy. So when she did leave us, it was hard to handle. I turned to God for help, and He did help me through the whole grief thing; He never left me alone. I don't know what I would have done without Him. He reminded me that even though she left us she was in a better and a happier place where she would not hurt anymore, but we could still feel her presence. I miss her and I still stay up at night sometimes thinking about her, recalling great moments we shared together. When I miss her, I try to remember that she's with God now. I look forward to seeing her again because I know the Lord, and I know I will go to heaven.

Sara York, 16, Antioch High School, Antioch, TN

*Father, when someone I love dies,
I want to be sure that we will see each
other again. That way I won't be quite as sad.*

let my people go

Afterward Moses and Aaron went to Pharaoh and said, "This is what the LORD, *the God of Israel, says: 'Let my people go, so that they may hold a festival to me in the desert.'"*

EXODUS 5:1

The other day I was thinking about this verse and it struck me that the story of Moses is similar to the story of George Washington. Moses led his people to freedom from slavery to the Egyptians, and they then celebrated in the desert. Washington led the people in a revolution, to establish a new country, and we celebrate every summer on the Fourth of July. They both courageously and humbly did what was asked of them or what they thought was right. It's easy to celebrate Independence Day and think that leaders like Washington, or even Moses, were extra-special. The reality is that these men were very human, imperfect, and prone to messing things up (just like you and me). Yet, they both led people to freedom because they weren't afraid to *act*, to *obey*, and to *be different*.

Laura Campbell, 17, Stillwater Christian School, Kalispell, MT

Help me to be the kind of person that isn't afraid to do Your will in order to change things, no matter how hard it may seem.

sparkly night

Now the Lord is the Spirit, and where the Spirit of the Lord is, there is freedom.

2 CORINTHIANS 3:17

Fireworks, a barbecue, friends, family, and a late, sparkly night…Today is our nation's birthday. So what is true liberty? What is freedom and where does it come from? Why do we celebrate it? God is the creator of freedom, and where He is there is genuine freedom. One of the things that I am reminded of is how the truth is what sets you free. John 8:32 reads, "Then you will know the truth, and the truth will set you free." Don't we all want freedom of some sort? People like to be free; it's as if we were made with the desire to be free…When Christ is living in and through us that is when we grasp true freedom. He gives us freedom from sin, freedom to obey, freedom to have hope, and freedom to choose how we live our lives. As we celebrate the freedom of our country, let's remember the Holy Spirit, within us and all around us, is what makes us truly free.

Danica Woods, 17, Nebraska Christian High School, Central City, NE

God, I want the freedom that only You can give me. Freedom on earth is nothing compared to freedom in You.

these small moments

Do not conform any longer to the pattern of this world, but be transformed by the renewing of your mind. Then you will be able to test and approve what God's will is—his good, pleasing and perfect will.

ROMANS 12:2

There are so many things teenage girls go through that most people don't understand. As I get a little bit older I am realizing that many things I thought were one way are actually another. And some of the things I thought were important really aren't. So much has already happened in my life, and I am only sixteen! God has used the experiences I have had to make me into who He wants me to be. I believe God has placed everyone on the planet for a purpose, and I am determined to walk in the purpose He has for me. Sometimes I wonder what that might look like next year or in five years...But right now part of His purpose for me is learning these lessons that he keeps putting in front of me. I know this will not always be easy, but I want so badly to walk in His purpose and plan for me, and I know no better way than doing it every day, in the smallest of moments. So, let's keep discovering what God's purposes for us in this day, this moment, might be.

Jazma Parker, 16, Martin Luther King Magnet School, Nashville, TN

Lord, thank You that You have a purpose for my life.
I would feel so lost without You!

July 6

being myself

Serve the LORD with fear and rejoice with trembling.

PSALM 2:11

I have struggled with knowing who I am. I didn't know what I wanted to do when I grew up. But then one day it hit me really hard. I wanted to be a singer. But what kind of singer did I want to be? I didn't know yet. I thought it wasn't cool to be a Christian artist. So I thought I had to be a secular artist, singing about how much I love this boy or how much I want to be with him. I started to become what I thought was "cool" in the eyes of the world. I didn't realize that in the process of trying to fit in with the world, I was losing my true identity in the Lord. I grew so far apart from Him that I didn't even recognize His voice. That scared me. I knew how important it was to listen to Him. My parents always told me to obey Him. But how could I obey Him when I couldn't hear Him. I had to stop what I was doing and turn back to Him. I had to find myself again. So I asked God for His forgiveness. Of course He forgave me, but I had to forgive myself. I had to know that I am who God created me to be. It took me a very long time to figure out what kind of singer I wanted to be. But now I know I want to be a Christian artist. I know it is going to be a hard way there. But I know now that I'm on the path God wants, and I trust he'll help me succeed.

Victoria T. Kaopua, 15, Kealakehe High School, Kailua-Kona, HI

Your way is the best way, Jesus. Help me to do Your will and not the will of the world.

dishwasher, plates, and meals

I can do everything through him who gives me strength.

PHILIPPIANS 4:13

Do you ever want to give up on life, to give up trying to be obedient, sharing, and being a true example of Christ. I wanted to give up when I was the one causing all the trouble in my family, even though I was trying so hard to have a true servant's heart. Being homeschooled has made it twice as hard. Basically when my family and I aren't doing mission trips, I am home almost all the time, oh, and this doesn't make me sheltered! I'm faced with most trials that every teenage girl goes through. With Christ's strength in me, even though it took, and still does, take time to learn that though we "always" do everything wrong and "never" seem to do anything right, God is in the midst of perfecting us, His precious beautiful daughters, into becoming strong women of character and righteousness. Once God gave me analogy, you have to use your imagination: *We, our lives are plates, life's trials and tribulations are the meals, and God is the dishwasher (except he never malfunctions and doesn't make that disgusting smell that my family's dishwasher does!). We go through one of the "meals" and it's sticking to us and making us feel unclean but once we go through the "dishwasher" we come out looking more pure and clean than ever before.* Do you understand it? Even though we always seem to get ourselves into a mess God still wants to clean us off and purify all the iniquities that seem to "stick" to us.

Jana Kroeker, 15, home school, Medicine Hat, Alberta, CA

Father, I just pray that You will make me clean.
Thank You for working to make me perfect even
when I feel like I'm doing everything wrong.

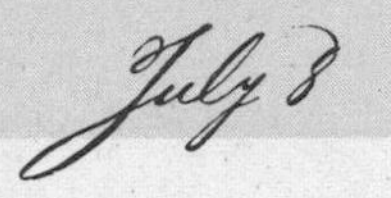

leave it all

As Jesus was walking beside the Sea of Galilee, he saw two brothers, Simon called Peter and his brother Andrew. They were casting a net into the lake, for they were fishermen. "Come, follow me," Jesus said, "and I will make you fishers of men." At once they left their nets and followed him.

MATTHEW 4:18–20

I was once in a conference for young girls and the speaker pointed out that God cannot use all of our lives unless we let Him. He desires us to be willing and devoted. The speaker continued to say that she had given her life, future, goals, and entertainment to Jesus. When she surrendered herself, God gave her an abundant ministry. She encouraged all of us girls to let God have all of our life so He could use it all for His plan. Right there, I decided that I wanted God's absolute best for me. However, it's easy to say that you're going to do His will only, but it's really hard to give up all of the fun that there is on earth. Daily, I find things that I still want control over in my life, but I have to tell myself that I am God's, made for His purpose ,and I am not in control of my own life. It was a hard struggle to let my entertainment and time go out of my hands into His, but every day my life grows sweeter as I drop my goals and wants and follow God. A lot of things are not important anymore because He is worth so much and everything is so much better living as His.

Hannah Reeves, 14, home school, Central, SC

Father, teach me to find the joy in living for You, the joy the surpasses anything I could have or do in this world.

p.u.s.h.

I pray for them. I am not praying for the world, but for those you have given me, for they are yours.

John 17:9

I met Laura in seventh grade. We were on the swim team together. I realized instantly that she was a really cool, really unique person. But after a while I started noticing cuts and bruises on her arms. When I questioned her, she would shrug off my questions. One day Beth from my church "met" with Laura and talked with her for me. Beth told me that the best thing I could do for someone who does not want to be helped is just P.U.S.H.: PRAY UNTIL SOMETHING HAPPENS. She said our most powerful words are those we use in talking God. She and I prayed for Laura for months. In ninth grade I moved to a swim team on the other side of town and no longer saw her. Sometimes we called each other on the phone, but after a while we stopped. I still thought about her and prayed for her and so did Beth. One year later I met Laura at a festival in town, and we were able to pick up just where we had left off. She told me she cut herself because of everything that was going on in her family... and that she had not wanted to open up because she was afraid. She had started visiting a church with a friend, and her outlook was changing. She was wrestling through what she did and did not believe. Being with her made me smile because of what God had done because I P.U.S.H.ed.

Michelle Palacio, 15, Alpha Omega Academy, Charlotte, NC

Lord, I want to believe in prayer enough to keep praying even when I can't see results. One day they will come, and I will see the great work You can do when I have faith.

wilbur

The LORD is…slow to anger, abounding in love.

PSALM 103:8

For a while, a canary-yellow cockatiel named Wilbur lived at our home. He was the most nervous and frightened bird that ever lived. It took about a year to get him to come out on my shoulder and not be afraid. After that, he turned into the most pathetically spoiled bird you have ever seen. My family loved him; I loved him. He and I were stuck together like glue; he took showers with me in the morning, ate from my plate, and rode on my shoulder all the time. One day I went out to feed my dog and when I came back inside, I saw Mom holding Wilbur. I knew he was dead, but I couldn't accept it for a long time. We buried him under a bald cypress tree. I was angry at God because I loved that little bird more than anything else in the world, and God had taken him away from me. I didn't pray to God for a few weeks; I wouldn't speak to Him. I was like a child whose parents said that she couldn't have a piece of candy. I couldn't understand why Wilbur's death had to be part of God's plan. But as I was sleeping one night, I saw Wilbur in a dream. A voice from someone I couldn't see called Wilbur, and he flew away. I somehow knew that God had sent me a message, telling me to not be angry at Him and that everything would be okay. I asked God to forgive me and He has. God is "slow to anger and abounding in love." I still go out to the tree that shadows Wilbur's grave, and I can feel God's love there.

Pamela K. Locke, 15, Walnut Grove Christian Preparatory School, Noblesville, IN

Father, I am so thankful that You don't get angry easily.
I get angry at You a lot, and I'm grateful that
You respond to me with love.

guilt trip

Their sins and lawless acts
I will remember no more.
HEBREWS 10:17

Guilt comes when you've done something you know is wrong. You don't want to get in trouble, but you also can't get rid of that awful feeling in the pit of your stomach. How do you get rid of that guilt that you are feeling? Tell God. Hebrews 10:17 says, "Their sins and lawless acts I remember no more." All we have to do is ask, and we will be forgiven. That is why Jesus came and died for us, so that we could have the chance to start over. Psalm 32:5 also says that when you confess your sins to the Lord, He will forgive you. But if you hide your sin and refuse to admit you were wrong, the feeling in your stomach will get bigger and bigger. Jesus loves us, so we should not be afraid of what will happen if we confess our sins. God does not want us to live with guilt. He wants us to feel free from our sins. Remember, if you ask, you shall receive.

Ali VanMinos, 15, Oconee County Christian Academy, Seneca, SC

Father, give me the humility to
admit my mistakes to You.
I want to be forgiven.

a different way (part 1)

For my thoughts are not your thoughts, neither are your ways my ways, saith the LORD. For as the heavens are higher than the earth, so are my ways higher than your ways and my thoughts than your thoughts.

ISAIAH 55:8–9 (KJV)

At birth, I was diagnosed with Spherocytosis, but I never had any major complications with my blood disorder. However, a few years ago, I became very ill when I had a common cold since my immune system was weak and getting weaker by the moment. My Mom worked during the day and went to school at night. We had no idea that my physical problem something greater than just a cold. As the week progressed, my fever began to rise and I started sleeping much of each day. In class, my teacher noticed my unusual behavior and sent me to the school nurse. Alarmed after taking my temperature, she called my mom and I saw the doctor immediately. Ironically, my doctor was on vacation and his new associate had to see me. He ordered blood work right away. I overheard him telling my mother that he'd never seen ANY thing like this in his life. After he saw the results from my blood work, he simply stated, "Get her to the hospital now, or she will not make it." I panicked. He elaborated that my immune system was shutting down and my red blood cell count was alarmingly low. I was dying. Was God there? Was He calling me home? Or was this a time of testing? These are times when we learn to trust HIM on the spot. He was in control and we knew it.

Danshelle Guy, 17, New Covenant Christian School, Pageland, SC

Lord, even when a situation looks completely hopeless and frightening, I want to trust You. I want to know You're in control.

a different way (part 2)

For as the heavens are higher than the earth, so are my ways higher than your ways and my thoughts than your thoughts.

ISAIAH 55:9 (KJV)

The doctor was surprised that I was hanging on, but, I thought, that was God! My grandmother had just died, not me, too. I was severely dehydrated and my first night was in the hospital was complete torture. I was assigned a *team* of doctors so whatever was wrong wasn't good. Blood had to be drawn from my foot. I went into cardiac arrest and the only option left was a blood transfusion, and my Mom freaked out. I could hear her refusing, but I could also hear the doctors telling her that without it, I would definitely die and with it there was a only 50/50 chance that I would accept or reject the blood. Looking at my odds, I stopped fighting and became furious with God for allowing such a thing to happen to me. What had I done to deserve this? I could hear my Mother on the phone with my pastor sobbing. I had already decided to just let it happen and I gave up, but I got better and was released in two days. My spleen was removed two months later and I am fine now. At that point in my life I felt abandoned by God. However, He had a plan for me and my life, and He never left me. He is there for you too. He will not abandon you in difficult circumstances. He just has a DIFFERENT WAY. It's our choice to go His way.

Danshelle Guy, 17, New Covenant Christian School, Pageland, SC

Father, I want to go Your way, even when it's the hard way, because I know You have a plan for me that is amazing.

locked into your memory

Thy word have I hid in mine heart,
that I might not sin against thee.

PSALM 119:11 (KJV)

What does it mean to hide God's word in your heart? When you memorize a verse, it is literally locked into your memory. One time I met an elderly lady that had had a stroke. Her husband said that right after the stroke, the only thing she could remember was the Lord's Prayer. Isn't that amazing! When we hide God's Word in our hearts, we can use it to share the gospel to others better, have a closer relationship with the Lord, and get many other blessings. How do we memorize scripture? I used to try to memorize a verse and would say it over and over, but then twenty minutes later it would be gone. I have found that meditating on the verse is what locks it into place. What is meditating? Meditating is thinking about what the words mean individually. I memorize and meditate by saying the first word, explaining what it means, then saying that word and the next one, defining the second, and so on. It really works! Also, for some people, writing the verse down helps. When you figure out a way that works for you, you will be able to store lots of God's words inside you. And having God's word in your heart will help you to know what is right and what is wrong.

Bethany Pearl Reeves, 15, home school, Central, SC

I want to know Your Word inside out,
Lord, so I will always have it with me,
and it will be a part of me.

July 15

moving to tennessee (part 1)

Such confidence as this is ours
through Christ before God.

2 CORINTHIANS 3:3–4

After several unsuccessful attempts to sell our house, my dad told me we were going to move—but I wasn't worried. I just kept telling myself, "Oh, it won't sell; it never has before." Was I wrong! The house sold, and soon after I finished my exams, my mom and I left for Murfreesboro, Tennessee, to live with my grandmother. My grandfather's health was bad, and we needed to be there for him and grandmother. At the same time, my dad had been called to go to Iraq. Mississippi had been my home for nine and a half years. I was a sophomore in high school with tons of amazing friends and a wonderful church, and I had just started dating a senior. This was the biggest trial I had ever faced. I began to pray and ask God to prepare me with strength and peace about moving.

Janelle Mitchell, 18, Siegel High School, Murfreesboro, TN

Lord, when I am worried about something,
help me to pray and ask for Your strength.
Talking to You will always helps.

July 16

moving to tennessee (part 2)

Such confidence as this is ours through Christ before God.

2 CORINTHIANS 3:3–4

God did give me strength and peace about moving, but it was still extremely hard. Changing schools in high school is one of the hardest things to do. Most juniors already have their friends and aren't looking for new ones. I missed my best friend from down the street at my old house…I didn't even have to knock on her door to go in. During this time of loneliness, I called on the Lord. My relationship with Him was strengthened. He gave me endurance, and perseverance to keep going. I had never lived near my extended family before, so I learned quickly that my grandmother would listen to my problems and pray with me whenever I needed someone. I don't know how I would have gotten through that year without the Lord and Him putting her in my life.

Janelle Mitchell, 18, Siegel High School, Murfreesboro, TN

Father, thank You for putting people in my life that support me and bring me closer to You. I couldn't make it without them.

sometimes it's hard to love

If your brother sins against you, go and show him his fault.... If he listens to you, you have won your brother over.

MATTHEW 18:15

I do not even know where to start! I have one sister and one brother and sometimes they can be so annoying that I wished they lived in Antarctica. Other times I am glad that they are here because I do not have to do all the chores by my self! Jesus says in Matthew 18:15, "If your brother sins against you, go and show him his fault.... If he listens to you, you have won your brother over." 1 John also says, "Whoever loves his brother lives in the light, and there is nothing in him to make him stumble." I do love my brother and sister...I just sometimes do not show it like I should. When I think bad things about them, these verses pop into my head, and I remember what Jesus said. I ask Him for forgiveness, and then I try to do better in showing them that I love them.

Ali VanMinos, 15, Oconee County Christian Academy, Seneca, SC

It's amazing how hard it can be to love people, Father. Please let Your Word guide me to love others even when it seems impossible.

July 18

when God says no

"Shall we accept good from God,
and not trouble?"
JOB 2:10

Think of a time (if you're like me, there have been many times) when you've wanted something really badly. You worked hard to achieve your goal; your hopes were up, expectations high. Then, for one reason or another, your parents said no. In the same way, when we ask God for things, His answer won't always be the one we hope for. More often than we want Him to, God says wait or even no. His plans are different from ours. I recently found out that my family would be moving to another state. Obviously, the plans I had for my life aren't the same as God's. On these occasions, my first reaction to God is like when my parents say no. I ask, "Why can't I have it? What's wrong with it? Don't you want me to be happy?" Our Heavenly Father does desire for us to be happy, but He also wants what's best for us. He'll give us the bad along with the good, not because he wants us to suffer, but because in the long run, we get more out of it. The question is, do we respect, love, and trust God enough to follow Him even when the answer is no? Coming to accept that God's plans are best, even when it doesn't seem that way, is something we'll only get better at the more we do it. As hard as it is, we have to trust that the unpleasant things God allows to happen are for our own good.

Emily Wilkin, 15, Walnut Grove Christian Preparatory School, Carmel, IN

God, next time, instead of asking why I
can't have I want, I pray that I will see what
You want for me and that I will accept it gladly.

faith?

Then he said to Thomas, "Put your finger here; see my hands. Reach out your hand and put it into my side. Stop doubting and believe."

JOHN 20:27

In 2001 my family was in India on a mission trip, and I saw many amazing things God was, and is still, doing in there in a country filled with lost people. One Sunday as we ministered in a local church we witnessed our living God at work as many came forward to be prayed with. One night there was a crusade going on with Impact World Tours. Afterward they gave the alter call for people who wanted to be healed of their diseases and ask Jesus into their hearts, and thousands of people rushed forward to accept Christ as their Lord and Savior! Having faith to believe that God is at work in such amazing ways is hard sometimes...it was hard for Thomas, in the Bible, to have faith and believe that Jesus rose from the grave and is alive! Jesus wants us to have faith and believe that through Him anything is possible. He wants to show us things and do miracles for us, but He also wants us to have faith in Him first. So have faith and believe!

Jana Kroeker, 15, home school, Medicine Hat, Alberta, CA

Lord, I want my faith in You to be strong so that I can see You working in the world, through me and around me, every day.

July 20

forever and always

Where you go I will go, and where you stay I will stay.
Your people will be my people
and your God my God.

RUTH 1:16

Loyalty is something imperative in the Christian life. We need to be loyal to God above all others. So if that is one of the most important things: Why is it so hard? I haven't really been tempted to turn on Christ since I go to a Christian school, but I can only imagine how hard it is for people in public schools! I pray my faith will remain strong once I leave our school and enter the "real" world. Christianity is so persecuted in the world today that is it just amazing. People don't seem to care whether or not they go against the Lord. I have been blessed with a wonderful family and wonderful friends that encourage me to walk with the Lord and never even think about straying. And, quite frankly, I don't want to. However…I know there's still room for improvement. I'm sure that when I do leave school and go out into the world that my faith and loyalty will be tested. Not only the loyalty to my Lord but my family and friends as well. Like Ruth, in one of the most poignant stories in the Bible, I will try to stay loyal to everything and everyone that I love.

Kelsie Nygren, 15, Covenant Christian Academy, El Paso, TX

I want to be a loyal person, Lord,
the kind of person people can always trust.
Help me to always keep my promises and never betray
the people I love—especially You!

but i don't want to obey!

He who obeys instructions guards his life,
but he who is contemptuous of his ways will die.

PROVERBS 19:16

Authority: something we teenagers naturally rebel against. It's something we're *known* for. I'd even go as far as to say that it's a fact of life. Most parents dread when their children become teenagers. We don't want to obey our parents or our teachers or even God! We want to live our life the way we want to, by our own standards and rules. Lately, I've found myself constantly challenging my mom and dad. I argue back, I'm sullen when they tell me to do things, and I just don't want to do what they want me to do. I often find myself thinking that I'm right and they're wrong. I might be right every now an d then, but most of the time, they are the ones that are correct. They are in control of my life, along with God. And despite what I want, what I'm feeling, I still have to obey my parents and God. God's the one in control of everything. He's the one who said for us to honor our fathers and mothers. He is in charge of our lives, no matter what we might wish. It's overwhelming, thinking that everything we do, everything we're going to do, is in the hands of an almighty God. But...it's also comforting. In a way, it truly is nice to know that we are forever protected, that we are cared for and loved. Knowing that, it's not *quite* as hard to accept authority.

Kelsie Nygren, 15, Covenant Christian Academy, El Paso, TX

I want to be right all the time, Lord, so please help me to remember that I don't know everything...even though it feels like I do sometimes. I want to obey my parents and You, no matter how hard it is.

July 22

the truth about lying

Everyone lies to his neighbor;
their flattering lips speak with deception.

PSALM 12:2

Liar. What an ugly word. One immediately wants to shrink away from it, to say, "No! I don't lie!" Well, that in itself is a lie. No one goes their whole life without telling a single lie. Me included, naturally. People want to cover up their faults, to say that they are good and perfect. Others merely want to please people by telling a "little white lie." I'll be blunt: I've told people that their new dress looks wonderful when it really doesn't. I'm guilty, just as everyone else is. We lie to our friends, our family, our neighbors. I think that we lie most to our parents; it's part of being a teenager, of wanting free reign. We don't want to get into trouble, and really, who would? And yet, hopefully, there is something to stop us in our tracks and to force us to tell the truth: guilt. Oh yes, that ever-so-lovely little reminder that we're doing something wrong. Personally, I'm afflicted by guilt a lot. And honestly: It's annoying. I want to be able to get away with these things, and yet that constant reminder that I'm doing wrong is always there. God despises lying. He wants us to be truthful, to honor our mothers and fathers (and I'm sure not being honest with them isn't exactly honoring). So, perhaps, next time something comes up that we are tempted to lie about, we should pause and remember that it *is* a sin. And also, not having to carry around a lot of guilt is a good thing too.

Kelsie Nygren, 15, Covenant Christian Academy, El Paso, TX

Father, I hate feeling guilty, feeling like I've let
You down. But please help me to remember that
awful feeling so that the next time I'm tempted to lie,
I'll make the better choice and tell the truth.

a quiet time

Walk in all the way that the LORD your God has commanded you, so that you may live and prosper.

DEUTERONOMY 5:33

Having balance in your life is very important. It can be so hard to remember to have quiet time with everything going on. There's always some homework that needs to be done, an instrument to practice, work, friends to hangout with. Just a little Bible time can waste that precious time, right? Wrong! Without Christ, where would we be? He's the One who created us and died for our sins! Shouldn't we spend the time to get to know Him? If you don't have a normal quiet time with God, you're missing out on who He really is. About four years ago I recommitted my life to Christ. I decided to discipline myself to get to know Christ better. I wish I could say I do it every single day, but I can't. I've gotten better at it, but I'm still working on it. When I do it every day for about two weeks, I feel this incredible peace. The more you search who God is and spend time with Him, the more He will fill you up. He is so anxious for you to come to Him just to spend time in His word and talk with Him. He always listens. He always cares. He is the perfect friend. One of my favorite characteristics is His unconditional love. No matter what, he will still love you! When it feels like everyone's gone, God is there to love you and comfort you. He is wonderful. I want to challenge you to spend time with God and make him an important part of your life. You will never regret it.

Danae Downs, 15, home school, Grand Junction, CO

Even these few minutes I'm spending with You to read these devotions are making a big difference, Father. I want to spend more time with You and get to know You even better.

July 24

tranquility

No temptation has seized you except
what is common to man. And God is
faithful; he will not let you be tempted beyond
what you can bear. But when you are tempted, he will also
provide a way out so that you can stand up under it.

1 CORINTHIANS 10:13

Hanging on.
Hanging by a tread I refuse to let go.
Quitting is not a choice.
Far below is an easy path if I fell I could be just like every-one else.
Without a mind, or a soul.
Unlike those that came before me I have one thing to keep me firm.
A bond of friendship that remains faithfully strong.
The only person that has stayed right there beside me.
The one person that I can tell the truth, and one person to keep me true.
I thought I was all alone, but now I know I have one rea-son to keep hanging on.

Rachel Crane, 14, home school, Lewisburg, TN

God, thank You for being my reason
to hold on when I feel like I can't.
I am so glad You are my unshakable foundation.

treasure hunting

I rejoice in your promise like one who finds great spoil.

Psalm 119:162

I am a hunter. A bargain hunter. The girls of our family all love a bargain. Just yesterday we found a great sale on jewelry at the mall. It thrilled me. I also found marked-down summer shirts, as well as cute fall sweaters on sale. I'm just sad I have to wait until warm weather to show off some of my new finds. I wish I was as determined and diligent to find treasures in the Bible as I am to snag a find in a great sale. This fall I've been reading through the Old Testament for the first time. I used to think it was only genealogy lists and odd rules for Israel, but now I've seen it's alive and applicable to me. I've learned from David and seen the qualities that made him a "man after God's own heart." God has shown me how merciful He was (and is) through His dealings with the Israelites. Like faithfully looking through a clearance rack to find clothes that fit, carefully reading the Bible, Old and New Testaments, is so worth the time it takes to locate treasures. Long after my clothes bargains wear out or are no longer stylish, these treasures will still be bringing me joy.

Christina Jensen, 15, Dogwood Christian School, Asheville, NC

God, I want to look hard for the messages
You have for me in the Bible. I want
to be dedicated to learning from every story.

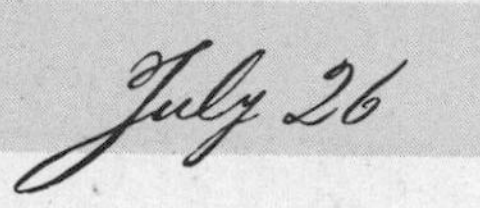

God is here

Where can I go from your Spirit? Where can I flee from your presence? If I go up to the heavens, you are there; if I make my bed in the depths, you are there. If I rise on the wings of the dawn, if I settle on the far side of the sea, even there your hand will guide me, your right hand will hold me fast. If I say, "Surely the darkness will hide me and the light become night around me," even the darkness will not be dark to you; the night will shine like the day, for darkness is as light to you.

PSALM 139:7–12

"God is here": I grew up in a Christian home, and for the longest time, I took those words for granted. Recently though, I found myself struggling with many things. Several difficult things in my life had me living in a constant state of fear. One night I confided in my sister about my fears and doubts. She took me to those three words. I said, "Yeah, can you tell me something that helps?" She went on to explain, and now I can't stop marveling at them. To understand, you have to take it one word at a time. *God*—who is God? He is righteous, loving, my protector and father, just, and all powerful, and the list goes on forever. *Is*—not *was*, not *will be*, *is*; God is here right now no matter what is going on. *Here*—how many places does here cover? Anywhere you are. He covers every place from church to the darkest street corner you've ever stood on. In places where He is not acknowledged or invited God is *still* there. *God is here*. Those words aren't *just* words to me anymore. They are comforting and life changing.

Carmen Dockweiler, 18, Nebraska Christian High School, Central City, NE

Dear Lord, I want to know You're always here.
I want to know it deep in my heart.

cats

Religion that God our Father accepts as pure and faultless is this: to look after orphans and widows in their distress and to keep oneself from being polluted by the world.

JAMES 1:27

It had become my passion early on in life to take care of stray cats (thought I'm a little saner about it now than I was then). Early in the morning, summer, winter, rain or shine, I would wake up to feed them, one by one, a feast of cold cuts, cheese, milk...whatever I could find. I would do anything in my capacity to make sure that every single one was happy. To me, they were the homeless people living out on the street, and I made it my responsibility to take care of them. These pets that tired owners had dropped off at my house had become my best friends after reaching out to them. Cats, however, are not the only ones who feel the sting of rejection. Often times, as Christians, we walk through our daily lives avoiding the "unwanted" or the "looked down on" in our society. Maybe it's the person in the lunch room who no one wants at their table, or maybe it's the girl who only owns two outfits because her family can't afford to buy her anymore. Whoever it is, don't you think that they deserve some love and attention? Would you be willing to reach out to those around you who are rejected by others? Christ's example was one of being around those who were rejected by His society. Take the time to reach out to those around you who are less accepted; this is true religion according to Christ.

Kristin Humphrey, 17, Houghton Christian Academy, Warsaw, NY

Lord, it isn't easy to be friends with people who other people have rejected. Kids might make fun of me...but I want to do Your will and not worry about what others will say.

July 28

we remain

The LORD is my strength and my song;
he has become my salvation. He is my God, and
I will praise him, my father's God, and I will exalt him.

EXODUS 15:2

Time slips by;
People fade away.
Stars that once shined brightly are dim, but we remain.
The sky around us falls, but we live on.
The earth is no longer under our feet, but we stand strong.
Guided by faith, we venture into the world.
When we have fallen, our quest goes on.
Listen to the World,
Listen to the World,
To those in pain,
The cry of the world as humanity slips away.
It's fading out.
Listen with all your might so you're not sent away.
Listen to what I say. Heed my words and never forget to
listen to the world,
Unless you want to fade away.

Rachel Crane, 14, home school, Lewisburg, TN

I want to hear people when they
cry for help, Lord. And when I hear them,
I want to help them. I don't want to ignore them.

sale rack

A gentle answer turns away wrath,
but a harsh word stirs up anger.
PROVERBS 15:1

Words affect me a great deal. If I get a compliment or encouragement after a long hard day, it always puts me in a good mood, no matter how horrible the day was. On the flip side, a harsh or discouraging comment from someone will take me right down, and it usually takes a whole lot of kind words to bring me back up again. I wish I could say that my own sensitivity to words has taught me to use them gently and wisely with other people, but that is not always the case. I have to keep reminding myself that I can either encourage someone or break them down, even in just a simple conversation. Our words are powerful, and they are like clothes on the final-sale rack: We can't take them back!

Lindsay Oliver, 15, Cedar Hall School, Nashville, TN

Words can hurt me so much, Jesus.
So please help me to save other people the pain
that I sometimes feel. Help me to say more
kind things and be less hurtful.

July 30

undivided devotion

An unmarried woman or virgin is concerned about the Lord's affairs: Her aim is to be devoted to the Lord in both body and spirit.... I am saying this for your own good, not to restrict you, but that you may live in a right way in undivided devotion to the Lord.

1 CORINTHIANS 7:34–35

We all want to love and be loved. Sometimes we satisfy that longing with our boyfriends, but then when we break up with him or get broken up with, and our need for love is still there. I am convinced that God wants us to be devoted to Him before anyone or anything else. He wants us to be satisfied in His love. For me, that means that I have decided not to date. For now, I want to commit my years of being single to undistracted service to God. It has been freeing to not have to wonder if I will date every other boy I meet. Deciding not to date is definitely not for everyone, but I think that trusting in the Father of Lights, from whom every good and perfect gift comes (James 1:17), is for everyone. When we truly start believing that, then we are no longer desperate for love from the guys around us. We are free to live in God's love and the promise of His goodness.

Bethany Pearl Reeves, 15, home school, Central, SC

I don't want anything to keep me from Your love, God. Not even a guy. No one can love me like You.

i want to be wise

"I, Wisdom, live together with good judgment. I know where to discover knowledge and discernment....

The LORD *formed me from the beginning, before he created anything else. I was appointed in ages past, at the very first, before the earth began. I was born before the oceans were created, before the springs bubbled forth their waters. Before the mountains and the hills were formed, I was born—before he had made the earth and fields and the first handfuls of soil.*

I was there when he established the heavens, when he drew the horizon on the oceans....

I was the architect at his side. I was his constant delight, rejoicing always in his presence. And how happy I was with what he created—his wide world and all the human family!"

PROVERBS 8:12, 22–27, 30–31 (NLT)

August 1

better or worse?

A righteous man is cautious in friendship,
but the way of the wicked leads them astray.

Proverbs 12:26

My friends are a huge part of my life. Some of my friends who are Christians have pushed me forward in life and have helped me grow in my relationship with Christ. They have kept me accountable by asking me the hard questions and by being there to remind me when I am getting it wrong. I have also had friends that have influenced me in some bad ways. With them, I have chosen to do things that I know are wrong, and when I am with them I become someone different than who I want to be. Have you ever thought about what a powerful influence the people around you have in your life? Whether we realize it or not, our friends push us to change, for the better or for the worse. They can encourage us or tear us down. What type of friends do you have? Are they bringing you closer to Christ or distracting you from Him? What kind of person are you becoming because of your friends?

Bekah Henderson, 17, Oconee County Christian Academy, Seneca, SC

Lord, give me the wisdom—and the strength—
to choose friends who will bring me closer to You.

a real friend

A friend loves at all times.

PROVERBS 17:17

Have you ever heard the saying "Friendship is one of God's most precious gifts"? God has blessed me with some incredible friends. When my family first moved to Grand Junction, God gave me friends right from the beginning, and they are still with me today. My friends encourage me, love me, and support me. We all need friends, and everyone needs to be a friend. So how can we be good friends? And how do we choose the good friends? There are three qualities that I think make any old friend a true friend. First is **Love**. Love is the foundation of a friendship: "Love your neighbor as yourself" (Matthew 19:19). Love isn't just a warm, fuzzy feeling inside that comes and goes; it sticks around even when you don't *feel* it. The second is **Listening**. Not focusing on yourself helps you to be a good listener. Sometimes just listening is the best way to love someone and show them that you care about what is going on in their lives. **Constancy**. No one wants a fair-weather friend. Being constant is being a friend that people can count on through *everything*. Love, listening, constancy: Your friends should have these qualities and so should you. When you do, your friendship is truly a gift from God.

Danae Downs, 15, home school, Grand Junction, CO

Please help me, dear God, to love my friends,
listen to them, and always be there for them.
And help them do the same for me.

August 3

you are God's art

God created man in his own image, in the image of God he created him; male and female he created them.

GENESIS 1:27

Why do we look at the girl next to us and wish we had her hair, nose, or thighs? Did God make a mistake when He made you or me? Sometimes it can seem that way. I used to feel awkward around people, which was weird since I am outgoing and love talking with new people. But during that stage I would retreat because I felt unsure around others. I was struggling with this when God showed me that I was paying more attention to what others said than what God says is true about me. Allowing the fear of people to rule my heart made me very insecure. I thought that the way people perceived me was how God must think of me too. WRONG! Read some of the truths in His word about you. He planned your body shape, chose the talents and gifts you have, and even knew where you would grow up and live. The enemy attacks God's artwork when he lies to us about our bodies, our personalities, and our lives. The only way to gain victory over insecurity is to trust in who you are in Christ. I started with reading and rereading Psalm 139. Learning who Christ is teaches you about who you are, because we are all made in His image. What an honor to be made in the image of the only perfect being that ever existed, to be God's artwork!

Chloé Truehl, 18, Adelaide, Australia

Is it true You made me, God?
Made me just the way I am? I'm just not sure I believe it.
Help me to believe today and feel it in my heart.

stepmom

Be kind and compassionate to one another, forgiving each other, just as in Christ God forgave you.

EPHESIANS 4:32

My parents divorced when I was three years old. My mom remarried when I was four and my dad remarried when I was about seven. I have always gotten along with my stepdad, but my stepmom is a different story. I blamed her for the divorce. I knew that one of the reasons my parents divorced was because my dad was cheating with another woman, and I had a feeling that my stepmom was the one he had cheated with. And so I was angry with her. I completely disrespected her. I talked back to her and told her she was ugly. Even though I did all those things, she was nothing but nice to me. She always bought me beautiful things, including my favorite necklace. I always wondered why she was so nice to me, when I was so awful. When I was about thirteen, my family started going back to church. The first Sunday we were there, the pastor gave a sermon about forgiveness. It was just what I needed and God knew that. Christ did not give up on me, and He has been changing my heart. I have finally found peace with my stepmom, and I know that without Christ I would probably still hate her. God wants us to forgive, and He will help us to do so, but we have to allow Him to work this gift in our lives. When we do, it is truly a beautiful thing.

Courtney Pinto, 15, Walnut Grove Christian Preparatory School, Fishers, IN

Father, thank You for people who are kind to me even when I treat them terribly. They teach me about You and Your love.

August 5

out of the depths

I can do all things through Christ
which strengtheneth me.

PHILIPPIANS 4:13 (KJV)

At the beginning of this year, I was depressed. It completely debilitated me and put my entire life on hold. I could not do anything by myself, and I did not want to be alone. Along with depression, I had obsessive-compulsive disorder and anxiety. It was hard to be seventeen and have these problems. I was supposed to be carefree, concerned with boys and friends and my schoolwork. Every day my parents and I prayed that I would get better. After a while, the depression got old. I slowly have gotten over all of it, except the fear of being alone. I have been on many different medications for about four months and a lot of them didn't really help me, but God has helped me tremendously. He is still helping me every day.

Brittany Plyler, 17, New Covenant Christian School, Pageland, SC

The best medicine when I'm not well,
Lord, is always You. Thank You for helping me get better.

separated

For what the law was powerless to do in that it was weakened by the sinful nature, God did by sending his own Son in the likeness of sinful man to be a sin offering.

ROMANS 8:3

When I was fifteen, my grandmother was diagnosed with cancer. We were living with her at the time, and she was in and out of the hospital, so I tried to help out more. It was hard, and I tried to keep up with cooking, paying bills, and shopping for food. It was exhausting trying to do these things in addition to school. My grandma started arranging for family members to watch us, which I hated. It was my home, and I didn't like other people coming in to look after us. I remember having to take my younger brothers to see the social worker and having to decide where we were going to live. My younger brothers were thirteen and eleven, and I don't think any of us really understood what was going on. The social worker said that we had to move because my grandmother wasn't able to take care of us because of her cancer. That just tore my heart out! I was separated from my older and youngest brothers and my older sister, and the following February my grandmother passed away. Even as I lost so many people that I loved, God stayed with me. Things are not easy, but He never leaves me.

Lissete Russell, 19, Redemption Christian Academy, Troy, NY

Thank You, Jesus, for never leaving me.
I am never alone as long as I trust in You.

August 7

what's the worst that can happen?

Do not be afraid of those who kill the body but cannot kill the soul. Rather, be afraid of the One who can destroy both soul and body in hell.

MATTHEW 10:28

Recently I headed out on a missions trip far from home. My mom is the kind of mom who worries about everything. To make matters worse, I am the youngest in the family, the baby, so she is even more protective of me than of my siblings. I have an intense passion for missions, and I take every opportunity I get to go on trips. On the night before my trip to New Orleans, my mom was looking very distressed, and I asked her, "What's the worst thing that can happen to me?" She just stood there, not saying anything. I proceeded to list various things that could happen to me (most ending in death), which probably wasn't the smartest thing to do given the situation. She looked as if she might cry. At that moment a song came to mind and I sang her the chorus. It talked about how our souls are secure in Christ, even if our bodies are hurt. I gently said to her, "Mom, I am in Christ and nothing will happen that is outside of His will." After this, she was able to let me go on my trip, believing that I was Christ's. I later realized that Satan cannot ultimately do anything to me. God can allow any number of things to come into our lives, but we are never outside His love or control.

Rebecca Brill, 18, Nebraska Christian High School, Aurora, NE

Thank You, Father, for Your constant protection. You keep me safe every single day.

He's first!

"Love the Lord your God with all your heart and with all your soul and with all your mind and with all your strength."

MARK 12:30

Have you ever liked a guy so much that you cannot stop thinking about him, no matter what you do? Maybe at first you kind of liked him and wondered if he would ever like you. Next, you are shopping near where he works to try and "accidentally" run into him. Before you know it, you're acting like a different person, just for his sake. I've definitely been there. My crush was so big and out of control. I spent more time in front of the mirror, thinking about him, and imagining scenarios with us together than anything else in my life. And then one day I woke up and I didn't have a crush on him anymore. It was so odd, almost like God had just removed my desire to please this guy. Since then, this desire has been replaced with the desire to please God. I am free to think and do other things not related to this guy, and mostly, I'm free to be my genuine self. Looking back, I believe that God wanted me to focus on Him more than anyone else. Maybe for you it's not a guy, but maybe it's sports, hobbies, or even school that takes all of your attention. I think that God wants us to learn to be wise and balanced with the time He has given us, and more than anything, He wants to always be first in our lives.

Lindsay Oliver, 15, Cedar Hall School, Nashville, TN

Dear God, when I feel really busy today (which I know I will), remind me that no matter how busy I am, I should always make time for You.

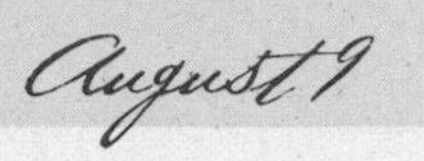

marco! polo!

Whether you turn to the right or to the left, your ears will hear a voice behind you, saying, "This is the way; walk in it."

Isaiah 30:21

I got into the car to drive to youth group and I felt like I should stop and eat my snack first. I admit it was kind of an odd thought, but decided there was no harm in stopping and munching on a few grapes before I pulled out of my driveway. Just as I was getting ready to leave for the second time, my mom came out to tell me that youth group had been cancelled. Now I know that it would not have been the end of the world to get to youth group, realize it was canceled, and drive back home. But, I think it's pretty cool that I listened to that nudging and it saved me the hassle. I don't know about you, but sometimes I don't hear God's nudgings quite so clearly. Often I feel like I am calling out "Marco" and endlessly waiting for God to respond back "Polo." God says we can hear His voice if we learn what to listen for, so maybe I am expecting the wrong sort of response. Listening well doesn't necessarily mean we will hear an audible voice. Maybe hearing God will come in the form of the idea to talk to a random person that we've never noticed before; maybe we will suddenly feel God's love in an overwhelming and real way; or maybe we will have a very clear direction about the decision we've been struggling to make. But however God chooses to reach out to us, I think that hearing God means being open to what HE wants to show us, instead of coming with expectations of how He should communicate. And then being willing to do what He says, even if it's something as small as eating grapes!

Maranatha Schulte, 17, Ben Lippen School, Columbia, SC

Keep me ears open, Lord Jesus, so that I can hear every direction You give. Show me what You want me to do.

awesome threesome

Not that I have already obtained all this…
but I press on to take hold of that for
which Christ Jesus took hold of me.

PHILIPPIANS 3:12

I am only sixteen, but so far, I have discovered three important/awesome things that help me keep my life on track.

1.) Self-esteem is awesome. Growing up isn't easy. In elementary school I was teased a lot, which made me cry. To shield myself from the pain, I developed a hard shell in middle school. It kept me from crying, but built up a wall that kept anyone from getting close. In ninth grade I recognized I needed God's help to get my self-esteem back and to break down the wall. Now if I get teased it doesn't bother me as much because I know who I am and I like it.

2.) Respect is awesome. Some of my friends don't know Christ yet, and I try to respect them no matter what they believe. I've learned that to be respected I must be the same person no matter who I am hanging out with. This is how Jesus acted towards people, and I want to be a good example to my friends so they will want to know Jesus too.

3.) Morals and Values are awesome. They guide our lives, affecting the decisions we make, and take a lifetime to grow. I know I am just beginning that lifetime, but I do not want to give up my morals and values for a good-looking guy who does not respect me. Because I have stronger self-esteem now, I can stick to my morals and values more easily (and not get so distracted by boys and other stuff). And when I do that, I earn respect from my friends and I am a good witness to them.

Candace K. Croston, 16, King's Fork High School, Suffolk, VA

Lord, lead me to the qualities and actions
that will make me a good Christian. I want to live
a life that is worthy of You.

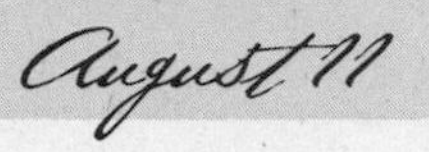

echoes in eternity

"Do not store up for yourselves treasures on earth, where moth and rust destroy, and where thieves break in and steal. But store up for yourselves treasures in heaven, where moth and rust do not destroy, and where thieves do not break in and steal. For where your treasure is, there your heart will be also."

MATTHEW 6:19–21

Being a senior and almost done with high school has really made me realize that this life goes by quickly. I keep asking myself if I have spent my time wisely. I recently read a poem that says, "Our one life twill soon be past and only what is done for Christ will last." That line struck me so profoundly. I have never understood so clearly that what I do now echoes in eternity. I want you to imagine with me a white rope so long it would go around the earth billions and billions of times. At the very beginning of that rope, the first inch is dyed red. That single inch is the length of our life on earth and all the rest of the rope is eternity. But even that little spot affects all the rest of the rope because the rope wouldn't be complete without it. I don't think very often about how the ways I spend my time now affect eternity. That is a scary, sobering thought because I feel like I have already wasted so much time! However, it is never too late to start living in a way that will echo in eternity.

Rebecca Brill, 18, Nebraska Christian High School, Aurora, NE

I don't want to waste any more time, God. Please show me Your purpose for my life and give me the desire to pursue it every minute.

the beautifier

Salvation is found in no one else,
for there is no other name under heaven
given to men by which we must be saved.

ACTS 4:12

This world is a broken and hurting place, and we are ALL desperate for God. I think it is easy to go through life and forget about the lonely, the hurting, the entangled, and the depressed people, when we are not in their midst. I forget that some of the people who are experiencing these things are people who know God. My prayer is that we will not forget to cry out to God in every hard situation we go through in our lives. It is only the love and grace of God that can touch the broken and wounded parts of our hearts. Psalm 103:3–4 reads, "God forgives all your sins, heals all your diseases, redeems your life from the pit and corruption and beautifies, dignifies and crowns you with loving-kindness and tender mercy." Wow! May we never forget to turn to Him and allow him to beautify and redeem our lives, through His loving-kindness!

Alexandra Truehl, 15, Adelaide, Australia

Thank You, Jesus, for making my life something beautiful. It is so incredible that You died for me!

bits and pieces

Now faith is being sure of what we hope for and being certain of what we do not see.

HEBREWS 11:1

What does it mean to have faith in something that we cannot see? I think that if we look closely enough, we will see bits and pieces of Him who we have faith in and hope for in the world around us. I get to know God better when I see my little sister singing "Jesus Loves Me," when I sit quietly and watch the sun slowly and brilliantly sink beyond the horizon, and when I remember that all the good things in my life are gifts from above. In order to see these little glimpses of God around us, we have to look with different eyes. Even with eyes of faith, sometimes we can't figure out how God is communicating with us. That is when we simply have to believe what we know to be true about our God. That is when we look at the amazing way He has orchestrated the world in the past and the incredible things He has planned for the future and say we trust Him, even though we do not see. I think it has to work like this because faith is not something to see and view from a distance; it is something to be experienced and lived out, every day, in our attitudes and our actions. And so, until we do see fully, until we are with Him face to face, we must keep looking for and believing in the glimpses of eternity that we get each day.

Michelle Palacio, 15, Alpha Omega Academy, Charlotte, NC

God, help me to see You in every part of my life so that my faith in You will grow stronger.

friend for life

Go in peace, for we have sworn friendship with each other in the name of the LORD.

1 SAMUEL 20:42

I have a really important friend, Katherine. She is one of the most considerate people I know. She is the type of person that will help you through anything. Whenever we're together, if anyone so much as bumps his or her toe, she is like, "Oh my gosh! Are you ok?" She cares about everyone and is always doing things for other people. I have never seen her really sad. Even when she is upset, she still seems to be smiling. I have never heard her complain—something I have a problem with. I remember the day we first met, at the playground of my sister's school. Pam, Kat's really nice sister, Kat, and I were playing on the merry-go-round. I was cold, so Kat gave me her gloves without me asking for them. That was when we were about nine; now we're fourteen. I've been at her house so many times that her family is like my family. We're inseparable! I am thankful that God has brought us together. He has used Kat to help me through a lot of hard times. God is such a wonderful Creator to bless people with great friends. Kat is one of my best friends, and I hope to know her for the rest of my life.

Sarah Lewis, 14, Walnut Grove Christian Preparatory School, Sheridan, IN

Really good friends are so amazing because they show me Christ's love. Thank You, God, for giving me the gift of friendship.

keep calling

*Now faith is being sure of what we hope for
and certain of what we do not see.*

HEBREWS 11:1

I wanted so badly to get into the Martin Luther King school! I was worried because my letter of acceptance was sent in late. When I turned in my letter, I was told I would be put on a waiting list, at number thirty-one. Despite this, I told my teachers at my old school that I would not be returning. At the time, I had no idea if this was true or not, but I just had a feeling that somehow, someway I would be switching schools and attending Martin Luther King next year. Every day I called to see if I moved up on the waiting list. I started to get discouraged because every day my name was still at number thirty-one. I called so often that the lady who answered the phones knew my name and exactly what I wanted before I asked. She could tell when I got frustrated, and she encouraged me to keep calling. Slowly, many, many calls later, the lady on the phone told me that I was number one on the waiting list. All I needed was one more spot to open up. I was very nervous because school started in just three days, and I still didn't know which school I would be going to. But God knew. The next day I received my letter of acceptance to MLK, and it reminded me of the importance of not giving up and of continuing to hope.

Jazma Parker, 16, Martin Luther King Magnet School, Nashville, TN

*God, I know that You want me to be
persistent when I want something.
Give me the faith to keep asking You until I get an answer.*

inferior?

May the God of hope fill you with all joy and peace, as you trust in Him, so that you might overflow with hope by the power of the Holy Spirit.

ROMANS 15:13

In physiology our teacher enthusiastically explained to us how one thing lower than another could be called *inferior*. For example, the heart is inferior to the brain because it is physically below your head. In science, inferior simply describes where something is located; it doesn't mean the heart, or any other "inferior" organ, is less important. "Inferior" should mean the same thing in people's lives. This last year, I wrestled with feelings of inferiority. When we moved, I compared myself to my new peers. During volleyball season, I mainly played on the "C team" even though I was a junior, while my friends played a level up. Granted, I hadn't really played volleyball before, but it still hurt. I began thinking of myself as inferior or not good enough. Thoughts like these persisted throughout the year. One night it hit me that I needed to depend on God for my self-worth, not others. Romans 15:13 helped me realize how the God of hope is the one who gives joy and peace. All through the summer, God kept showing me that I was still perfect to Him even if I was "lower" than some of the people around me. Feelings of inferiority still plague me, but I have to remind myself that I am special, even if I sit the bench. I may not be the captain or all-star player, but I play just as important a role in God's plan as anyone else. Even though the heart is inferior, the brain wouldn't be able to function without it. The same is true for the body of Christ!

Laura Reimer, 17, Nebraska Christian High School, Central City, NE

Father, thank You for making me a part of the body of Christ. I love that I am so valuable to You.

August 17

bumpy friendship (part 1)

Pursue peace with all men, and holiness, without which no man will see the Lord.

HEBREWS 12:14 (KJV)

During my sophomore year, I met a girl and we instantly clicked. We quickly became close friends and true confidants. Then, after a while everything in our friendship started getting really weird. She stopped talking to me and acted like she didn't want to be around me anymore. I don't think rejection ever feels good, but in this situation it was even harder because I did not know why she was rejecting me. I had three ways that I could have chosen to respond to her: 1.) retaliate and snub her, talk about her to other friends, in an effort to get back at her; 2.) confront her and ask bluntly what her problem is; 3.) pray for her and choose, as a willful act, to forgive her. I chose option number two, which blew the situation up into an even bigger problem. I was so confused, frustrated, and angry. I still did not know what I had done wrong in the first place to cause my friend to treat me that way. It got so bad that we could not even stand to see each other. I felt like it was hopeless and that I had run out of God's grace. Thankfully, His grace never runs out…but I hadn't figured that out yet.

Maranatha Schulte, 17, Ben Lippen School, Columbia, SC

God, help me to remember that Your grace never runs out, no matter what.

weeds and healing (part 2)

Follow peace with all men, and holiness,
without which no man shall see the Lord.

HEBREWS 12:14 (KJV)

I knew that God wanted me to forgive my friend and move on, but I really didn't want to. I had been told before that un-forgiveness is like fertilizer to weeds of bitterness. Where un-forgiveness remains unchecked, bitterness eventually takes over, until it is impossible to enjoy being around anyone anymore. It was a hard thing to do because I was still hurt, but I asked God to give me the love I needed to forgive her. His answer was a process. He asked me to do several, deliberate acts of kindness for my friend, to soften my heart towards her. I learned to redirect my thoughts when I began to get angry at how she had treated me. I started praying for her and for myself. And I had to accept responsibility for whatever part I played in the break down of our friendship. As I took those steps of obedience, the healing process began. God has restored my relationship with her, and though it is not the same as it once was, we have truly forgiven each other and moved on. When your own journey finds you in a battle to forgive or not, remember that God is waiting to give you the grace to walk through it His way, if you are willing to humble yourself and obey.

Maranatha Schulte, 17, Ben Lippen School, Columbia, SC

Forgiving is so hard, Father.
Teach me how to do it even when it
seems like it isn't possible.

the simple life (part 1)

"This, then, is how you should pray: 'Our Father in heaven, hallowed be your name.'"

MATTHEW 6:9

Life was simple when I was little. I got up, ate some Apple Jacks, went to "school," where I took a nap and made crafts, went back home and had dinner, made a mess for mom to clean up, and then went to sleep. This was the basic daily cycle. For me, even a relationship with Christ was easy to attain. It was as simple as saying my ABCs. I was told, "Tell God that you are sinner. Believe that Jesus is God's only Son. Commit your life to God, and ask Him to fill you up with His love." Yes, things used to be simple. Then, slowly in the beginning and then more rapidly, life began to change. I got my driver's permit and then my license, and I got a lot more freedom. I began filling every waking moment with activities and people and places to go. My life became complicated and confusing, and sometimes it was even scary, although I didn't want to admit that! The truth (that I am usually "too busy" to pay attention to) is that simplicity and silence are so necessary. Christ longs for us to spend time just being with Him. He doesn't make pursuing a relationship with Him hard, but it does require that we stop our busyness and focus on Him. I think He is waiting, hoping that each one of us does this.

Hope Hamilton, 17, Donelson Christian Academy, Donelson, TN

Things can get so complicated. Help me, dear Jesus, to see that You are the only really important thing. The rest is just clutter.

the simple life (part 2)

"This, then, is how you should pray:
'Our Father in heaven, hallowed be your name.'"

MATTHEW 6:9

God doesn't make us jump through a bunch of hoops in order to know Him and to serve Him. He even tells his disciples (and us) how to pray. There are so many ways to worship God. Sometimes worship is singing along to a CD as you drive to school. Sometimes it is thanking God for everything that you can think of that He has given you. Sometimes worship is being curious and astonished by the creativity and diversity you see in nature. My life is so complicated and hectic that I struggle to give God my time. I want to uncomplicate my life, and in a sense this is impossible, because the world and sin are always confusing and complicating things. But we can simplify life some by focusing on what is essential. I have been learning to stop filling up every moment of every day with activity. I have been leaving space in my life to let God in. I have been asking if the ways I spend my time and the things I do will matter in five years, or in a couple of months, or even tomorrow...When I do this, suddenly the pressure I put on myself dissipates. I begin to see what matters—and that is Christ. It overwhelms me that GOD *wants to be with me all the time*, 24/7! As much as I love my friends, I sometimes get tired of them after spending a lot of time with them, but God never gets tired of us!

Hope Hamilton, 17, Donelson Christian Academy, Donelson, TN

You really want to be with me all the time?
That's almost impossible to believe. But I want
to believe it, and I pray that You will help me do it.

what's joy?

Consider it pure joy when you face trials of many kinds, because you know that the testing of your faith develops perseverance.

JAMES 1:2–3

What is joy? *Joy* is one of those words we hear a lot, but don't really understand. When the God tells us to consider the hard things in our lives pure joy, He cannot be talking about the bouncy, cheerful kind of joy that laughs at everything. Does God really mean that we should be joyful and laugh when a loved one dies or when parents get divorced? God's idea of joy must be different than what we initially think of. The dictionary defines *joy* as great pleasure or happiness; a source or object of pleasure. As Christians, we have a great happiness (joy) in all things because of what God has done for us. He sent His only Son to die for our sins, and because of this, we will live forever with Him. This is why Jesus wants us to be joyful no matter what circumstance we are in. Because, ultimately, we *do* have the best reason in the world to be joyful.

Ali VanMinos, 15, Oconee County Christian Academy, Seneca, SC

Father, I want to celebrate You every second.
I want to be happy because I know You.
I want to show the world the joy You have given me!

no one said it would be easy

Do not conform any longer to the pattern of this world, but be transformed by the renewing of your mind. Then you will be able to test and approve what God's will is—his good, pleasing and perfect will.

ROMANS 12:2

I have never heard anyone say that growing up is easy. For me, going from elementary to middle school was a big change, but the biggest change was going from middle to high school. On the first day of my freshman year, I felt intense pressure to dress "right," act "right," and talk "right." I remember feeling terribly awkward around the "popular" kids. I was afraid that if I messed up or said something stupid, I would be made fun of and forever put in the lame category. But the transition to high school brought with it some good changes along with the hard ones. I started to grow in my relationship with God, and as I did, I slowly began to care less about what anyone and everyone else thought of me. I started caring more about what God thought of me, and I grew less afraid of being just who I was. I began to make friends that love me for who I am, who don't make me try to be someone I am not. I am thankful for the person I am, and even for the tough process it has been to get here.

Katelyn Westfall, 15, Dover High School, Dover, OH

You never said the right road would be the easy road, Lord. Help me to learn from hard times rather than just feeling sorry for myself.

a joyful job

If anyone serves, he should do it with the strength God provides, so that in all things God may be praised through Jesus Christ.

1 Peter 4:11

I am usually a fairly happy person. More often than not, I have some song stuck in my head that I can't seem to help singing. But the one thing that is guaranteed to change my mood and make me stop my singing is getting assigned a long list of jobs to do around the house. When this happens, I am definitely not a joyful person inside. Sometimes I feel like bluntly refusing to do what my parents tell me to do, but usually, I trudge ahead, making even the simplest chores into the hardest jobs known to humans. I really long to have God's joy in everything I do and say, whether I am hanging out with friends, babysitting, or doing the gnarliest of chores. One of these days I want to shock my parents by singing, "The joy of the Lord is my strength..." while cleaning the bathroom. I know that my parents would be flabbergasted. I still have a lot to learn about doing my chores with a joyful heart. I can just imagine the difference it would make in my own life and in other people's lives if I was joyful all the time. I am beginning to believe that joy is a choice. And I want to choose it.

Jana Kroeker, 15, home school, Medicine Hat, Alberta, CA

Today, when my parents ask me to do some boring chore, I want to do it with joy, Lord. It will surprise them in a really good way.

like a fawn

As the deer pants for streams of water,
so my soul pants for you, O God.

PSALM 42:1

A deer's best line of defense is its swift, powerful, and slender legs. It is always alert, watching, listening, and sniffing, ready to bolt if danger is near. Sometimes following the fleeing instinct would be a death sentence for fawns because they are not strong enough to withstand a long run. It is better for them to hunker down and lie motionless, hopefully evading detection. If a fawn were to grow impatient, hop up, and run for his life, he would be easy prey for a coyote, a mountain lion, or whatever predator was stalking him. It may seem like an odd comparison, but I think that we can learn a lot from deer, fawns in particular. I think that people have a similar instinct to continually go and be actively pursuing something all the time. Like the fawn, sometimes we need to stop running and allow the Holy Spirit to care for us. There are times when we are too weak to fight temptation or to run, and instead of trying, perhaps we need to hunker down and rest in the arms and shield of God. So, let's be more like the fawn, remembering that our instincts are not always the best option and that patience is vital our lives as Christians.

Carrie Lewis, 14, home school with tutorial, Clemson, SC

I know I need You, dear God, so much.
Make me thirsty for You alone.

easier said than done

So, if you think you are standing firm, be careful that you don't fall! No temptation has seized you except what is common to man. And God is faithful; he will not let you be tempted beyond what you can bear. But when you are tempted, he will also provide a way out so that you can stand up under it.

1 Corinthians 10:12–13

Saying no to temptation is not easy because we are not tempted by things that aren't appealing or attractive to us. For me, drugs were a big struggle for me. It seemed like everyone was doing them, and it was hard to be different, to not give in. Looking back, I see that I was in a shaky place in my relationship with God, and the people I hung out with were not the friends I thought they were. They accepted me because I was just like them, and it felt good to be a part of the "in crowd," to be accepted by them. But when I finally stopped doing drugs, my friends suddenly stopped accepting me or liking me at all. They liked the person who I was pretending to be, but not the real me. It took a while for me to realize that they weren't my friends at all; their friendship was conditional. Now I know that real friends are there no matter what, and they will love you for *the real you*, not for being who they want you to be. In my temptations and struggles with drugs and friends, I see that God was with me in all of it. He showed me that there was a way out, a way to be who He made me to be.

Sara York, 16, Antioch High School, Antioch, TN

God, when I turn to other things besides You, show me the way back to You. Because that's where I really want to be.

to bethel

I can do everything through him
who gives me strength.

PHILIPPIANS 4:13

When I was seventeen, I got pregnant. My mom learned about a place called Bethel Bible Village. It is a home for children from broken homes, and a home and training center for unwed mothers. We decided to look into the possibility of me going there after I graduated from high school. My mom struggled with feeling like she was giving me up to the state. I felt unsure about moving to Bethel because I knew it would be hard. Once I moved there, I think we both realized it was the best place for me to be. At Bethel, I have changed a lot, spiritually and emotionally. God has been so faithful as I work through a lot of pain from my past, in the company of others in similar situations. I am hopeful about the future and confident that God will provide for me and for my son. God has shown me that He truly is our refuge. NOTHING, not even pregnancy out of wedlock, is too big for Him, if we call upon Him.

Rachel Eggensperger, 19, Bethel Bible Village, Hixson, TN

You can tackle anything, Jesus. Absolutely anything. Thank You for being bigger than my biggest mistakes.

receiving God

Whosoever shall receive one of such children in my name receives me: and whosoever shall receive me, receives not me but him that sent me.

MARK 9:37 (KJV)

Sometimes it's difficult to live with my siblings and to love them. It would probably be easier to love them if I didn't have to live with them (or to live with them if I didn't have to love them)! I remember one long car trip in particular. We had been driving about six hours already and had nine more to go. My little sister, understandably, began to get a bit restless and irritated. At first I got annoyed with her, but then I realized it would do none of us ANY good, especially since we were going to be in close quarters for nine more hours! I made a choice to not let her annoy me. A few minutes later, my mother came up with a game that had everyone laughing and enjoying each other once again. Often my siblings are simply irritating, and most of the time I can't figure out why. Sometimes it feels like they just like it! But then I start to wonder how they are doing. Maybe they are having other problems, or maybe I have bothered them recently. Even if I cannot figure it out, it helps the situation so much when I simply choose not to be bothered. Siblings are probably the hardest children to receive, as the verse tells us to. But when I think about the promise in that verse, that when we love others we receive God, it makes it a little easier to love my siblings.

Hannah Reeves, 14, home school, Central, SC

Jesus, You have called me to love others because by loving them, I am loving You. Help me to remember that the next time I get mad at someone.

mock trial

These things I have spoken unto you,
that in me you may have peace. In the world
you will have tribulation; but be of good cheer.
I have overcome the world.

JOHN 16:33 (KJV)

Last year I got to play the part of a punk piano player for a mock trial at my school. I had so much fun, and the only hard part was that I could never be completely prepared for the cross-examination. I prepared a testimony from our information, but at the mock trial, the other schools did the cross examinations. They always seemed to bring up something unexpected. I soon found out how easy it was for the cross-examiners to manipulate my words and make me look like I was very biased and even that I might be lying. Even though this trial was completely an act and not real in any way, I had to keep reminding myself that it was okay if I messed up or didn't have the most articulate testimony. It was comforting to remember that in the midst of the real trials and tribulations in life that I didn't have to be perfect either. I know in the real thing, God is the One in control, not me, and after my experience at the mock trial at school, I realized that is a very good thing.

Calista Turner, 17, Donelson Christian Academy, Nashville, TN

Thank You, Father, for being in control.
If I were in control, I'd mess things up a lot.
I'm so glad You are taking care of me.

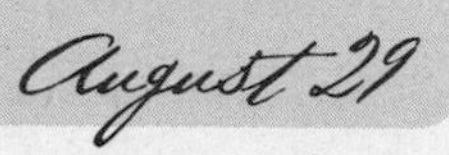

a fresh verse

"For I know the plans I have for you,"
declares the LORD.

JEREMIAH 29:11

I'm in my senior year of high school. Things are rapidly changing in my life and I feel pulled in a million different directions. I have to apply to college and for scholarships, think about my major, potential jobs...my life is taking a new road that is exciting, but overwhelming. Often I find myself sitting with a furrowed brow and tense shoulders, and I am having trouble sleeping or just relaxing. My mind has been too preoccupied to concentrate on my friends, family, or simply having fun. The questions and doubts seem unending: What if I don't get accepted into college? What if I don't have enough money to pay for college? What if I don't enjoy my major and change it several times? A few days ago I was reminded of Jeremiah 29:11. I had heard this verse so many times, but it struck me so personally this time. My whole life I have depended on my parents to feed me, clothe me, and take care of me. Just as I depended on my parents for everything a few years ago, I am learning to depend on God in a similar way. He has a perfect plan for my life. And if I trust Him with my goals and dreams, my life, then He will show me His way and direct my steps.

Hannah Howerton, 17, home school, Greenville, SC

You know the plans You have for me.
So why do I worry? Teach me to trust You.

perfect girl

Man looks at the outward appearance,
but the LORD looks at the heart.

1 SAMUEL 16:7

I think we all can picture the girl at our school who is perfect. She is oh so pretty; good at everything she does; and has a really hot boyfriend (who is, of course, the captain of his team). Compared to her, it's easy to feel bad. For me, an average girl who has never had a boyfriend and isn't particularly good at anything, it feels like I could never even begin to measure up. But for a long time I tried to do just that. I concentrated on getting a boyfriend so much that it became obsessive. I began to care about what I looked like more than anything else. I stopped paying attention to the kind of person I was and focused on how I portrayed myself to others. Eventually I realized that there is another way of looking at myself that is so much more important, and that is looking at what's going on inside of me. Paying attention to my heart means that I think about other people more, I am less concerned with what I look like, and I am getting to know God better. It helps me to feel more confident about my answer to a very important question: "Am I pretty on the inside?"

Megan Bordenkircher, 16, Nebraska Christian High School, Central City, NE

Teach me, Lord, to look inside first when I'm
judging my own beauty. I want to see what You see.

August 31

i want to be gentle

A gentle answer turns away wrath, but harsh words stir up anger.

The wise person makes learning a joy; fools spout only foolishness.

The LORD *is watching everywhere, keeping his eye on both the evil and the good.*

Gentle words bring life and health; a deceitful tongue crushes the spirit.

Only a fool despises a parent's discipline; whoever learns from correction is wise....

The LORD *hates the sacrifice of the wicked, but he delights in the prayers of the upright.*

PROVERBS 15:1–5, 8 (NLT)

my biggest enemy

Charm is deceptive and beauty is fleeting,
but a woman who fears the LORD is to be praised.

PROVERBS 31:30

I have an enemy that has been around for as long as I can remember. My enemy is the mirror. But even though I say that I hate mirrors, I don't think I could live without one. I love looking at my face in the mirror, both to admire how I look or stare at myself in disgust. When you are shopping, do you ever sneak a quick glance at your reflection in the passing mirror or window to make sure everything is perfect? I do that all the time. Jesus made us women to want to feel beautiful. He put that desire in our hearts, which is fine, but our inward beauty is also something we should be concerned with. The Bible confirms that outward beauty does not last forever and that charm can deceives us, but nothing compares to the inward beauty that the Father gave us. Psalm 45:11 says, "The King is enthralled by your beauty!" Take care of yourself on the outside, but don't be obsessed. Instead, work on being who Jesus made you to be, full of life and righteousness—because that is the kind of beauty He's really enthralled with. I suppose wrinkles will always take over someday, but the beauty of a relationship with God will continue to grow.

Katie-Lee Kroeker, 16, home school, Medicine Hat, Alberta, CA

Lord, do You really think I'm beautiful?
I want to believe that. I really do!

learning hope

The LORD delights in those who fear him,
who put their hope in his unfailing love.

PSALM 147:11

A friend of mine was in a horrific car accident, and she had major damage to her brain and went into a coma. The news from the doctors was discouraging; the said she probably wouldn't make it through the night. Her family was discouraged and quickly lost hope. Friends came and shared with them numerous verses in the Bible. The verse in Psalm 147 particularly stood out to them, and after they heard it started to hope again. My friend made it through that night and all the other nights afterwards. After about six months of waiting and praying, her family was told that she was waking from her coma and she would live. After leaving the hospital my friend went through months of rehabilitation and physical therapy. It wasn't easy, but now she drives and does all sorts of average teenage stuff. My friend's story reminds me that hope is such a necessary ingredient in life, and it is because of Jesus Christ's death on the cross that we have hope. I long to have the kind of hope throughout my life that my friend's family exercised during the months she was in a coma. That kind of hope is real; it is an earnest expectation for what is to come.

Laysha Powers, 17, Maranatha Academy, Oakwood, GA

Lord, I want to be hopeful. I want to believe
that good things can happen. Help me to have that belief.

school, please?

For the LORD *searches every heart and*
understands every motive behind the thoughts.
If you seek him, he will be found by you;
but if you forsake him, he will reject you forever.

1 CHRONICLES 28:9

I have been homeschooled most of my life. I didn't mind it because my mom was a good teacher, but I really wanted some friends. I took dance classes and joined clubs and organizations to try and make good friends, but none of it seemed to work. I wanted to be a part of all the school happenings. I was going to start high school in the fall, and I really didn't want to be homeschooled anymore—so I started praying. One night when we were having dinner with some friends, the subject of schools came up. Our friends, who had also been homeschooling, had found a private school that used the same curriculum as we did. I was thrilled! My parents looked into the school and said I could attend! God knew my desires and answered my prayers. I've been at my school for a few months, and it feels so normal, like I am exactly where I need to be. I am so thankful that God listens to my heart and answer my prayers.

Keegan Nitz, 15, St. Ambrose Christian High School, Meridian, ID

Father, I just want to praise You for the way You make things work out. Sometimes life just fits together like this perfect puzzle, and I can see Your great work. Thank You!

September 4

his way is perfect

As for God, His way is perfect.

Psalm 18:30

Recently I went through a time when I was very discouraged and felt like I had very few friends. I had just been through a tough breakup, and through that I lost my best friend. I didn't really know who I was or how to begin to discover myself. But I did know that I had to turn to God, and the things He taught me at the beginning of that time were very humbling. At one of my lowest points I read Psalm 18:30 in a devotional, and it said to replace God's name with Love, for He *is* Love. When you do that, the verse reads, "As for Love, His way is perfect"! I cannot begin to tell you how that encouraged me. It gave me hope that in the future there is something that God has planned for me that is perfect. I tried so long to do it my way, but my way is nowhere near perfect. This verse made me redirect my thinking, and I began to look forward to God's perfect way.

Rachel Thurman, 17, Cedar Hall School, Rockvale, TN

Father, help me to realize
that what I want is not always what
I need. Even when I can't see the reason
for what You're doing, I want to trust that
Your way is the best way…the perfect way.

pillows of love

His never-failing love protects me
like the walls of a fort!

PSALM 31:21 (TLB)

I'm fifteen and my only sister is nineteen. We're best buddies. Most everything in life is much more fun when we're together. We have many shared friends and interests, and we especially love to go on trips, jog, and play cards together. Last week she moved to college. We had a fast, fun, but bittersweet final week together that included waxing her jeep, physicals, shots, and getting our ears pierced. Even though the week's activities were fun, a cloud of sadness and dread followed me. Friday we loaded her Jeep and my parent's car…my sister and I were quiet during the drive to her school. We set up her dorm room, and it looked odd to see her stuff in a strange room. After telling her good-bye, my parents and I had a droopy drive home. We came with four people and left with three. That evening our house felt abnormally empty because someone was missing. A verse that God has used to help me in this experience is Psalm 31:21 "His never-failing love protects me like the walls of a fort." The verse makes me think of myself and my cares snuggled between pillows of His love, even when I feel alone without my sister around. I know I still have to endure this adjustment, but I'm glad God's helping me through.

Christina Jensen, 15, Dogwood Christian School, Asheville, NC

Father, I pray that I will always know You're
there for me even as the world changes around me.

letting go

Now I commit you to God
and to the word of his grace.

ACTS 20:32

Where is your brother?" demanded the impatient choir director. I looked at her, quite bewildered, because I had no idea where he was. It was twenty minutes into our choir period, and he should have been at school. I glanced out through the frosted windows and saw the snow coming down in torrents. I tended to be a worrier, so images of my brother lying in an overturned car by the side of the road flashed through my brain. My thoughts ran away with me in this direction, and silent tears started to stream down my face. My brother eventually showed up, confessing that he had lost track of time and then had to drive slowly because of the snow. This experience reminded me that my big brother, the one who is in almost every memory I have, was graduating and going off to college soon. I wasn't going to know where he was all the time, and that scared me. I knew I couldn't handle this alone, so asked God to help me. He reminded me that He would always know where my brother was, and that reality brought me peace. I am now in my second year with my older brother away from home. When I start to miss him, I simply send a little prayer up and know that God is listening and watching over my brother, wherever he is.

Karis Horton, 17, Houghton Christian Academy, Houghton, NY

Lord, thank You for watching over those
I love who are far away from me. I miss them,
but I'm glad that You are with them, even if I can't be.

mission impossible

Be perfect, therefore,
as your heavenly Father is perfect.

MATTHEW 5:48

We all have role models and celebrities in our lives that we constantly desire to be like. We study their actions, attributes, and words. I confess I have my own heroines that I scrutinize. There is nothing quite wrong with this, as long as we consider the One who should be the ultimate person we follow. He is God Almighty. He should be our aim of perfection. You may be wondering, "Well, I thought that it was impossible to be like God." This is absolutely true. It is an impossible mission. But it's also impossible to become that gorgeous actress we love so much. Yet, that doesn't stop us from cutting our hair like her, buying clothes like her, reading articles about her. So we should seek even harder to be like God, seek with all our heart, mind, and soul, even though we know we'll never make quite succeed. We should want to look like Him and read about Him even more than we want to read about that famous actress. We are told in Ephesians that we are to be imitators of God. While imitating someone famous gets us nothing more than new hair or new clothes, imitating God gets us an eternity in heaven.

Caroline J. Hornok, 15, Veritas Academy, Texarkana, TX

I know I can't be perfect, God, but I want to
try as hard as I can anyway. I know You'll help me.

God hears

The righteous cry out and the LORD hears them;
he delivers them from all their troubles.
The LORD is close to the brokenhearted and saves
those who are crushed in spirit.

PSALM 34:17–18

Have you ever felt like God has forgotten you? Did you feel like he was not hearing you out? Well I have. I recently had a friend go through open-heart surgery. Some things in the surgery went wrong and we almost lost him. I just kept crying out to God and asking why he was letting this happen to my friend, why He wasn't healing him, why God wasn't intervening and showing the doctors how it was really done. I just remember begging and pleading with God to make His presence known to me, to show me that He cared and to heal my friend. After a while God did make His presence known. He gave me strength for myself and to give to others. And I realized through everything He was really there. The doctors said that there was no way my friend should have lived through the surgery. God used the situation to put our full attention on Him so we wouldn't miss his miracle. It's okay to plead with Him. But just remember to praise Him and thank Him for what He has done. And when it feels like He's forgotten you, just remember He is there.

Danae Downs, 15, home school, Grand Junction, CO

God, I never want to forget to thank
You for the amazing things You do in my life.
I ask You for a lot of help, so I want to
show You that I appreciate what You've done.

making your morals your own

"Watch and pray so that you will not fall into temptation. The spirit is willing, but the body is weak."

MATTHEW 26:41

College kids are notorious for partying. We are "let loose" in college and (drum roll please) freed from our parents! We can finally make our own decisions, and we don't have to answer an angry parent when we get home at three in the morning. When we're young, our parents basically established morals for us. For example, I was not allowed to watch R-rated movies or have coed sleepovers. But now I am on my own—I make my own decisions! And that is where the chaos can begin. As new college students, we must ask God to show us Biblical guidelines to follow; important things that we will not compromise on. We need to figure out how to make good decisions without our parents watching us, so that we can be good Christians and live a good example for others to see. 1 Corinthians 8:9 says, "But beware lest somehow this liberty of yours become a stumbling block to those who are weak." God wants us to have fun and be crazy sometimes, but not to the point where we're causing ourselves and others to get into trouble. We should enjoy the freedoms of college, but not allow those freedoms to drag us away from the true freer—God.

Amber Van Osdol, 18, Hanover College, Hanover, IN

I have learned a lot about You from other people, Lord, and I am glad. But help me to live these lessons even when I'm on my own, with no one to keep me accountable.

who would you pick?

O LORD *my God, I called*
to you for help and you healed me.
PSALM 30:2

If you could have a conversation with anyone who has ever lived, who would you pick? Would you pick Abraham Lincoln? Or perhaps your favorite author, so you could ask them a hundred questions about the characters in their books. Have you ever thought about what it would be like to talk to Solomon, the wisest person who ever lived? I wonder what you'd talk about...Whatever the topic of conversation, I am sure it would be unforgettable! I have never thought of the Bible as an exceptionally fascinating book, but then I realized that, among a lot of other things, it contains the thoughts and ideas of the wisest person that ever lived. That's kind of exciting, and it definitely makes me a little more motivated to read it. It's not quite the same as talking to my favorite musician or king or writer, but it's still pretty exciting if you ask me.

Hannah Reeves, 14, home school, Central, SC

Lord, I am so thankful that You have given me
Your Word to read and learn from every day.
Help me to take advantage of this gift.

God is there

Thy mercy, O LORD, is in the heavens;
and thy faithfulness reacheth unto the clouds.

PSALM 36:5 (KJV)

A few days ago, I was thinking about when the World Trade Center towers fell in New York City on September 11, 2001. I remember thinking that is was really strange that all the people suddenly put up signs in their yard saying "God Bless the USA." I mean, they should have those signs up all the time, but we usually don't appreciate what we have until something terrible happens. It seems like we do the same thing with God, only remembering Him when we are faced with trials or when something bad happens. Then, when we are all fine and dandy, we just forget about Him altogether. God loves us so much, and he wants us to remember Him through all times. Psalm 36:5 tells us that God's love is neverending, and his faithfulness to help us in times of trouble is unfailing. We may forget about Him, but He never forgets about us.

Ali VanMinos, 15, Oconee County Christian Academy, Seneca, SC

Lord, it seems like I only turn to You when
I have a really big problem. I pray that You will be
a part of my life every day, and not just when I'm in trouble.

new zealand

Don't let anyone look down on you
because you are young, but set an example for the
believers in speech, in life, in love, in faith and in purity.

1 Timothy 4:12

I spent three months in New Zealand with an evangelism outreach team. I remember one night in particular where I was brought to tears when I prayed for the people who didn't know God. I was crying out for mercy, for God's intercession, and that was the night that God birthed in me the desire to pray on behalf of others. I was only thirteen, but I became bold when I prayed during those months in New Zealand. I yearned for closeness with God, and my fears of what other people thought of me totally disappeared. When I returned home to Canada I slipped into my old ways and began, once again, to be overly concerned of what people thought of me. My boldness evaporated, and in its place came fear. When I let fear rule me, thoughts like, "Oh no! She's talking about me!" or "Is my hair okay?" or "Do these pants make me look fat?" consume my mind. I think we all have questions like these at some point, but I am longing to begin again to be what God has called me to be, not what I think people want me to be. That is what I am longing for and what I am praying for.

Jana Kroeker, 15, home school, Medicine Hat, Alberta, CA

Lord, I pray that I won't be afraid
to be the person You made me to be.

my miracle

Wait for the LORD; be strong
and take heart and wait for the LORD.

PSALM 27:14

Several years ago I developed a minor health problem that could be fixed with surgery. I didn't tell anyone because I was scared to have surgery, but the problem only got worse. I began lying to my parents, to try and hide the problem. I was in constant pain, praying for a miracle. Months went by and no miracle happened. I thought God just didn't care about my life, my prayers, or my pain. Instead of asking for help, I distanced myself and tried to be tough. Finally, one night I cried myself to sleep. I prayed and talked to Him for a long time, pouring everything out to Him. I knew I had to tell my parents. When I told my parents they were worried that some major problems had developed, since I had waited so long. I prayed for another miracle, and this time, He answered. I had my surgery, which was not nearly as bad as I imagined it would be, and there was nothing major that was wrong with me. Now I am completely healed, but this process taught me that sometimes you have to wait for God to answer your prayers. He always hears us, but sometimes His answers come in different times and ways than we expect.

Katelyn Westfall, 15, Dover High School, Dover, OH

God, help me to learn that Your answers to
my prayers are even better than the ones I imagine.
I want to trust that Your solutions are the best ones.

remaining true to my purity

Who may ascend the hill of the LORD?
Who may stand in his holy place?
He who has clean hands and a pure heart.

PSALM 24:3–4

When I turned thirteen years old, (the beginning of my fearsome teenage years), my parents gave me a purity ring. The ring is silver, has a small diamond, and fits my ring finger perfectly. I've worn it so much that my hand feels naked without it. This ring means a lot to me. It represents my faith and my standards. It's not only a ring, but a symbol, not just for me to see, but for my peers and strangers to see. Whenever I slip the ring on my finger, I'm reminded of my future spouse and my promise to him that I will remain pure. I am also reminded to pray for him and his purity. I don't have a boyfriend presently, but that doesn't mean that I won't ever be tempted. My purity ring is a great reminder that when I'm tempted, there will always be a way of escape. My promise to my future spouse not only protects my body from sexual sin, but it protects my heart and my mind. And that is pleasing to the Lord. The commitment to remaining pure is not an easy one, but it's definitely worth it in the long run.

Rebecca Wilson, 18, Maranatha Christian Academy, Oakwood, GA

You are preparing one person to be my husband, Lord? How amazing is that? Teach me to follow the right path so that I will find the one You intend for me to be with.

sticks and stones

How beautiful you are, my darling!
Oh, how beautiful!
Song of Solomon 1:15

Sticks and stones may break my bones, but names will never hurt me"? What a lie! Names and labels that cut down who you are DO hurt! I remember second grade when I was called fat by one of my "friends." It took me till junior high to realize Satan was trying to attack and destroy my self-image. I continually compared myself to my sister and other people until I found out that I am made in a very beautiful and creative way by my Creator, Jesus Christ. He made me with my own beauty, gifts, and talents. I wasn't made to look like, or be like, anyone else, except Jesus Himself. I am still going through the process of finding out who I really am. Trying not to let people's words cut me down is tough, but God's words—"How beautiful you are, my darling! Oh, how beautiful!"—are more powerful than anything anyone else could say.

Jana Kroeker, 15, home school, Medicine Hat, Alberta, CA

Father, You look down at me from heaven and see nothing but beauty. All my flaws are erased, all insecurities gone. It is so amazing to know that someone sees me that way!

September 16

far-away adventures with God (part 1)

I am convinced that neither death nor life, neither angels nor demons, neither the present nor the future, nor any powers, neither the height nor depth, nor any anything else in all creation will be able to separate us from the love of God that is in Christ Jesus our Lord.

ROMANS 8:38–39

The verse above is one of my favorites because it provides assurance. I don't know about you, but I like doing things that make me feel good. But if there is one thing that I have learned so far, it is that not everything you do is going to make you feel good. Sometimes we have to do what is right to get the best result (like swallowing gross medicine to get better when we're sick). I grew up in the Amazon and that is where my heart and home remain. I never knew how lucky I was to live there until I had a complete change of lifestyle. My life was turned upside when my parents said, "We're going to Australia!" I thought, "Well, Australia has kangaroos...so yeah I'll go." Really, I had no choice since I was only twelve, so I had to make the best of it. Everything I had heard about Australia was good and that was encouraging, but there were many surprises waiting for me. I found myself making English-speaking friends in an English-speaking primary school, even though my first language is Portuguese. I needed the reassurance of Romans 8:38 to remind me that though I was far away from home, I was not far away from God.

Sasha Truehl, 19, Concordia College, Adelaide, Australia

No matter if I move half way across the world, You will always be there, Lord. Thank You that there is not one place I can be where You aren't!

far-away adventures with God (part 2)

I am convinced that neither death nor life…
nor anything else in all creation will be able to separate
us from the love of God that is in Christ Jesus our Lord.

ROMANS 8:38–39

Oh, did I have a lot to learn when I moved to Australia! The lessons began when I had to pick a new favorite color because brown apparently didn't count in Australia! I was different from everyone else, very different. I have been to about fourteen schools in twelve years and eaten monkey for dinner on more than one occasion. However, it was "coming to Australia" that I struggled with. I cried myself to sleep for months, and that doesn't exactly feel good. My relationship with our Father in heaven is where I found strength for going through the pain, in order to grow and eventually get to a better place. I now know why God brought me through six challenging years in Australia. I have met incredible people, some of whom will remain my lifelong friends. I've had a great education and have grown in every way. I know that God will use all He has taught me to bring out His plans for my life. I want to remember that there is always a bigger picture, even if I cannot see it. There is no depth deep enough or place far enough where God's love isn't able to reach.

Sasha Truehl, 19, Concordia College, Adelaide, Australia

It is amazing how much You know and how far Your love
can reach, Lord. All I can do is be in awe of You!

genuine service

These have come so that your faith—of greater worth than gold, which perishes even though refined by fire—may be proved genuine and may result in praise, glory and honor when Jesus Christ is revealed.

1 PETER 1:7

Sometimes as Christians, it is easy to get trapped by other people's expectations. We set a standard for life based on other people's lives, rather than on what the Bible says. Being a preacher's daughter has taught me a lot about this. No matter what others say, I have to live my life for Christ because I love him and trust in him, not because my father is a pastor. If my service to Christ is not genuine then it is meaningless. It doesn't really matter if we are a preacher's kid or if we are the only Christian in our family. God cares about the desires of our hearts, no matter what our circumstances. If we live our lives for Christ, people will see it. A life lived for Christ will have a greater impact that we may never fully see until we are able to lay our crowns at the feet of Jesus.

Ally Powell, 17, New Covenant Christian School, Pageland, SC

Father, when I'm in heaven, I want to be able to look down and see that my life made a difference in the world. But I can only make a difference if You help me. Please help me!

faith in college

Let us hold unswervingly to the hope
we profess, for he who promised is faithful.

HEBREWS 10:23

During my senior year, I looked over college catalogs trying to find the perfect fit. In order to do that, I realized that I had to go where God led me and not decide my entire future based on pictures and statistics inside brochures. The most essential question was "Where does God want me?" I prayed that God would open my eyes to His will so that I would see the college where I could do the most work for His kingdom. I was lucky enough to find the answer. In many cases, students move away from God once they start college because of all the changes they face. However, that was the one steadfast thing for me to cling to during those adjustments: my relationship with God. In all of the changes, He has been my Rock. With God in my life, there is always someone to talk to and someone who takes care of me. He is available every minute of every day and after all He has done for me, including giving me new friends, a church family, and the education I am receiving, there is no possible way I could give up my faith. He has done so much for me, and it is all thanks to Him that I can encourage everyone else to hold tightly to their faith.

Jennifer Caudill, 19, Hanover College, Hanover, IN

Father, when I have to make big decisions,
remind me to pray for Your guidance. Too often I try
to make choices on my own when I should be asking You.

two's company, three's a crowd

For we are God's workmanship,
created in Christ Jesus to do good works,
which God prepared in advance for us to do.

EPHESIANS 2:10

One in a world of twos! Have you ever felt left out because *all* your friends have "significant others"? Your best friend has a boyfriend now, so even though she doesn't try to push you away or anything, you feel like you don't belong in that circle anymore? These couples now share an emotional connection that naturally excludes you and everyone else. My problem is that I somehow feel *less* because I don't have a boyfriend like all my friends. I know, how lame is that, right? It's not that I necessarily *want* a boyfriend, but to know that someone likes you goes a long way. Yet I've been so stupid, looking for someone in the world when God is right there. We are God's workmanship. Have you ever seen an artist who didn't treasure something that he'd sweated over and made perfect? I like to write and I know that I get pretty protective of my work! How much more does God love us? He has created us to do good works and He knows what we'll do. That means we don't have to worry about finding a guy *now*. God will take care of us. Think about Adam and Eve in the garden. Adam wanted someone to share life with him, but he didn't go looking for a wife by himself. He knew that God would provide someone for him. God will take care of us. The hard part is waiting for His timing.

Laura Campbell, 17, Stillwater Christian School, Kalispell, MT

God, thank You for loving me
and for sending other people to love me.
Teach me to know that You will take care of all my needs.

sisters

A friend loves at all times,
and a brother is born for adversity.
PROVERBS 17:17

My younger sister and I are twenty-one months apart in age, and we could not be more different. I like to cook and work with beads. She could care less about those things and would prefer to simply eat the food and wear the jewelry. I prefer to spend time with a few close friends, while she is very social and likes to have a lot of friends at the same time. I am very opinionated, and she has trouble making even very simple decisions. My sister and I are together most of the time, but we have not gotten along since we were little kids. We are in the same high school class at a very small school, we go to church and youth group together, we are in the same Bible studies, and, of course, we live together. It is not an issue of not loving or respecting my sister, because I do! But that hasn't made being together so often any easier. This summer it seemed to hit both of us that I am going to be gone to college next year. We have both been reevaluating our relationship and learning to treasure the time that we do have with each other. Our times together have begun to be more enjoyable for us both. Our relationship as sisters is definitely not perfect, but now I know that I would not give up on it—especially what it will become in the future—for anything in the world.

Rachel Thurman, 17, Cedar Hall School, Rockvale, TN

Sometimes the people in my
family are the hardest ones to love, Lord.
Give me the strength to love them the way I should.

the sting

Where, O death, is your victory?
Where, O death, is your sting?

1 CORINTHIANS 15:55

One day I received one of the hardest phone calls I had ever gotten. A very close friend of mine was killed in a terrible car wreck. I didn't believe it at first. I just stood there saying, "There's no way, there's no way." Jonathan was only eighteen years old and was finishing up his freshman year of college. After it sank in that he truly was dead, I started crying and calling all of my friends to get the details. What I gathered was that he had been thrown from the car, which had been going about 90 mph around a curve. It hit a telephone pole and Jonathan hit the pavement. At the funeral, the church was packed with friends and family who were just as shocked as I was. He was only eighteen! He loved life and had big plans for his future! Why did God take him so young and so suddenly? I don't have an answer for that, but it made me realize that if death could come to Jonathan, it could come to anyone, even me. I was reminded that as a Christian, death has lost its sting because Jesus died so that I may be saved from eternal death. Jonathan's death reminded me that life is short and that my purpose in life is to know Jesus and to make him known to the world.

Hannah Howerton, 17, home school, Greenville, SC

God, I don't want to fear death, and because of You,
I don't have to. You are an awesome God. Amen.

persevering in the irish dance

A wise man keeps himself under control.

PROVERBS 29:11

Irish dancing (what the people in Riverdance do) has taught me some important lessons about life. The dance has two forms that require two different types of shoes: soft shoes and hard shoes. Soft shoes, called ghillies, are made from black leather, have long laces, and look like ballet shoes with really cool little patterns. When new, they are very tight and painful to wear because they are supposed to be so formfitting. You have to wear them a lot. I slept and walked around in mine for days before they actually fit comfortably. It definitely takes self-discipline to break them in. Hard shoes are made of leather and have a hard toe and a hard heel. When you walk, they make loud clicking noises. It takes a long time to make a distinguishable "click-ety-clack," and you feel very clumsy while still learning. It takes flexibility, agility, and endurance to complete a full reel or jig (dance), slip jig, treble reel, and hornpipe in Irish dancing. The steps are confusing and complex to remember and execute, not to mention staying on time, keeping your arms at your sides, head up, toes pointed, and smile in place. It takes an incredible amount of patience to do all of it at once! To overcome the difficulties of Irish dancing, you must have control of your emotions and actions. It is easy to become frustrated, angry, and upset while learning. But it looks so cool (just watch Riverdance some time).

Kerstin Jones, 17, Stillwater Christian School, Kalispell, MT

God, I want to have the strength and self-control to overcome difficulties. Because, when I'm honest with myself, I'm most satisfied by the things I have to work hardest for.

taking a shower in the rain

Then they cried out to the LORD in their trouble, and he brought them out of their distress. He stilled the storm to a whisper; the waves of the sea were hushed.... Let them give thanks to the LORD for his unfailing love and his wonderful deeds for men.

PSALM 107:29, 31

While on a summer mission trip, we traveled by bus and canoe to the rain forest to serve a native tribe. Our team held a worship service, played with adorable children, and helped the tribe to build a path to their school. Working in one-hundred-degree weather, we were hot, sweaty, and started calling dibs on the shower! On our canoe ride back there was a storm that even tipped the boat ahead of us over. We got soaked by the rain, but it was refreshing and God cooled us off! The rain poured even harder and the wind was blowing more violently. Our boat started to take on water, even as we sang worship songs and prayed that God would protect us, and we tried not to be too scared. Other canoes pulled up beside us and some of us climbed into them. We ended up making it out of the storm and back to shore. God cooled us off when we were hot and showed me that even in the midst of things that we have no control over, when we're afraid, He is right there with us to keep us safe.

Holly Scott, 18, North Buncombe High School, Weaverville, NC

When I am hot, You cool me off. When I am afraid, You make me feel safe. You are everything I need!!

can you be saved and still have fun?

And my God will meet all your needs
according to his glorious riches in Christ Jesus.

PHILIPPIANS 4:19

You can be saved and enjoy life. At first it seemed difficult because I really didn't know what I was getting myself into. All I knew was that I had given my life to God and that living a Christian life means living differently. But I have started discovering that God wants us to enjoy life, and the most amazing part is that now I enjoy life even more than I did before I was saved. When I first wake up, I thank the Lord for allowing me to see another day. When I talk to Jesus in prayer, I ask for His forgiveness and for Him to guide me in the right direction. I am so amazed at the response I get. I have accomplished so many goals (spiritual, academic, and athletic) that I would never have been able to reach on my own. I never had the faith to think that I would get a full scholarship to attend boarding school where I can actually start off with a fresh reputation and a brand new slate of grades. Being saved, I have much more fun. I actually have friends who will be there for me. It is good to know that the Lord is my savior, my protector, my provision, and my guide. God meets my needs and makes the rough times easier. And that definitely helps me enjoy life!

La'Nice Dominek Kibler, 17, Redemption Christian Academy, Troy, NY

Lord, I don't want to feel like being a Christian
is boring or restricting. I gained so much more than
I lost when I accepted You. And I want to remember that.

splurging

See how the lilies of the field grow.
They do not labor or spin. Yet I tell you that
not even Solomon in all his splendor was dressed
like one of these. If that is how God clothes the grass of the
field, which is here today and tomorrow is thrown into the
fire, will he not much more clothe you, O you of little faith?

MATTHEW 6:28–30

Okay, so my family definitely isn't poor, but we're not rich either. I'm not the type of girl that can go on shopping sprees every weekend and splurge on shoes and purses. But I'd love to...really love to. And I'm always jealous of girls who can. When my best friend gets a new pair of pants, it takes everything I have to be happy for her. I am happy, but I want a pair too. Contentment is a lesson I'm convinced I will never fully learn. I'll struggle with it my whole life. But the apostle Paul seemed to have a good grip on it. Think about it. The guy was in prison more than once and was persecuted, and yet he was still able to sing and be perfectly satisfied with his situation. That was all because Paul wasn't concerned with his material possessions. I highly doubt he compared his rags to the ones his cellmates were wearing. He focused on things of eternal value. And he believed that God would always provide for all of his needs—which he faithfully did for Paul and promises to do for us. Sometimes it really isn't easy being content with what He provides for us, and my friend's new jeans will probably always be appealing. But I just have to remember that the things God gives me are way better than a new pair of jeans.

Grace Bricker, 16, Jonathan Edwards Academy, Greenfield, MA

God, I want to be thankful for what
I have rather than just wanting, wanting,
wanting more, more, more. You give me all I need.

i'm leaving on a jet plane (part 1)

Cast all your anxiety on him because he cares for you.

1 PETER 5:7

"I'm sorry, what did you say?" I stared at the airline clerk through glazed, sleep-deprived eyes, silently begging her to take back her words. I had gotten off a plane from the Philippines, leaving my missionary parents, to come to school in the States. In case leaving home for the first time wasn't enough stress, the airline clerk had to throw a curveball. "Ma'am, you can only check two fifty-pound bags and one carryon, plus a purse." Those words are the worst to hear when coming from an international flight. I had three suitcases, a backpack, and a violin. I frantically poured all my clothes out onto the floor and did my best, with my shaking hands, to fit it all into two suitcases. All I could think was how it wasn't fair that I had to go through this on such a long trip. I was so tired and stressed that I forgot that God would take care of me, which is so easy to do when I feel overwhelmed.

Bethany Christensen, 18, Houghton Christian Academy, Houghton, NY

God, when I my mind is too full of worry to remember that You are there, please remind me.

i'm leaving on a jet plane (part 2)

Cast all your anxiety on him
because he cares for you.

1 PETER 5:7

Eventually I ended up with two very full suitcases, a massive backpack, clothes sticking out of my violin case, and butterflies in my stomach. After flying from Spokane to Seattle, Seattle to San Francisco, San Francisco to Chicago, and finally, Chicago to Buffalo, I was royally in need of sleep. Sometimes the cheapest route is not always the most direct. As I navigated the endless streams of traffic in the airport and tried to stem the tide of tears that was threatening, I remembered the Bible verse that says, "Cast all your anxiety on him because he cares for you." I tend to stress over details so I have to constantly remind myself that God is in control. I am nothing without Him and it is only by His strength that I made it through all the chaos and surprises of that trip.

Bethany Christensen, 18, Houghton Christian Academy, Houghton, NY

Life can be so stressful. But it feels
so wonderful when You show me a way to get rid
of that stress. Thank You for helping me not to worry.

no matter what

"Because he loves me," says the L*ORD,*
"I will rescue him; I will protect him,
for he acknowledges my name.

PSALM 91:14

I was feeling so lonely one day because my friends were mad at me. When I went to church that night, what do you think my youth pastor talked about? He said that even if my entire group of friends left me, God would always be there. I really didn't think about it at that time, but later it hit me that God loves me no matter what! Even if I were the ugliest, or the most horribly hated girl in the school, He would love me just the same. The other girls and boys would probably pay no attention to me. They would treat me like I was worthless. But Psalms 91:14 tells me that if I love God, He will rescue me from the things that I am having a hard time with. He loves me so much that He sent His Son to die for me and for everyone that has lived, is living, and ever will live. It is so awesome how one person can have that much love for someone like me! He loves you, too, and He will always and forever.

Ali VanMinos, 15, Oconee County Christian Academy, Seneca, SC

I love how You can make a
church sermon speak directly to my problems,
Lord. You know when I need to hear Your voice.

September 30

i want to draw from the well within

Though good advice lies deep within a person's heart, the wise will draw it out.

Many will say they are loyal friends, but who can find one who is really faithful?...

Even children are known by the way they act, whether their conduct is pure and right.

PROVERBS 5–6, 11 (NLT)

All that we were—our sins, our guilt,
Our death—was all our own:
All that we are we owe to Thee,
Thou God of grace, alone,
Thou God, of grace, alone.
Thy mercy found us in our sins,
And gave us to believe;
Then, in believing, peace we found;
And in Thy Christ we live,
And in Thy Christ we live.

Horatius Bonar (1808-1889)

it's all my fault!

Can a mother forget the baby at her breast and have no compassion on the child she has borne? Though she may forget, I will not forget you! See, I have engraved you on the palms of my hands; your walls are ever before me.

ISAIAH 49:15–16

Divorce feels like total rejection and complete abandonment. Feeling that kind of pain makes it hard to open up to people. It seems like no one is trustworthy and that everyone is going to ditch you. My friend's parents just got divorced, and she's been confused because she can't find a logical explanation for *why* it happened. She blamed herself for her parents' breakup. One day I just told her bluntly that it was NOT her fault at all! That she is not the problem. It's hard to believe because the answer to the "Why did this happen?" question is still hidden. But in the midst of this question, my friend is starting to turn to God. He knows all about everything that happens in our lives. Even though He might not reveal in black and white to my friend why her parents are divorced, just praying to Him is comforting to her. My friend has reminded me of something so important. God has all the answers, and when we turn to Him, He does what is good. He will NEVER EVER forsake us.

Stephanie Sherwood, 14, St. Ambrose Christian High School, Boise, ID

When I can understand something,
that's when I need to turn to You the most.
I don't have all the answers, but I know that You do.

i want to be loved (part 1)

I have loved you with an everlasting love.

JEREMIAH 31:3

How many times have you liked a guy? The sight of his smile makes your heart skip, the glance of his brown eyes leaves you weak-kneed, and he consumes your every thought. You find yourself floating on air at the slightest hint that he knows you exist, but where is God in the midst of these crushes? We innately desire to be loved, not just liked, but passionately and undeniably loved. Many of us have pined away for guys who did not return our affections, and that is painful. If only we would turn to God first! He will never turn away from us; on the contrary, He chases and woos us. Most of us will probably get married, but that is a long ways off. When it seems like all my friends have boyfriends, I usually slip into self-pity. But I think that God does care about this time before we are adults and before we get married. To Him, it is a blessed time of singleness. He wants us to draw close to Him because He knows us more intimately than any one else ever will. Singleness is blessed because you get to be just you! You are a beautiful creature created in God's image, created to enjoy Him. My words may not be enough to convince you, but here's what the Maker has to say, "*I* have loved you with an everlasting love; *I* have drawn you with loving-kindness." (Jeremiah 31:3) The Master of the universe desperately loves you. As your relationship with Christ grows, He will fill your desire to be loved and give you marvelous peace, whether or not there is a guy in your life.

Jessica Runk, 19, Patrick Henry College, Purcellville, VA

It's so hard to realize that the love of a boyfriend won't fix all my problems.. Help me to see that only Your love can really be enough for me.

i want to be loved (part 2)

I will instruct you and teach you in the way you should go; I will counsel you and watch over you.

PSALM 32:8

Many nights I have cried myself to sleep, wishing I could stop the stinging pangs within my heart. Having your heart broken is an experience a lot of us have probably had. I wish that we could just wrap our arms around each other and cry together. How do we move past the rejection and the bitter pain? I think it honestly starts with something simple. We must run to Jesus and share our pain with Him. Another part is encouraging each other, because most of us are having similar experiences in relationships and in life. We were created to love and to long for our love to be returned. But I know for me it is easy to look for that love from someone who doesn't really care for me or who can never completely satisfy my heart. There are so many other ways to use our emotions and gifts, besides obsessing about guys, like spending time with people, reading good books, or developing friendships with people who are lonely. The pain of crying myself to sleep those nights with a broken heart cannot be forgotten, but I am beginning to learn from it. Difficult experiences of many kinds refine our hearts, bringing us into closer communion with God, and helping us relate to others facing similar adversities. Recently, I began to pray, "Lord, please use the tough things in my life to help me love and encourage others." That is a prayer that Jesus will answer, if we are willing.

Jessica Runk, 19, Patrick Henry College, Purcellville, VA

Lord, I want to pray what Jessica prayed:
Please use the tough things in my life
to help me love and encourage others.

forgiveness is a choice

Forgive as the Lord forgave you.

Colossians 3:13

Last year I was a bitter person, but now I don't even recognize the girl I was. My Dad cheated on my mom and left her for another woman. That woman is now my stepmother. Throughout my childhood, my stepmom has been very verbally abusive, and I hated both her and my father for the way they treated me. My dad had abandoned me and my stepmom cut me down with her words. Hate and bitterness consumed me, and I had to learn to forgive. Maybe you're thinking, "Wendy, you don't know what has happened to me," and you're right...I don't. But God does, and He has commanded you to forgive. He never commands us to do the impossible (though it may feel like it at times). God doesn't say to forgive if we feel like it; He says, "Forgive as the Lord forgave you." Forgiveness is a choice. Don't wait until you feel like forgiving because you may never feel like it. Forgive amidst your hurt. Forgiveness isn't letting someone walk over you. If you are being hurt or need help, tell a trusted adult and get godly counsel. Ask the Lord to reveal to you the people you need to forgive, and then pray this prayer:

Lord, I choose to forgive ________ for ________
and for making me feel ________. Help me to
love them as You love them.

Wendy McCain, 17, Grace Academy, Asheville, NC

lies vs. truth

Fear of man will prove to be a snare,
but whoever trusts in the LORD is kept safe.

PROVERBS 29:25

I have tender emotions that make me very vulnerable to Satan's lies. He tells me things like "You don't look pretty" or "Your friends don't really like or care about you." I think these are lies that most girls face, but it's so hard to see that they are not true. So what do we overcome them? First of all, tell the devil that he is liar and that you will not believe him anymore. Secondly, pray and read your Bible, because God will refresh you in the water of His Word (Ephesians 5:26). You can find strength and reassurance in every single book, even the ones you wouldn't expect. Like, when I read the Song of Solomon, it reminds me that I am the bride of Christ. God wants us to go to Him for fulfillment. He knows what our troubles are even before we tell Him, and He knows the lies that we can't seem to stop believing. And He is always waiting to have compassion on us and is eager to tell us the truth.

Bethany Pearl Reeves, 15, home school, Central, SC

The world is full of lies,
Lord, and they are so easy to believe.
But I want to believe Your truth.

when the answer is no

"Everything is permissible"—but not everything is beneficial. "Everything is permissible"—but not everything is constructive.

1 Corinthians 10:23

I have grown up being taught that some things are good to watch, listen to, or read and that some are not. Even so, I have sat through sketchy parts in a movie and later on regretted that I even watched it. I am learning that even if my friends, including Christian friends, watch a movie, it doesn't automatically mean that it is okay for me to watch. I remember watching a movie at a friend's house that her mom said was okay, but afterwards I felt uncomfortable with it. It is a bit scary to realize that it is up to me to stand up and walk out of the movie theater, hit the stop button, or close the magazine. Even though some people may think I am stupid to say no to things that everyone else is doing, I know that in the long run I will be glad. Who knows? Maybe my friends will even respect me for acting with integrity and taking a stand. This may seem weird, but I have started asking the question, "Would Jesus watch this?" When the answer is no, I am learning to walk away.

Jana Kroeker, 15, home school, Medicine Hat, Alberta, CA

I like being independent, but it's kinda scary that I get to make decisions on my own. Lord, help me to make good ones!

edge of existence

Show me, O LORD, my life's end and the number of my days; let me know how fleeting is my life.

PSALM 39:4

I'm standing on the edge.
My whole existence behind me.
All of creation lies before me.
I feel the presence of people all around me,
  but I stand alone.
I can see nothing but blinding light,
But I see the world more clearly now.
I hear a distant sound it has a peaceful ringing
But I feel a chill approaching.
Dark is colorless around me smothered by the light.
I am stranded in the mist of time.
I fear nothing, but I can sense the danger ahead.
Time is short I must move on, but where can I go I'm
  standing on the edge of existence.
Something lies before me I can feel it. I must reach
  my destination, or else be stuck
standing on the edge of existence.

Rachel Crane, 14, home school, Lewisburg, TN

I'm only on this earth a short time,
Lord, but right now I'm young, and I don't
feel the urgency of making every moment count.
Help me to start making the most of my life now.

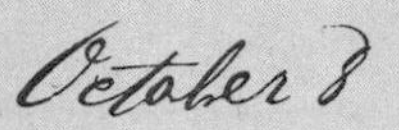

skin and eyes

I also want women to dress modestly,
with decency and propriety, not with
braided hair or gold or pearls or expensive clothes.

1 TIMOTHY 2:9

Whenever I go shopping for clothes, I always try on pants that are too tight, or shirts that are too low-cut, or skirts that are just a bit too short. I am tempted to buy them. I am surrounded by ads that encourage me to wear suggestive clothes and girls everywhere who do. Because I want to fit in, I feel like I have to dress that way. I try to explain it by thinking, "Well, who is this bothering? I feel great." But then I stop and think about why I am wearing these clothes. Is it really to fit in? Is it so that guys will notice me? I begin to wonder if that's the kind of attention I want from guys. Do I want them to talk to me because of how I look or because of who I am? My friends who are girls don't like me because they think I am hot or like the brand of jeans I wear. My friends are true friends precisely because they don't care about what I'm wearing or what I look like. So why should we want guys to like us for that reason? There is something else, though, that I rarely consider. Guys really struggle when a girl wears immodest clothes. Maybe he does want to get to know her, but the shirt that she's wearing is distracting him from getting to know her past what she looks like. By wearing provocative clothes we encourage guys' minds to wander, hurting both them and ourselves. Someone told me to consider whether my outfit is drawing attention to my face or another part of my body. When I get dressed, I ask myself, "Does this honor God and my brothers in Christ?"

Grace Bricker, 16, Jonathan Edwards Academy, Greenfield, MA

Lord, is what I'm wearing right now
honoring You? Did I even think about that
when I got dressed? I pray that I will from now on.

it's my turn now!

Trust in the LORD *with all your heart and lean not on your own understanding; in all your ways acknowledge him, and he will make your paths straight.*

PROVERBS 3:5–6

Perhaps you know this verse by heart, but I wanted to share it with you because it gives me a lot of peace. I'm blessed beyond what I can imagine, and I'm fortunate to have grown up in an amazing Christian home. At seventeen my life got pretty crazy, even though my life is easy. Looking ahead at my life, there are things like college, relationships, and getting a job that are hitting me right in the face. I know these are things that I have to deal with, and I know the Lord knows my heart and needs better that I do. The thing I've had the most trouble handing over to God is… the boy department. I've never had a boyfriend, and at seventeen that can get pretty frustrating. There have been boys that I've liked a lot and prayed about, but the Lord's answer has always been no or things just haven't worked out. Sometimes it hurts when I see my friends who have those perfect guys and I wonder what my problem is. But that is when I turn to Jeremiah 29:11which says, "For I know the plans that I have for you, declares the Lord, plans for welfare and not for calamity to give you a future and a hope." Then it always hits me that I'm silly to worry over having a boyfriend. God has a perfect plan for my life, full of hope. I know He's protecting my heart, and I know I'll find the right relationship if and when He wants me to.

Claire Englehart, 17, Cedar Hall School, Bell Buckle, TN

God, give me peace. I worry so much.
I want to trust in Your plan and be at peace.

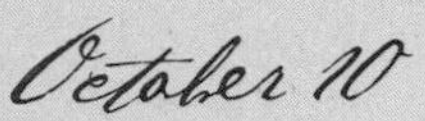

the happiest little dog

There is a time for everything, and a season for every activity under heaven: a time to be born and a time to die, a time to plant and a time to uproot.

ECCLESIASTES 3:1–2

Well, tonight our fifteen-year-old dog died. She was very old and couldn't really walk well, but she was always the happiest little dog who loved her life. I don't know if you've ever lost a pet, but for my family it was really hard. My brother and sister are both having a hard time with it. Death is such a tough thing to deal with, and everyone tends to deal with it differently. Death is especially hard when it's a family member, friend, or even a neighbor. I know when my grandmother died; it took me awhile to accept that it was true. But the crazy thing about death is that we know about it, but it still surprises us. We all know in the back of our minds that one day we will die, but dealing with the reality of death when it actually comes is the tricky part. I know that there's no way to make death easier, but God still walks with us when we are dealing with it. I know that my brother and sister will be alright eventually and will be able to remember our sweet little dog, Hope, with a smile. Relying on God when death does occur is much easier said than done (believe me, I have been through it), but He is the God who experiences and lives our pain with us.

Holly Scott, 18, North Buncombe High School, Weaverville, NC

God, thank You that You feel my pain with me.
It is so great to know that I am not alone when I'm hurting.

the play that changed my life

God made Him who had no sin to be sin for us,
so that we might become the righteousness of God.

2 CORINTHIANS 5:21

A few years ago I went to a Mission Adventures summer camp. It was something cool to do in the summer, since (if you can believe me) living in Hawaii was getting boring for me. I was excited to meet people my age from a bunch of different places. At first it was just a whole lot of fun as we started getting to know each other, and even though we were all really different, we were all there because there was not much to do back home during the summer. The second night things started to change and get a bit more serious. The staff preformed a play depicting the Crucifixion of Jesus. Watching what Christ did suddenly became so much more real to me. It hit me that Jesus died on the cross for my sins. I realized that all the things that I ever did and all the things I was doing now that were wrong could disappear in one night. All I had to do was ask Jesus to forgive me. I dropped to my knees and did just that. I asked Him to forgive me for everything I had done that didn't make Him happy. I cried because this Man was the only One who could do this for me. He died so that I could live. Jesus wanted us to see God in a new way, in the right way. God wants us to come to Him just the way we are, and He takes care of everything else.

Victoria T. Kaopua, 15, Kealakehe High School, Kailua-Kona, HI

Father, when I really think about Jesus dying
on the cross, I am so amazed. He suffered so much
so that I could be with You. Thank You for sending Him!

flip the switch

I am the light of the world.

JOHN 9:5 (KJV)

Have you been in class when the teacher's words fade slowly away and that fly buzzing around the room becomes more interesting than Antarctica's geography? During one of those afternoons, my perspective on life changed. I sat in a wooden desk between four white walls staring up at the ceiling. One florescent light bulb was flickering on, then off, with no predictable rhythm. Just when I thought it was out for good, it flashed back on, brighter than ever. The challenges of my junior year were suffocating me. I was struggling with things I had been warned would come, but they were the kinds of things that you cannot understand until you actually go through them. That year, I had watched many close relationships disintegrate into ashes. I knew that God was there and would help me out, but I impatiently wanted to know when. I read the story of Joseph and though I had heard it hundreds of times, this time it seemed different. Joseph was seventeen, my age, when his own brothers sold him. While facing turmoil, he had no clue that God would bring so many great things into his life. He just had to stick it out. In that classroom, I discovered that life is like the flickering light bulb. It is scary when things get dim, and we are not sure what might happen. But we must stick it out. God has plans to make us stronger and brighter. All we have to do is breaking out of our daze and watch as God flips the switch on.

Charity Yost, 17, Oconee County Christian Academy, Seneca, SC

You can use anything to teach me about
You, God. Absolutely anything. I just have to be
open to Your lessons, and I will find them everywhere.

the big, horrible, little-girl-eating cow

What time I am afraid, I will trust in thee.

PSALM 56:3 (KJV)

When I was younger, my friend and I went on an adventure across the pasture to visit his grandmother. When we looked ahead we saw the cows. His mom said that we were going to have to travel through the cows, but that they would not bother us. My little heart began to race, and sweat started forming on my brow. I knew, right then, that I would not live to see the other side of the pasture. As we began to pass through the cows, I looked to my right and there, standing at ten-feet tall, was the largest cow I had ever seen. It had big red eyes and smoke pouring out its nostrils. My whole five-year-long life flashed before my eyes as I almost collapsed on the spot. At school we learned a verse for every letter of the alphabet. That week we had learned the W verse, Psalm 56:3: "What time I am afraid, I will trust in Him." My teacher encouraged us to repeat verses like prayers when we were scared. So my little quivering self started to pray that verse that I had just learned, over and over. Christ gave me peace that I can't describe and that I still remember- like He wrapped me in His arms. I wasn't afraid anymore. Needless to say, I survived the little-girl-eating cow with red eyes…Ok, so perhaps it didn't have red eyes, smoke trailing out of its nose, or a taste for little girls. But God answered the prayers of this little girl, teaching her to trust Him completely. It is so comforting to know that God is always there for us and He will never let us out of His arms, even in the face of cows who eat little girls.

Kaity Flynn, 16, Nebraska Christian High School, Palmer, NE

What time I am afraid, I will trust in You.
What time I am afraid, I will trust in You.
What time I am afraid, I will trust in You.

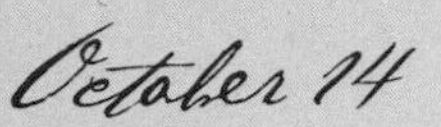

the master builder

And in him you too are being built together to become a dwelling in which God lives by his Spirit.

EPHESIANS 2:22

My younger brother is an amazing builder. Whenever I look into his room, he's always using his hands to put something interesting together. One day it will be a castle with turrets, and then the next day I'll find a deep-sea submarine or an original space ship. I admire him for his exceptional talent and his ability to use mundane toys to make such creative objects. There is no way I could ever match his skill at building things. I think life is much the same. Sometimes I get so discouraged because I can't seem to be the person I want to be. No matter how hard I try, I can never be quite good enough. My own attempts at fixing myself just make matters worse. Often when close to giving up, I am reminded that Christ is at work in my life, just as my brother is always at work on his designs. Only God can accomplish what I have tried and failed to do so many times. Jesus has already lived the perfect life for me, and in Him I am able to become what I was truly meant to be. I have to trust that the Master Builder is completing the work in my heart, and His finished product will be infinitely better than anything I could have ever imagined.

Meredith Koontz, 17, North Buncombe High School, Weaverville, NC

Thank You, God, for building me
into the person I should be.
I know what You have planned will be incredible.

one little piece of paper

You are the light of the world. A city on a hill cannot be hidden. Neither do people light a lamp and put it under a bowl. Instead they put it on its stand, and it gives light to everyone in the house.

MATTHEW 5:14–15

Come on, girls—it won't be that bad," Vinnie encouraged us. "You two come with me," he added, pointing at Stacey and Chrissy. They disappeared into the shadows of Darien Lake to hand out tracts to the people still in the park. Shinaé and I were left behind to evangelize the people leaving. As soon as Vinnie and the girls were gone, Shinaé and I looked at each other with raised eyebrows. "Are you going to do this?" she asked. "Are you kidding me?" I replied. "I'm not doing that!" Instead, we stood around and talked until it was time to leave the park. At the time, my decision didn't seem bad. I didn't want to hand out tracts to a bunch of people I didn't know, so why should I? Looking back now, I wonder why I didn't take the opportunity. I wonder why I'm so afraid to share my faith with people I don't know. We are told that we should be living a Christian life and setting a good example for people, but what about the people we may never meet again? One little piece of paper with the gospel message could change their entire life. Next time I have the opportunity to hand out tracts, I hope I won't let my fear control me. I hope I will have the strength to hand somebody that one little piece of paper that could make an eternal difference.

Sarah Brautigam, 16, Houghton Christian Academy, Houghton, NY

God, I don't want to let one opportunity to share You with someone pass by. Help me to take advantage of every one.

our temporary home

So we fix our eyes not on what is seen, but on what is unseen. For what is seen is temporary, but what is unseen is eternal.

2 CORINTHIANS 4:18

I grew up in my parent's home until I was seven. My mother was Korean and learned enough English to get by. My dad married her when he was a sergeant in the army, commissioned to Korea. My mother was lovable, but she wasn't used to being a mom and did not expect to take care of my brother and me. In Korea, the custom is for a grandmother to take care of the children while the mother worked. Up until the time I was eight, social services frequently checked up on us. It seemed like just a part of life, and I didn't think twice about why these people kept coming to our home. One day, I was pulled out of public school and learned that both my brother (who is two years older than me) and I were going to temporarily live with my aunt and uncle. After settling in, a few more months went by with more visits from social services, and we found out that we were going to live permanently with my aunt and uncle. As I have grown older and learned more about Christ, I realize that even this is still temporary. Through the process of getting to know God, I've realized that this earth is just a temporary stop on the journey to heaven, and that what we do now with what we've been given affects our life in heaven.

Virginia MacKinnon, 15, Jonathan Edwards Academy, Turners Falls, MA

Father, I love thinking about when I will be in heaven with You. I am so thankful You have made an eternal home for me!

a heavy burden

"Fear not, for I have redeemed you;
I have summoned you by name; you are mine."

ISAIAH 43:1

It's so easy for me to fall into shame and guilt! Shame, because I haven't held up the standards I feel I must meet. I began to grow tired because of the heavy weight that I feel I must carry. Guilt, because sometimes I don't want to do anything but watch a movie and sleep. I don't want to feel guilty anymore, but I can't get away from it. Thoughts keep coming to me about how I did something wrong or how I messed up over there, and I can't forget about it! These feelings of guilt and shame flood my whole body, and I want to run to my bed and cry. "Why can't I do anything right? God must be disappointed with me!" I feel like there is no way out from this hole. I feel I can't go to God because there is no way He will forgive me again! But these are lies, not the truth, and I don't have to be entrapped by the guilt anymore! Christ has taken all the guilt and shame on Himself. He carried it all to the cross and buried it, so it will never be found! I don't have to carry the load on my own, and the fact is, I can't. Christ has redeemed me and delights in me. And God accepts because of Christ. It is true that I am a rotten sinner, but I have freedom in Christ and in Him I am guiltless and free.

Hailey Howerton, 16, home school, Greenville, SC

Don't let me get caught up in being
ashamed and guilty, Lord, because this keeps
me from doing work for You. When I ask You
to forgive me, I want to believe I am truly forgiven.

be patient, God has a plan

Many are the plans in a man's heart,
but it is the L*ORD's purpose that prevails.*

PROVERBS 19:21

As a senior in high school, I find myself questioning whether my plans for my future are really my plans or God's plans. This past summer, I thought I wanted to be an orthopedic surgeon or nurse. I was invited to attend a National Leadership Forum of Medicine where I would have the opportunity to mirror physicians in different fields for ten days. As it turned out, the trip never took place. I attended a Christ In Youth conference with my youth group instead. Does this means that God doesn't want me to go into the medical field? Does this mean that He's closing that door? I don't know, but Proverbs says, "Many are the plans in a man's heart, but it is the Lord's purpose that prevails." At Christ In Youth we touched on the subject and I realized that I have to be patient, pray, and be still so that I may know the direction that God has planned for me. Daily I will pray for Gods direction in my life. I know in my heart that all things happen in God's time, and that when I graduate from high school, I still may not have a peace about where God is leading me. That's okay, because I must learn to be patient and wait for His timing. Matthew 7:7 says "Ask and it will be given to you; seek and you will find; knock and the door will be opened to you. For everyone who asks, receives; he who seeks, finds; and to him who knocks, the door will be opened." Each day I shall pray for God to open that door.

Shelbie Lutz, 17, Seaman High School, Topeka, KS

Lord, open the door You want me to walk through.
Show me where to go. I want to be led by You.

you get out what you put in

Do not be deceived: God cannot be mocked.
A man reaps what he sows. The one who sows to please
his sinful nature, from that nature will reap destruction;
the one who sows to please the Spirit, from the Spirit will reap
eternal life. Let us not become weary in doing good, for at the
proper time we will reap a harvest if we do not give up.

GALATIANS 6:7–9

It's a fact: If I never studied Spanish, never talked in Spanish, never wrote in Spanish, never thought about Spanish...I'd never learn Spanish. Relationships are the same way. You get out of them what you put in. The Lord convicted me that if I don't read the Bible, pray, memorize, or meditate on scripture, or think about Him, then I will never learn to love Him with all my heart, soul, mind, and strength, as He commanded. It's the same in our relationship with our siblings. If I never talk to them, spend time with them, or do things for them, if I don't care enough to ask what is really going on inside them, I will never learn to love them and we will never become friends. A relationship is something that takes constant work to keep up. Girls, we need to invest some energy in our siblings, and really learn to love them. The two most important relationships to invest in are your relationship with God and your relationship with your family. Your siblings will be with you for a long time, and God will be with you long after that.

Nina Lewis, 18, home school with tutorial, Clemson, SC

God, help me to invest as much
as I can in my relationship with You.
I get so much from You, so I need to give a lot too.

time's up!

"Let the little children come to me,
and do not hinder them, for the kingdom
of God belongs to such as these."

LUKE 18:16

I was at a leadership camp where we learned how to share Christ with others. As part of that training, the staff decided to take our camp onto the streets of the city where we were. I was assigned to a softball complex. As we boarded the bus that Thursday evening and looked around, my group realized that we were going to be the last dropped off and the first to reload. By the time we had driven everyone else to their destinations, we were bound to get thirty minutes at the tournament. How unfair! This was the highlight of the week and we were being cheated out of the full time! Some people began to sing and I joined in, but was rather half-hearted. When we finally arrived, I headed to the picnic tables. I talked with some people, but didn't get anywhere near the gospel. Deciding that maybe the children would be more receptive, my partners and I migrated toward the playground. As we played with the kids we made sure they knew about sin, and who Jesus is. I turned around to my partner, Lindsey. She asked me if I would pray with this little boy to receive Christ. I was so excited I forgot to ask his name before we prayed. I prayed after him, and I had to stop and ask him what it was! Just when I had counted God out because of time, He showed up and called one of His little children to Himself.

Danica Woods, 17, Nebraska Christian High School, Central City, NE

God, I love sharing Your gospel with others.
I don't want to hold anyone back.
I want to bring them closer to You.

florida lessons (part 1)

And we know that in all things God works for the good of those who love him, who have been called according to His purpose.

ROMANS 8:28

On July 21, 2002, I answered the phone to hear my grandfather's choked voice asking us to come over immediately. Silently pondering what event triggered this, we drove the two miles to hear that my aunt and fourteen-year-old cousin, Elisha, were in intensive care after an automobile accident. The situation was complicated further by another cousin, Micah, being immobile and in excruciating pain from having had a twenty-four-inch rod inserted in his back on July 11. Instantly our lives turned upside down. My younger sister, my mom, my grandparents, and I left immediately for West Palm Beach to offer what help we could give. I left my relaxed summer of play practice and sleeping in to take charge of cooking, cleaning, and laundry for nine people. Since all the drivers were at the hospital daily, we were stranded. Soon Elisha came home and my sister, Christina, and I did our best to help our recovering cousins, although we often were unsure what the best was. Once Micah got stuck on the floor and we didn't know whether to laugh or call 911! The weeks in Florida were good in many ways...God taught me lessons from the eight weeks there. He showed me that I am not in control of my life and schedule. We grew closer to our cousins and saw God answer prayers as He helped my aunt recover beyond any hope. God helped me grow up and realize He alone is in control.

Maryanna Jensen, 19, North Greenville College, Asheville, NC

Lord, sometimes it takes a really drastic situation to teach me to trust You. Help me to never forget the lessons I learn in hard times.

florida lessons (part 2)

By this all men will know that
you are my disciples if you love one another.

JOHN 13:35

Although my aunt, uncle, and cousins had moved from Southern California to West Palm Beach less than a year before their 2002 accident, their church in Jupiter (more than an hour away) came to our aid immediately. Other neighbors and Christian friends also showered us with Jesus' love. Every day their church family would bring us a delicious meal (sometimes driving four hours roundtrip). We had so much the refrigerator would not hold it, so they cut back to bringing meals every other day. When my aunt came home to recover a month after the wreck, their small home was extremely crowded. A church family invited my grandparents to stay with them and also took us four teens to church on Wednesday nights. Their neighbors fried fish, loaned us a blow dryer, and checked on us often. Reba, a close family friend, took my sister and me on a one-day beach trip that was an oasis in a desert of laundry and dirty dishes. Phone calls from concerned friends and family from all over the country kept me busy the first few days. These calls and loads of mail continued for weeks to encourage our entire family. I hope I will always remember how valuable loving actions were to us in our crisis. When others around me have their world turn upside down, I want to be there for them with a meal, a phone call, or an outing.

Maryanna Jensen, 19, North Greenville College, Asheville, NC

God, thank You for the people
who give so much to help me when I need it.
I pray that I can be that selfless when someone needs me.

some friendly advice

Above all, love each other deeply....
Offer hospitality without grumbling. Each one should use whatever gifts he has received to serve others, faithfully administering God's grace in its various forms.

1 PETER 4:8–10

Going to college is a wonderful time in your life, but it is also really hard! And I'm not just talking about school work. You have to face so many things you never have before. Like what to do if you don't get along with your roommates. Sometimes personalities clash and make dorm life a trying experience. The best advice I can give is to remind you of the verse that talks about patiently bearing with one another in love (Ephesians 4:2). And what do you do when you get bad grades? Do not lose heart when you receive a less-than-pleasing grade—it will happen! Low grades, however, can be averaged out and as you adjust to the college workload, you will see the reward of hours of studying. And what do you do if you are homesick? If you are really homesick, call your family often and write your siblings letters—they will miss you too! Also, I encourage you to spend time with families from a local church; in general, the family atmosphere is very encouraging. And also remember to think of your classmates and go to them for support. Chances are that they struggle they are struggling too and you can help each other get through it.

Jessica Runk, 19, Patrick Henry College, Purcellville, VA

I have some big challenges ahead, Lord.
Help me to listen to the advice of others so that I can learn from them instead of having to learn form my mistakes.

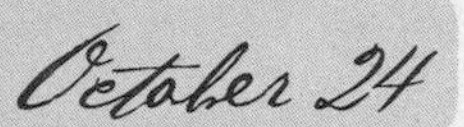

a starting missionary

Therefore go and make disciples of all nations, baptizing them in the name of the Father and of the Son and of the Holy Spirit. and teaching them to obey everything I have commanded you. And surely I am with you always, even to very end of the age.

MATTHEW 28:19–20

God called my family three years ago to be missionaries and to travel to India. Since then we have been to six different countries and are planning to travel a lot this year. It is hard sometimes, not having money when you need it, always pouring what you know into other people. Sometimes it's scary being in countries where just about everything is dangerous. But honestly, I am happiest when I am serving others and holding starving kids in my arms to love and comfort them. I am most excited when I am in squatter huts helping homeless and hurting people. I love giving my time up for them. However, just because we travel around and go places most people never get to go, you are just as called as I am. We are all called to be missionaries, whether you live in the U.S. or abroad. Jesus gave us all the Great Commission. You too can be a missionary right where you are by reaching out to hurting and lonely people. To be a missionary, show them that you actually care. Show Jesus by your actions. People will see the difference. We all need to start somewhere.

Katie-Lee Kroeker, 16, home school, Medicine Hat, Alberta, CA

God, can I really be a missionary right here in my town? Show me people nearby that I can witness to so that they will know about Your love.

what to wear?

Do not conform any longer
to the pattern of this world, but be transformed
by the renewing of your mind.

ROMANS 12:2

When you wake up in the morning you have a choice to make: what you will wear that day. For a lot of girls, this is a big choice, and a tough one, because we want to look pretty. But when we are Christians, we have more to consider when we get dressed than just what looks good. We are God's beautiful creation and He commanded us to dress in a way that honors Him. 1 Timothy 2:9 says to dress moderately and discreetly. Okay, I know what you're thinking: "Do I have to wear rags?!" No! God wants us to feel and look beautiful, but in a modest way. You girls may not know this, but you are all extremely gorgeous! And since you are so gorgeous, when you wear clothing that is revealing or tight it can make boys look at you in ways they shouldn't. What we do can cause others to sin, so we need to be careful. When you wake up in the morning ask yourself, "Am I honoring God with what I'm wearing?"

Janelle Mitchell, 18, Siegel High School, Murfreesboro, TN

God, I want You to approve of everything
about me, even the clothes I wear.
Help me to make good choices—Godly choices.

big God

Cast all your anxiety on Him because He cares for you.

1 PETER 5:7

Have you ever had a problem that was too big for you? Well, I have some really obvious but really important news for you: NO PROBLEM IS BIGGER THAN GOD. Is that comforting or what? I know that we're all supposed to know that, but we forget it all the time. But even when we forget Him, God knows *everything* that goes on in our lives. He created us and has a plan for us. God will never give you more than you can handle. But if you feel that you are too small and the problem is too big, then give it to God..He is so much bigger! He cares for you so much! Don't worry. Ask Him to fix your problem. Then ask Him if there is anything that you need to do. Sometimes there is; sometimes He'll take care of it all. So "cast all your anxiety on Him because He cares for you." He is bigger than any problem, and He will not make you deal with it on your own.

Stephanie Warner, 14, Walnut Grove Christian Preparatory School, Carmel, IN

I know You are bigger than all my problems, Lord.
But I get so caught up in things that I forget.
Help me to remember.

material girl

Do not store up for yourselves treasures on earth, where moth and rust destroy, and where thieves break in and steal. But store up for yourselves treasures in heaven, where moth and rust do not destroy, and where thieves do not break in and steal. For where your treasure is, there your heart will be also.

MATTHEW 6:19–21

We've all heard the lyrics to the song "Diamonds Are a Girl's Best Friend." Part of this is true: We are living in a material world. Girls and women these days are stereotyped by men (and themselves) to love shopping and love material things. We are led to believe that in order to have a happy life, we must have the biggest house, the nicest car, and the most stuff. But God tells us something different. It does not matter what we have here on earth. What matters is what treasures we have stored up in heaven. In Matthew, we learn that our possessions here on earth are only temporary, for moth and rust destroy them and thieves to break in and steal them. I know right now it seems like we need to have the best clothes and shoes and accessories, but we can't take those things to heaven with us. There will be things there that are so much better we'll forget about all the earthly stuff we used to think we *had* to have.

Brittany Behler, 17, Chattanooga School for the Arts and Sciences, Hixson, TN

I think I have to have so many things.
But the only thing I have to have is You.

really forgiving

"Come now, let us argue this out,"
says the Lord. "No matter how deep the stain
of your sins, I can remove it. I can make you as
clean as freshly fallen snow. Even if you are stained
as red as crimson, I can make you as white as wool."

ISAIAH 1:18 (NLT)

I was reading a book a couple of months ago, and there was a chapter devoted to forgiveness. When I was reading it, I thought I had already forgiven everyone that had done something wrong to me in the past. But when I prayed about it, I realized I hadn't. God brought to my attention several people I had never really forgiven. During that week I had forgiven a handful of people that had hurt me in some way, but I realized all I had *really* done was push those memories to the back of my mind and try to move on. When I forgave them, I felt a peace inside because it was for real this time. I realized that I can't expect God to forgive me if I don't forgive those who hurt me. Are you harboring unforgiveness in your heart? Ask God to help you forgive and forget, then move on with your life for Christ.

Katelyn Westfall, 15, Dover High School, Dover, OH

God, who do I need to forgive today?
Who am I holding a grudge against?
Teach me to forgive as You do.

one thing makes a big difference

Esther won the favor of everyone who saw her.

ESTHER 2:15

A tropical depression in the Atlantic Ocean turned into hurricane Katrina, a national disaster. Starting out as something small, she grew as strong as a category-five hurricane before crashing into America's Gulf Coast at category-three strength with devastating affects. Small things can turn into big disasters, but small things and "small" people can also make a huge *positive* difference. Esther started out as an ordinary girl who made a big difference in the lives of her people. Esther's Uncle Mordecai said, "Who knows that you have come into royal position for such a time as this?" Esther thought about what her uncle said, and finally told King Xerses about Haman's plot to kill all the Jews. After hearing this, Xerses had Haman hanged. Esther was an ordinary girl who became the one who saved all of her people. She started out small, but she affected many more people than anyone thought. If you know someone who isn't a Christian or who is just having a bad day, one thing you say to them could make all the difference. Don't be afraid to be used by God. No matter how small you are or how insignificant you may feel, God has a BIG plan for your life.

Ali VanMinos, 15, Oconee County Christian Academy, Seneca, SC

God, sometimes I feel powerless to change anything. But I know that You can use something as small as a kind word to change lives. Thank You for making my small actions so big.

4 a.m. terror

For our struggle is not against flesh and blood, but...against the powers of the dark world and against the spiritual forces of evil in the heavenly realms.

EPHESIANS 6:12

I am honestly not very excited to write about this subject. In fact, it is the one subject I hoped to avoid, but it has continued to be a part of my life in ways I cannot deny. In the past few years, I have had many confrontations with evil. I don't know why Satan wanted to frighten me so badly, but night after night and I was filled with an unexplainable terror. I didn't know what to do to get him to stay away. I felt helpless because I knew he had power. But it didn't take me very long to figure out that I knew Someone with more power. I knew that Jesus had conquered Satan, and that He had the power to protect me. One night I was scared, and I prayed and cried until I finally fell into an exhausted sleep at 4 a.m. That was the beginning of my escape. The next night I laid in bed in the dark, and I could feel a dark, evil presence in the room with me. I was petrified, but I was prepared with a promise that God had given me—the use of His name. That night, I commanded Satan to leave me and never come back. I commanded him in the name of Jesus. I can truthfully tell you that since that night, I have never been visited by Satan's evil again. There have been times that I know he wants to get at me, but I can always feel God surrounding me, protecting me with His power and love. Because I trust in Jesus, Satan cannot control me. Thank you, Jesus, for always protecting me, for always being there for me.

Kimberlee DeGroot, 14, Petra Academy, Bozeman MT

God, sometimes I'm really, seriously afraid.
Not just worried but genuinely scared.
Comfort me then, so I'll remember You always keep me safe.

i want to say the right things

Timely advice is as lovely as golden apples in a silver basket.

Valid criticism is as treasured by the one who heeds it as jewelry made from finest gold.

Faithful messengers are as refreshing as snow in the heat of summer. They revive the spirit of their employer.

A person who doesn't give a promised gift is like clouds and wind that don't bring rain.

Patience can persuade a prince, and soft speech can crush strong opposition.

PROVERBS 25:11–15 (NLT)

When doubts and fears arise, teach me Thy way!
When storms over spread the skies, teach me Thy way!
Shine Through the cloud and rain, through sorrow, toil, and pain;
Make Thou my path-way plain,
Teach me Thy way!

B. Mansell Ramsey

November 1

different kind of beauty

Charm is deceptive, and beauty is fleeting;
but a woman who fears the LORD is to be praised.

PROVERBS 31:30

I remember searching desperately for beauty when I was just a young girl. Those were probably the worst years of my life. I was the chubby, long-haired, freckled, buck-toothed little girl that no one wanted to befriend. I cried and prayed myself to sleep every night. I wanted so much for people to look past my outward appearance. I was forever on a diet, sometimes even skipping meals. All I wanted was to fit in and belong. Although I knew Jesus at the time, I did not realize what beauty means to Him. I finally discovered the truth in Proverbs 31:30. After reading this verse, I saw that physical beauty truly does not matter in God's eyes. I know that is an easier concept to say than to believe, but it is so true. I finally made peace with myself and my body as I realized that what makes someone beautiful is God shining through them. I look at people so differently now. I do not say that a girl is beautiful unless I see her inward beauty. Now, I can honestly say that I am beautiful, because God has opened my eyes to what that means. I hope and pray that every girl learns to see herself through God's mirror, because it is impossible to love others if we cannot love the way God made us.

Jessica Gordon, 16, New Covenant Christian School, Pageland, SC

I don't want insecurities to keep me from
loving others. I want to really like myself, so that
I can be free to love others and let them love me back.

the choice

But among you there must not be even a hint of sexual immorality, or of any kind of impurity, or of greed, because these are improper for God's holy people.

EPHESIANS 5:3

As teen girls growing up in a sex-oriented world today, we have an important choice to make: to choose to remain sexually pure until marriage as God commands us, or to abandon God's commandment and give in to our desires. It would be much easier for us to honor God's commandment if we lived in the times of the Puritans or something, because sex wasn't as big a deal in their culture as it is in ours. Sex is more openly talked about now, so it makes it harder for us to avoid it. But as girls who strive to reflect God in their lives, we must make our own personal choice about sex. Personally, I have chosen to remain abstinent until marriage. On my left ring finger, I wear a promise ring that looks like a wedding band. This ring represents my promise to God, myself, and my future husband that I will remain sexually pure. In Ephesians 5: 1–3, God tells us why we should remain pure. If we are His holy people, we have to obey His Word and not let sin hold us back.

Brittany Behler, 17, Chattanooga School for the Arts and Sciences, Hixson, TN

Lord, my purity is a promise
I don't want to break because it's a promise
I've made to You. Help me to keep it.

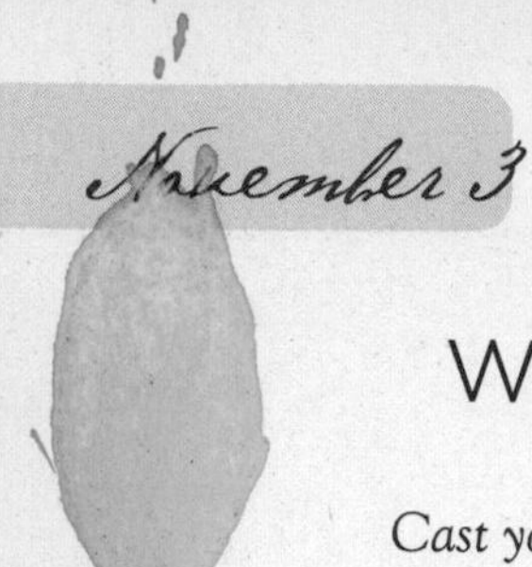

wide enough

Cast your cares on the LORD and he will sustain you; he will never let the righteous fall.

PSALM 55:22

Senior year. I can hardly believe I've gotten to this point. All my life, I've looked forward to this time with great anticipation, and now it's here, it seems so unreal. It definitely isn't what I expected. Everyone in the past has said that her senior year was the best out of them all, but right now it's hard to imagine feeling that way. The weight of responsibility is dragging me down—I have so much to do all the time without a spare moment in sight. Homework is a constant companion, and my senior project hangs like a rain cloud over my head. All I want to do is sit down. Today, my anxiety was like a blaring trumpet, a great pressure in my chest. After a while, I felt the need to read my Bible. Lately, I hadn't taken as much time to pay attention to my devotions, but this afternoon was special. I could feel God talking to my heart through the Scriptures, and He told me He *loved* me. My eyes filled with tears. Even though I feel so overwhelmed sometimes, God is stronger than all of my trials. While I'm straining to carry all of my worries, Jesus is reaching out his hands, saying, "Let me carry that, beloved. My shoulders are wide enough." Of course, everything won't be easy in the days to come, but with the right perspective, I know that this last year will be a time to grow closer to God and make lasting memories for the future.

Meredith Koontz, 17, North Buncombe High School, Weaverville, NC

Lord, when I feel like I can't take it anymore, bring me to the Bible. I know Your Word can help me get through anything.

jealousy

When Rachel saw that she was not bearing Jacob any children, she became jealous of her sister.

GENESIS 30:1

Jealousy has been a problem for me. My older sister gets to do everything first. My younger brother never gets blamed for anything—if we fight, I get in trouble. The list is endless. Reading the story of Rachel and Leah helped me realize that being jealous only makes you bitter inside, and you start to despise your sibling. We should be thankful for our siblings, not jealous of what they can do that we can't. God gave us older siblings to look up to for guidance or younger siblings to set the example for. I never realized how much I loved my sister until my brother started treating me like I treat my sister. If we keep up the view of jealousy, then we, like Rachel, will begin to grow bitter and start to wonder why everyone likes our siblings better than us. If you are a new older sister, then you may think your new sibling is stealing all the attention away from you. But we need to love our siblings, not be jealous of them. God made us who we are, so there's no reason to be jealous of anyone. It really helps to read this passage and find out how Rachel reacted. We should ask God for help with this, so that He can help us through it.

Kristen Isaac, 14, Covenant Christian Academy, La Union, NM

God, I want to love my siblings, not be jealous of them. Teach me to be happy with what I have.

November 5

are you a slave?

Then you will know the truth
and the truth will set you free.

JOHN 8:32

Jesus answered them, "I tell you the truth, everyone who sins is a slave to sin" (John 8:34) What is freedom? Have these verses changed your perspective on freedom? I used to think freedom was doing what you want when, you want until one day in Bible class when I read these verses. I realized freedom was a totally different thing than what I had thought. All true believers are free if they are following God. Freedom isn't doing what you want but rather being the person God has created you to be and living in obedience to Him. WOW! That changes perspective. So why would someone want to become a slave once they are free? Now that's an obvious question: No one wants to be a slave. But you know, in the second verse it says if we commit sin, if we make a habit of sinning, then we are slaves to sin. No one is perfect. We will sin. But if we want to keep from being slaves to sin, we have to fight against our nature and ask for God's help, so that we can be truly free.

Tiffany Heetderks, 15, Petra Academy, Bozeman, MT

Father, I want the freedom only You can give me.
I want the freedom that comes from serving You.

encouraging others

And we urge you, brothers,
warn those who are idle, encourage the timid,
help the weak, be patient with everyone.

1 THESSALONIANS 5:14

Throughout the first two months of school, the reality of this world's problems seemed to slap me in the face. People tend to think that Christian schools are perfect and everyone who goes to school there has a wonderful life, but that is not true. Among all of these struggles, I have realized how important it is to trust in God, give your life to Him, and be there for your friends. I know some students who struggle with suicidal thoughts. One friend deals with family problems and another struggles with a true Christian faith. God put me in their lives to be an encouragement to them. I feel so often that I don't know the exact words to say to make things better. I am just there to listen, to care, and to pray for them. As I hug them while we are both praying and crying, we work at trusting in God. I don't know the answers, and I can't fix all of the problems, but I can encourage them with a note, some yummy chocolate, a prayer, or even a smile. I remind them that they are important and special in God's eyes and how important a relationship with Him is. I am not at all perfect, but I use the ability God has given me to strengthen others.

Stacey Krieger, 16, Nebraska Christian High School, O'Neill, NE

God, I know I can't solve everyone's problems,
but You have given me the gift of prayer, of listening,
and of love to help them. So please help me use these gifts.

making decisions

Whether you turn to the right
or to the left, your ears will hear a voice
behind you, saying, "This is the way; walk in it."

ISAIAH 30:21

Everyone knows that the teenage years are a time of a lot of important decisions. As I entered my sophomore year of high school, I suddenly began panicking because I needed to start thinking about college. This constant worrying and anxiety drove me crazy. I got little sleep, and the sleep I did manage to get was filled with giant college applications chasing me around and around. I would wake up more exhausted than when I fell asleep and still not be any closer to knowing what I wanted to do for college. I wondered if I would be able to keep up good grades. I wondered if I should stay in my hometown and attend Montana State University (Yea Bobcats!) or venture out to the East Coast. And what on earth did I want to major in? I talked to one of my teachers, and she encouraged me to pray, pray, pray. After all, since God knew exactly what He wanted to do with my life, all I had to do was figure out what he wanted and follow Him. That night as I was reading my Bible, I read Isaiah 30:21. It jumped off the page at me. All I had to do was pray, and God would really help me in my decisions. Thank you, Jesus! No matter what I do, I know you will be there helping me.

Kimberlee DeGroot, 14, Petra Academy, Bozeman MT

God, guide me to what You
want me to do. Please show me what I
should do with my future that will please You most.

a time for apologies

There is a time for everything,
and a season for every activity under
heaven:...a time to tear and a time to mend.

ECCLESIASTES 3:1, 7

One of the hardest things for me to do is to apologize. In order for me to do it, I need to get rid of my anger against that other person, set aside my pride, and admit that I was wrong. Unfortunately, even though I hate it, I find myself apologizing all of the time. When I am mad at a classmate and avoid him all day, I have to apologize, and it is sooo hard. But as Christians we have made an agreement with God to put off our old nature and take up a new nature. That means getting rid of my anger and pride—and being willing to apologize. Just this weekend I had to apologize to a close friend for how immaturely and rudely I behaved when I got mad over a small issue. That really hurt—it was not easy for me, but God was there behind me every step of the way, making sure I handled the situation correctly and didn't leave anything out. Talk about supervision! As the author of Ecclesiastes says, there is a time to tear and a time to mend. When I hurt others by my words or actions, I have the responsibility to make it right, to mend the relationship. Sometimes it is easier than expected; other times it is extremely difficult, but God expects me to make the effort to fix the problem I have made.

Kimberlee DeGroot, 14, Petra Academy, Bozeman MT

Admitting I'm wrong is one of my least
favorite things to do, Lord. So please teach me
to be more humble so that I can forgive and be forgiven.

a week in eagle, alaska

For everything that was written in the past was written to teach us, so that through endurance and the encouragement of the Scriptures we might have hope.

ROMANS 15:4

Every year my youth group travels twelve hours on a bus to a teeny tiny town known as Eagle, Alaska. Once there we spend a week leading vacation Bible school for the kids. It's one of our most exciting and rewarding trips every year, and because it takes on so many different angles, it becomes an amazing opportunity for everyone who goes. It's great because we spend part of our time working with the kids and serving the Lord in any way possible; and then the rest of the time we're able to relax and hang around with each other, building stronger relationships that have a common bond in Christ. This year our lessons focused on the Lords prayer found in Matthew 6:9–13, and each day that we spent with the kids, we would look at a different aspect of our Heavenly Father. I was teaching the fourth through sixth graders and it was amazing to look at these verses over and over and learn something new every time. It's Scripture that I know by heart and have said numerous times, but I realized that there's a difference between simply knowing something and teaching it to someone else. Being able to spread the Word to younger kids who were so excited to hear about it was an incredible experience for me. The best feeling in the world is to know that God is using you, and whenever I'm in Eagle teaching the kids there, I know that I'm being used for his glory. And that feels awesome.

Adrian Thistle, 17, Houston High School, Willow, AK

I want to know that You are using me, dear Jesus. I want to be the person You work through to reach people who don't know You.

a new experience

And Jabez called on the God of Israel saying,
Oh that thou wouldest bless me indeed,
and enlarge my territory, that thine hand might be with me,
and that thou wouldest keep me from evil, that I may not
cause pain. And God granted that which he requested.

1 CHRONICLES 4:10 (KJV)

Almost a year ago, my family and I moved away from the home I had known for eight years. I had moved once before, but I had been only five and didn't remember much. Although I wasn't scared, I was sad and wondered what was going to happen. We already owned a house where we were moving and had visited it twice. I had a lot of things to look forward to: a new mall, my own room, a bigger city, but what about my friends? Would we still be friends after I had been gone a while? Would we write as often as we said we would? Would we remain friends as we grew up? What was going to happen? I couldn't really cry because I was driving in a car with a family friend. As I watched the miles disappear behind me, I started praying to God, asking for help and guidance. About an hour later the rain cleared up and everything looked beautiful. I had strength and all of a sudden I knew I would always keep my same friends; this was just a new way to make more. Although I haven't been gone a year, I have made new friends and kept in contact with my old ones. I love where I live now, and I know that God has blessed me, answered my prayers, and enlarged my circle of friends.

Keegan Nitz, 15, St. Ambrose Christian High School, Meridian, ID

Thank You, Father, for bringing blessings
I don't expect. Just when I think I couldn't
be sadder, You give me a reason to be happy.

never let go (part 1)

For I am the LORD, your God,
who takes hold of your right hand and says to you,
Do not fear; I will help you.

ISAIAH 41:13

Have you ever felt as if your world is trying to fall apart? As a young teen, I was like any other girl. I devoted a lot of my time to physical activities like dance and cross country, and everything seemed to be fine. Then I began to have unusual health symptoms that caused my physician to be concerned, so I went through a few tests to determine the problem. Soon after, at the age of fifteen, I was diagnosed with Crohn's disease. At the doctor's pronouncement, I felt numb, cold. *Could this be happening to me? For real?* I was told that Crohn's is a chronic condition that is treatable, but no cure is available. I felt like I had been punched in the stomach. *But I'm so young,* I thought. I never thought about something like this would happen to me. And I never thought something so bad could teach me so much about God and His love for me.

Meredith Koontz, 17, North Buncombe High School, Weaverville, NC

Father, it so amazing how an illness can
be a blessing if I trust You. Give me the faith
to see even sickness as a way to grow closer to You.

never let go (part 2)

For I am the LORD*, your God,*
who takes hold of your right hand and says to you,
Do not fear; I will help you.

ISAIAH 41:13

Since I found out I have Crohn's disease, I've had to learn to cope with doctor visits, medications, mood swings, pain, tears. Sometimes it's really hard to keep going, to keep smiling. Despite all of that, I have an amazing source of strength and hope. Jesus has been there with me through every trial, and because of Crohn's, we have grown much closer over the past two years. He is my shelter from the storm, my constant comforter and helper. Without Him, I don't know where I would be. I do long for healing, but it's up to God whether it will happen on this earth or in heaven. What matters most is that I have a lifelong Friend who will *never* let go of my hand.

Meredith Koontz, 17, North Buncombe High School, Weaverville, NC

Thank You, Jesus, for never letting go of my hand.
I am so grateful that You walk with me every step of the way.

my rainbow

We are hard pressed on every side, but not crushed; perplexed, but not in despair; persecuted, but not abandoned; struck down but not destroyed.

2 Corinthians 4:8–9

God, *You have known me from the beginning, and You know my end. You see my tears. I'm stuck, lost, hopeless, and I feel like everyone has given up on me, as if I've disappointed the world. I realize how I got here , which is a big step for me because I don't always understand. I sit and watch people comprehend and take notes and absorb the things they are taught. I don't understand that. But I do understand this:* God, *I blamed You. I blamed You for the wrong in my life, the troubles I got myself into, the stupid things I did. And You took it, You dealt with it, You watched me make mistakes, You watched me take the wrong path; You tried to grab my hand, but I jerked it away. You saw me, and You cried. I heard You, but I ignored You. I heard Your voice, and I tried to drown it out with anything I could get my hands on....music, friends, movies, cigarettes, books, anything to silence the sound echoing in my head. I'm sitting here wishing this all would end, and You are sitting right next to me, holding my hand, drying my tears, and You hug me. You never promised life would be easy or that I wouldn't feel broken, and ashamed, but You did promise to ALWAYS be there for me.* God, *You are my only source, my only hope, my all. You promised that You are the one waiting with open arms and the biggest smile on Your face because another child has returned home.* God, *You promised me a rainbow.*

Shannon Fitzgerald, 17, Maranatha Christian Academy, Oakwood, GA

pure eye, pure heart

The eye is the lamp of the body.
If your eyes are good, your whole body
will be full of light.

MATTHEW 6:22

I love movies. I love going to the movie theater with my friends, eating popcorn, and watching a movie. It's something that has become ingrained in our culture. Lately, I've been convicted about the movies I watch. Once I went to a friend's birthday party. I didn't know she had rented a couple of movies that were R-rated and full of gore, swearing, violence, and sex. I felt disgusted as I sat there before the television. I felt paralyzed, forced to watch these terrible images and hear sounds that would be burned into my mind forever. And then the movies began to take the Lord's name in vain…over and over. My spirit felt grieved. I wanted to stand up and say something. All my other friends there were Christians, and here we were sitting and watching a movie that cursed our Savior and ridiculed everything we believed. But I just couldn't. I could not make myself stand up and make the suggestion to turn off the trash. I was afraid. I pretended like I was falling asleep so I didn't have to watch the screen. Once at home, I cried on my dad's shoulder. Why am I ashamed? Why could I not stand up for the name of my Lord? After seeing those movies, I decided on something: I will honor Jesus' holy and precious Name, even in the movies I watch. Now I'm very careful about the images I put into my mind. I'm sure you've heard the phrase "You are what you eat." I like to say "You become what you watch."

Rebecca Wilson, 18, Maranatha Christian Academy, Oakwood, GA

God, I know that the things I watch and read
can have a real effect on me if I let them. Help me
to stay away from things that You wouldn't approve of.

playing for Jesus

Praise the LORD with the harp;
make music to Him on the ten-stringed lyre.
Sing to Him a new song; play skillfully, and shout for joy.

PSALM 33:2–3

Can you imagine a day without music? What would sleepovers be like without crazy dancing in our PJs? What would driving be like without the radio on? How fun would movies be to watch without a soundtrack? Music is a major part of our lives! God has given it to us to enjoy...it's a gift. He also wants us to enjoy it in our worship of Him. If we have music in every other area of our life, why not in our Spiritual one too? We can use our musical gifts to worship Jesus, and praise Him with song! Gulp. This isn't as easy as it sounds though, huh? Play in FRONT of people, no way! Playing the flute at my church has been a challenge for me, but I have learned that it's not about me after all. I don't have to worry about what people think because they are not who I am playing for. Jesus, and only Jesus, is my audience. It doesn't even matter if I sound nervous or choke a few times (which has happened not just once or twice) because whatever I do in worship is music to God's ears. And when we do get nervous? I wish I could say it never happens, but it does. No matter what we do, playing in front of people can be scary. Just remember this: Jesus is by your side the whole time. Pray for His peace to surround you as you play. Don't think about yourself or what people will think. Focus on why you are playing...it's a song of worship to your God. You are playing for Jesus.

Hannah Reed, 16, Jonathan Edwards Academy, Greenfield, MA

Thank You for the gift of music, dear God.
I want to use it to praise You, whether I am
listening to it or playing it.

rise up and be a pure generation

Don't let anyone look down on you
because you are young, but set an example for the
believers in speech, in life, in love, in faith and in purity.

1 TIMOTHY 4:12

I'm sure many of you have grown up being told that you need to stay pure until marriage, but I'm not talking about just the no-sex kind of purity. I'm talking about every aspect of your life being pure: your words, your actions, what you put into your mind, what comes out of your mind, and what you wear. That is what is meant when we're told to stay pure until marriage. Yes, not having sex is a major part of it, but if you aren't putting clean things into your head, if you're not putting a pure and modest signal out to the guys, if you're not acting in a pure way, then you can't really consider yourself pure. I challenge you to not only be pure in how far you go with a guy, but also be pure in every other aspect of your life. Get a ring to symbolize this commitment of purity and then stick to it. Another suggestion I would make is to think about what kind of guy out there is worthy of dating the princess of God. You're incredibly special to God, and He only wants the absolute best for you. Make a list of what you want in a guy, underline the important things (like strong character, Godly, honest, etc.), and then stick to it. Don't waste your time on a guy that you know is not good enough for you. Set your standards high because you are a princess of the King.

Holly Scott, 18, North Buncombe High School, Weaverville, NC

Lord, I want to seek purity in all my life.
I want to think of what would please You,
dear Jesus, and then I want to do it.

growing up

"I tell you the truth, anyone who will not receive the kingdom of God like a little child will never enter it."

LUKE 18:17

I have always been afraid of growing up. When I was little, I didn't play marriage and house with everyone else because I loved being exactly the age I was. It got confusing when I got older; I wasn't so sure of myself anymore. I wanted to grow up, have a career, get married...but I still wanted to be able to climb trees, run, and play. I was worried because I knew I could not stop getting older. I started praying to God and talking to my mom. I realized that getting older didn't mean I had to leave my childhood self behind completely. I could become more mature and still be a kid in my heart. There is nothing wrong with an adult who climbs trees and loves to laugh. (Actually, life would be really boring if adults didn't act like kids once in a while.) God has made me sure of myself again by showing me that growing up doesn't have to be a scary thing.

Keegan Nitz, 15, St. Ambrose Christian High School, Meridian, ID

God, I never want to lose my childlike desire for and awe of You. No matter how old I get, I want to receive You like a little child receives her Father.

a perfect fit

"For I know the plans I have for you,"
declares the LORD, "plans to prosper you and
not to harm you, plans to give you hope and a future."

JEREMIAH 29:11

I went out with a guy from my church recently that I have known for a couple of years. We went to a movie and had a great time. But after the date, the guy seemed to avoid me. When we talked he said he felt he wasn't ready for a girlfriend, which was fine with me. Even though all of our friends had us "dating" already, we just decided to be really good friends for now. In today's society, magazines, media, and music portray girlfriends or boyfriends as the absolute must-have accessory—but I can't go shopping and buy my future husband from the clothes rack and make the relationship fit *perfectly*. I want someone to see me as special and like me for who I am, seeing my inward beauty as well as my outward beauty. And finding that person can require more patience than we're used to sometimes. In Bible study we talked about relationships and dating, and I learned God's timing is everything. I can't rush into something that is not there and expect perfection. God will open the door when He feels I'm ready. Until then, I must learn to be content.

Shelbie Lutz, 17, Seaman High School, Topeka, KS

Teach me patience today and every day,
Lord, so that I can happily wait until You bring me
my perfect fit, the one man You have chosen just for me.

He cares about it all

But how can I bear your problems
and your burdens and your disputes all by myself?
DEUTERONOMY 1:12

If family members are having problems with each other, it affects everyone in the household. Whenever I have family troubles, I get depressed. Sometimes when you're depressed, you can cause more trouble by being grumpy and causing arguments. This leads to more stress when there's already tension. God doesn't want us to be unhappy. I don't know about you, but when I'm depressed, everything seems worse. Sometimes the only way you can survive is by asking God for help. Remember, God is merciful and won't give you more than you can handle. Whenever life gets hard, ask God for help and strength to make it through. Trust me; I used to think God never cared about the little things, like when there's something you want, but it's not in the budget or when you have little petty arguments, but He cares about it all—big or small. He wants us to be happy. Just remember, God can fix anything, especially with prayer.

Sarah Lewis, 14, Walnut Grove Christian Preparatory School, Sheridan, IN

I know You want me to be happy, Father.
When I feel sad, please lift me up with Your spirit.

encouraging the best of 'em

[Say] only what is helpful for building others up according to their needs, that it may benefit those who listen.

EPHESIANS 4:29

I love my guy friends. When all your girl friends have their own emotional turmoil, the guys are the ones with the shoulder to cry on. They cheer you up and make you smile. However, it never crossed my mind that they might desire my encouragement and respect as much as I love their stability and sensitivity. I've been learning that part of being a good friend is *encouraging*, and I've been discovering I don't do it nearly enough. I'm a very sarcastic person, and I love to tease. As much as I hate to admit it, the phrase, "Oh, get over yourself!" or "You're so full of it!" are never far from my lips. I've noticed every time I say something to put a friend down, even though I consider it humorous, the recipient winces. I had always excused it as, "Well, they know I'm kidding," but I've begun to understand that even if made in a teasing manner, those comments cannot be justified. Your guy friends need your praise and encouragement more than anyone. One of my friends had just spoken in front of a large crowd, and I knew how nervous he had been. Afterwards, I told him what an amazing job he did. He lit up, and it hit me that my little comment meant more to him than I would ever know. If we honor and encourage our guy friends, we show them how much we love them. And that, ladies, is something we should always try to do.

Mary Kaylin Staub, 16, Heritage Academy, Flowery Branch, GA

Please don't let me forget that people need my encouragement, Lord. I want to be the one that lifts them up when they feel scared or sad.

ter 21

living for the Lord

Trust in the LORD *with all your heart and lean not on your own understanding; in all your ways acknowledge him and he will make your paths straight. Do no be wise in your own eyes; fear the* LORD *and shun evil.*

PROVERBS 3:5–7

Being a Christian teenager in today's society is very difficult. The world wants us to live what their idea of a life is: immorality, rebellion, lying, cheating, impurity, and many other things that do no please the Lord. There is a lot of peer pressure on teenagers to do things like smoking, drinking, drugs, and having premarital sex in order to "fit in." To live a pure and Godly life we definitely have to resist this peer pressure. When someone tempts you with something that you know is wrong, you can recite a Bible verse in your heard, pray a prayer for strength, or even just sing s hymn. Do whatever it takes to get your mind off of the sin, even if you have to leave. Another thing that you must do to live for the Lord is give every part of your life to the Lord. Proverbs 3:6 says: "In all your ways acknowledge Him and He will make your paths straight." That means in everything—your social life, your dating life, your entertainment choices, absolutely everything. It is so important to stay in God's Word and pray on a regular basis. If you are not hiding God's Word in your heart, and you do not know what He wants for your life, then when you are faced with a temptation, you will not be able to resist it. Pray that the Lord will give you strength and endurance to live for Him through everything you do. Also, pray that He will allow you to know His will for your life so that you can accomplish it.

Emily Malone, 15, Oconee Covenant Christian Academy, Seneca, SC

Lord, help me to build a really strong foundation in You so that when I'm faced with temptation, I will have the strength to say no.

He's always there

The LORD will keep you from all harm—
he will watch over your life; the LORD will watch
over you're coming and going both now and forevermore.

PSALM 121:7–8

A little over a year ago, I was really struggling with knowing God was always with me, watching over and protecting me. I felt spiritually alone, and I prayed every night for God to show Himself to me in some way, as did my mom. One night three of my friends and I were traveling around to several graduation receptions in my friend's compact car when we got lost looking for a house. We were enjoying ourselves, just having fun. Suddenly we went through an intersection and hit some loose gravel, and the car went into a ditch. My friend, who was driving, lost control and overcorrected, causing the car to roll once and land right side up. Ten feet more and we would have hit a light pole, or if we had gone to the other side of the ditch, we would have gone through a barbwire fence. We scrambled out of the vehicle and called for help. We were rushed by ambulance to the hospital; one girl had a concussion, but the rest of us were fine. We went to see the car the next day and saw that the whole frame had shifted on the roof and all of the windows on my side of the vehicle had been smashed out, totaling $10,000 in damage. We weren't protected because of seatbelts. God's hand was holding that car the entire time. That potentially deadly accident was exactly what I needed to see that God would always be present.

Erica Freeman, 17, Nebraska Christian High School, Central City, NE

Father, thank You for all the times
You have protected me and the people I love
from harm. I am so grateful that You watch over us.

thanksgiving

Let us come before him with thanksgiving,
and extol him with music and song.

PSALM 95:2

Thanksgiving is the time of year when friends and family come together to celebrate and worship God. This tradition started when the pilgrims came over from England and gave thanks to God for providing them with the necessities of life in the new world. Psalm 95:2 says, "Let us come before him with thanksgiving,and extol Him with songs and praise." Psalm 100:4 also says, "Let us enter his gates with thanksgiving, and his courts with praise." So we should give thanks to the Lord through all things. When we give thanks to the Lord, it shows Him how much we love him and appreciate the sacrifice He made for us! So in everything we do and say, we should try to thank God for all things.

Ali VanMinos, 15, Oconee County Christian Academy, Seneca, SC

Lord, I want to thank You for everything.
Every single thing. For notebook paper and couches
and trees. All of it, everything I take for granted,
is a gift from You.

alexa and Jesus

"The King will reply, 'I tell you
the truth, whatever you did for one of
the least of these brothers of mine, you did for me.'"

MATTHEW 25:40

When I was fourteen, I had the opportunity to go with my youth group and minister at a women and children's rescue shelter in downtown Orlando. There were many underprivileged people, and it was a culture shock for the kids from our upper-middle-class church to see just how little these people really had. The kids at the shelter had very few clothes and not many toys. Compared to us, they were pathetically poor. I "adopted" a little Hispanic girl, Alexa, who was at the shelter with her mother. There was bad blood between her mother and her father, and I doubt whether she got to see her father very much, if at all. Alexa and her mother lived in poverty, and I felt bad for them, but I also saw how I could help them. All Alexa really needed was somebody to hug her and let her know that Jesus loved her, and I had the privilege of being that person for a week. I haven't seen Alexa since that time, but I constantly meet people like her. They may not be physically poor, as she was, but they need Jesus. I have the opportunity to treat them kindly and show them Christ in my life. I know that when I am kind to someone who doesn't have as much as I do, I am really honoring Christ. I hope I won't turn down the opportunities to help others and show them the light of Christ. God wants to use us no matter how young we are. We just need to be willing to be used by Him.

Sarah Brautigam, 16, Houghton Christian Academy, Houghton, NY

Lord, showing Your love to someone
can change their lives. Help me to do that
today for someone who really needs to know You.

emily

I will never leave thee nor forsake thee.

HEBREWS 13:5 (KJV)

I wanted to try something new for my junior year of high school, so my parents and I decided that I would be homeschooled. I started going to a tutorial every Monday. At first I hated it because everybody already knew everyone else in the group and I didn't, so I had no friends there, which is a big deal for a teenager. There was one girl, Emily, who would always say hi, and she would give me a hug every week. There was just something amazing about her, like when her friends were having a bad day, she could tell, and she would try to cheer you up. One night I found out that Emily was in a car accident, and she had been killed. I was completely shocked. After a lot of crying and praying, I realized that she had lived her life to the fullest and is in heaven now. God was there for me, as well as all of Emily's friends, and He helped me, and them, to be stronger and to look to Him during that hard time. He helped me realize that I want to live my life to the fullest and not take life for granted. Have you made a decision to follow Christ and to live your life to the fullest? We never know when God will call us home, but we can leave a powerful lifestyle behind that might make a difference in the lives of some of our friends.

Bethany Musgrove, 17, home school, Hermitage, TN

Lord, when I leave this earth,
I want to be able to say that I lived for You every day. Help me to really do that.

God honors work

For even when we were with you,
this we commanded you, that if any would
not work, neither should he eat.
2 THESSALONIANS 3:10 (KJV)

Volleyball is a blast! We have improved so much, and we went from having a losing season year before last to having a winning season last year and being conference champions this year. We finished second at state last year and might win this year. We also made a huge improvement in basketball. We went from being 2-15 to 15-10 and third at state. These leaps were not made without a cost. Our teams worked very hard, and God honored that work. I have learned that if I try to please God in all that I do and if I work to the best of my ability, God will bless my work. He expects my best, and I shouldn't do less than that. I also learned that some who don't want to work hard can hold a team back. Playing time has to be earned, and those who don't pay the price often sit the bench. I don't want to sit God's bench. I want to be a worker for Him.

Melanie Helm, 15, New Covenant Christian School, Pageland, SC

Lord, like any really good thing,
being a Christian takes work.
Please give me the desire to work hard for You.

a truly great spring break

Be careful for nothing; but in every thing by prayer and supplication with thanksgiving let your requests be made known unto God.

PHILIPPIANS 4:6 (KJV)

During spring break of junior year in high school, I traveled to Venezuela for a truly life-impacting mission trip. The communities we visited and worked with lived off the two-square-mile dump of Maracaibo. I experienced firsthand the sight of people rummaging through the garbage for anything to eat, drink, wear, or build houses with. The last night in the community, we walked around to the different houses and passed out bags of food. At each house we would ask if they had any needs that they would like us to pray for, and when I asked this one lady; she graciously answered that her family knew Jesus and that was simply all they needed. That was truly remarkable that someone who has no electricity or running water can say that, when we still complain even with all the things that God has blessed us with.

Haley Martin, 17, New Covenant Christian School, Pageland, SC

God, it never ceases to amaze me how selfish I can be. Help me to realize that I am truly blessed to have all the things that I have and that there are people who live happily with far less.

lonely

Whom have I in heaven but you?
And earth has nothing I desire besides you.

PSALM 73:25

There are many times in my life where I have felt very lonely. I have felt as though I have no one to turn to. Sometimes I feel as though I can bear anything in the world rather than loneliness. I have been through times where all I want is a friend, someone I can be completely open with and who I love being around, a person who really understands me and who is excited about the things I am excited about and who loves the things I love. I have thought that if only I could find that perfect friend, then I would not be lonely. Then I realize who I am describing! Of course I know that friend! He is Christ! He is my best friend! He is the only one who will always be there no matter what is going on in my life. I know now that there are times when I will be truly lonely and when I may not have a good friend here on earth. But this is okay. God made us to need friends, but ultimately He is all that will last, and He alone will satisfy. Another thing God has taught me in the lonely times is that I should appreciate those natural friends I have had since I was born, my family! God gave us our family so that we can lean on each other as we strive for the cross. To me that is very exciting. And it is true that we may not always have our family around, but Christ will never forsake us. He is our everlasting and perfect friend. I pray that God will teach me to be content in Him as I strive on in this journey of life. Even in the loneliest of times!

Hailey Howerton, 16, home school, Greenville, SC

God, I get lonely a lot. I can't feel Your presence,
and I think I have no one to talk to. I pray that I will
never forget that You are there waiting to keep me company.

grieving our losses

I will life up mine eyes unto the hills,
from whence cometh my help. My help cometh
from the LORD, which made heaven and earth.

PSALM 121:1–2 (KJV)

Many times when we lose loved ones, we tend to question and blame God. My grandmother died when I was young, but I still question why I had such little time with her. The Lord has plans for everyone, and we can't even being to fathom what he has in store. Instead of questioning, we should turn to Him for comfort. He is the source of our strength in hard times. He is our help. The devil will try to tell us that God is against us and wants to make us suffer, but we have to stand against these accusations. Steadfastly reading God's Word and praying will help us to rely on Jesus for help.

Angela Hendrix, 15, New Covenant Christian School, Pageland, SC

Father, I can really question You sometimes.
Help me to trust You more and question You less.

i want to be bold as a lion

The wicked run away when no one is chasing them, but the godly are as bold as lions....

People who cover over their sins will not prosper. But if they confess and forsake them, they will receive mercy.

PROVERBS 28:1, 13 (NLT)

His name is Jesus, Jesus,
Sad hearts weep no more.
He has healed the broken hearted,
Opened wide the doors,
He is able to deliver evermore.

Composer Unknown

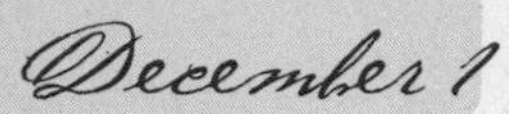

learning obedience

Everyone must submit himself
to the governing authorities, for there is no
authority except that which God has established.
The authorities that exist have been established by God.

ROMANS 13:1

Why should we obey our parents? In Romans 13:1 Paul tells us to be subject to, or to obey, authority. Since God placed us in our particular families with our particular parents, if we disobey them, then we are disobeying the authority God has put over us. It's really hard for me to accept this when I think my parents are wrong about something. But really, the only good reason not to obey my parents is if they tell me to do something that goes against God's word. Other than that, if I have a different opinion on something or really want to do something, that is not an excuse to disobey. If we are truly serving God, we should be obeying our parents. And if we cannot obey our parents, who we can see, how can we obey God, who we can't see?

Tiffany Heetderks, 15, Petra Academy, Bozeman, MT

I know I should obey my parents, Lord.
People tell me that all the time. Help me to not
roll my eyes when I hear this. Help me to really
respect my mom and dad.

nothing is lost

Now faith is the substance of things hoped for,
the evidence of things not seen.

HEBREWS 11:1 (KJV)

Several times I have lost items that were really important to me. Once it was my purse. I knew I had left it at a park while I was with my friends. However, when we drove back, it was gone. I started getting upset because I had hoped to buy my brother's birthday present with the money I had in it. We were also moving soon, and I had all of my friends' school pictures in there. Because I didn't have any identification in my purse, I didn't think anyone would bring it back. After praying to God for hope, I received a call from the police who had found my mother's Petco card inside my purse, which someone had found and turned in! Nothing was gone but a few dollars. God had answered my prayers. Another time when I was being careless, I dropped a ring my grandmother had given me for my birthday. It had been loose on my finger, and I didn't feel it fall off. I was so upset. I retraced my steps several times, all the while praying to God to show me where it was. After an hour, my mother told me to take a break and look later. Because I felt that taking a break was giving up, I searched on. I tripped on a chair and landed right next to my ring. It was found! Thanking God, I ran in to show my mother. I couldn't believe I had found it right there where I had walked a hundred times.

Keegan Nitz, 15, St. Ambrose Christian High School, Meridian, ID

God, it's so amazing how, when something
is really upsetting me, You bring me a little
miracle to make it better.

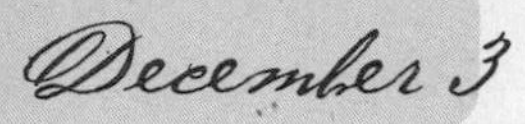

don't worry!

"Therefore I tell you, do not worry about your life, what you will eat or drink; or about your body, what you will wear. Is not life more important than food, and the body more important than clothes? Look at the birds of the air; they do not sow or reap or store away in barns, and yet your heavenly Father feeds them. Are you not much more valuable than they?"

MATTHEW 6:25–26

Do you worry? Are you anxious about school, your style, or the way you look? Almost every day at school we hear or say, "Do I look okay?" "Is my hair okay?" "I'm so nervous about this test!" We do it so often that we don't even think about it anymore. But Christians do *not* have to worry. We need to concern ourselves with things of God, not worldly things like style, grades, looks, and anything else like that is not something with real importance. This does not mean that you should not care about your body, though. God says, "Your body is the temple of the Holy Spirit who is in you." We need to take care of it, but at the same time, not be overly obsessed about the way we look. Also, we should not be absorbed with our grades. We should just do the best we can. If we try our hardest and are not satisfied, then we need to talk to God about it. You should not worry, for God will watch over you. He has a plan and purpose for you. You should not be anxious with your looks or your grades. Just trust in the Lord.

Katie Davis, 15, Jonathan Edwards Academy, Millers Falls, MA

Father, I worry a lot. All the time. I just can't seem to remember that You've got everything under control. Please help me to trust You more and worry less.

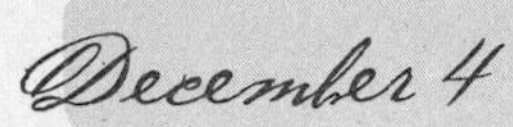

on telling the truth

Whoever loves discipline loves knowledge,
but he who hates correction is stupid.

PROVERBS 12:1

A fortune made by a lying tongue is a fleeting vapor and a deadly snare" (Proverbs 12:1). The Bible spells it out for us pretty clearly—LIARS NEVER PROSPER! So why do people lie? Do we think that in some way we'll be better off if we don't tell the truth? Mostly, I think that we lie because we are afraid of the consequences if we do tell the truth. I tell lies all of the time, and it certainly doesn't help me at all. I have a hard time telling the truth! A lot of the time, I beat myself up over it. But we're teenagers, and let's face it: We mess up all the time! We need discipline to get anywhere in life. And since discipline is something we really need, we should try not to hate it. I like how the Bible actually says that those who hate correction are *stupid*, because they really are. People who are afraid of the consequences shouldn't have been doing those bad things anyway. Telling the absolute truth is so much better than lying! If you tell a lie, the lies just build up, getting bigger and bigger, one after the other. Soon, the lie will involve many people and might get everyone in trouble. When you tell the truth, you don't have to remember any elaborate story that you made up, you don't have a huge burden to carry, you won't feel guilty, and you can start to live the life that God wants you to live. The truth really will set you free!

Kerstin Jones, 17, Stillwater Christian School, Kalispell, MT

Father, when I lie, there is no excuse for it.
Give me the strength to always tell the truth,
no matter what.

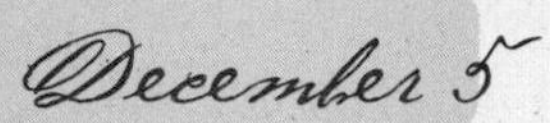

what's your idol?

"You shall not make for yourself
an idol in the form of anything in heaven
above or on the earth beneath or in the waters below."

EXODUS 20:4

In Exodus we find a list of the Ten Commandments. Some people, when reading these commandments, think that they only break a few. That is, just the ones like lying or coveting. They don't believe that they worship false gods. But in actuality everyone worships false gods sometimes. We are not supposed to worship anyone or anything besides the one and only true God. God tells us that He is a jealous God. He wants us to worship Him and only Him. What are some of the idols we worship? It depends on the kind of person we are. Some people worship celebrities, sports, food, race cars, or their looks. Whatever it is, it is wrong. What are some of the ways we worship idols? If we watch football every Sunday instead of going to church, we are worshiping an idol. If we watch shows and read magazines about celebrities everyday instead of thinking about God, we are worshiping an idol. If we devote lots of time to thinking about these earthly things instead of thinking about God, we are breaking the second commandment. Maybe none of these things is your idol. But something is, so figure out what it is. And whatever it is, try to stop worshiping it. Put the things of the world behind you and follow Christ.

Katie Davis, 15, Jonathan Edwards Academy, Millers Falls, MA

Father, I may not bow down
to a golden calf like people in the Old Testament,
but I do have idols. Please help me to never give
something on earth more praise and attention than I give You.

"you shall not covet"

"You shall not covet your neighbor's house. You shall not covet your neighbor's wife, or his manservant or maidservant, his ox or donkey, or anything that belongs to your neighbor."

EXODUS 20:17

What is one of a girl's favorite places to go? The mall. Why is that? Shopping! What is the greatest sin we girls commit when we're shopping? Coveting. Probably every girl has gone to the mall and coveted numerous things. Coveting is wishing for something you don't have. Whether we covet clothes, makeup, or another girl's features, it is still a sin. Maybe you never thought of it as a sin or you didn't know you were doing it. I know a certain girl who I went shopping with, and it was amazing how many times she said, "I wish I had..." It is one thing to go to a store and buy stuff, but it is another thing to go around and say, "Oh I wish I had that and that and that." That is coveting, and it is something God commanded us not to do. We need to be thankful and content with what we have. This is the way God wants us to be. Wishing we looked different or had different stuff is saying to God, "I don't like the way you made me. I want to be different." Next time you find yourself coveting, stop. Thank God for everything that you do have. Maybe make a list of all the things He's blessed you with. Then You can see in black and white how lucky you are and why shouldn't wish to have anything else or be anyone else.

Katie Davis, 15, Jonathan Edwards Academy, Millers Falls, MA

God, today I will make a list of all the amazing things You've done for me and given me. I pray that writing all these things will help teach me to appreciate what I have.

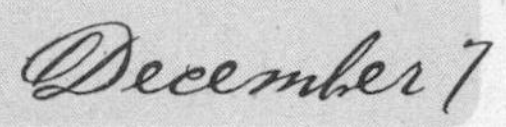

fear of the Lord

Charm is deceptive and beauty is fleeting,
but a woman who fears the LORD is to be praised.

PROVERBS 31:30

Much can be said about girls and beauty. We all need a regular reminding that being beautiful is not the most important thing. The wise man's words in Proverbs are often used to diminish beauty's importance, but seldom is the second half of his advice addressed. What precisely does it mean to fear God? Is it the same as fearing failure, pain, or even death? Fearing God needs to be clarified. Fear in this context means recognizing that you are beneath God, that He is greater than you. It's letting God have dominion over you. I'm afraid of snakes, and that fear does let the snake control me (I'll run away as soon as I see one). Bu my fear of God, though similar in a way, is also very different. It should be about being in awe of His power and greatness. I tend to concentrate mostly on God's goodness and friendship. I forget that He's so great He created the universe and all the stars just for His own glory. Fearing God is submitting to Him, obeying Him, and being in awe of Him. I often lose sight of this awe and slide God into the Unimportance Corner. Yet He should be the first thing I think of and the one person I try to serve and glorify. So what precisely does fearing God look like in the life of an average girl? He's kept in my thoughts and decisions. He's the priority in my life, and I let Him reign over me. Fearing God should be our ultimate purpose, but because while what we look like will change, what we do for God lasts forever.

Caroline J. Hornok, 15, Veritas Academy, Texarkana, TX

Father, today I want to stop being afraid I look ugly.
I want to have a new kind of fear, a king that isn't about being
afraid but is about knowing how truly awesome You are.

companionless?

The LORD himself goes before you and will be with you; he will never leave you nor forsake you. Do not be afraid; do not be discouraged.

DEUTERONOMY 31:8

My slightly cold omelet matched the dull conversation. On this Saturday night all my girlfriends were at the school dance. There I sat in a booth at IHOP with a few bites of egg left. My dinner companions were two guys who couldn't get a date, my youth pastor, and, Grace, my seventh-grade sister. The night had been a flop. I'd opted not to go to the dance and decided to spend the evening at a local Christian concert. The music was not all that wonderfully talent filled. *So much for Christian convictions against high school dances.* I panned the table and thought, *Why on earth am I here?* Was this how life was going to be for the rest of high school? Were my friends really blowing it by spending a night dancing and watching compromising movies? Were my personal standards going to ruin every weekend? I concluded miserably that my days were going to be gray. But it wasn't much later that I snapped out of it and rediscovered a simple truth: God is with me. He is omnipresent and all knowing. He is with me when I'm awake and when I'm asleep. He is with me on my good days, and He is most assuredly there with me on my loneliest days eating IHOP omelets. This truth encourages me when I'm lonely and helps me see that in the grand scheme of things, that sticking to my standards really is the best choice.

Caroline J. Hornok, 15, Veritas Academy, Texarkana, TX

God, when I feel like following You is keeping me from all the fun, please help me to see that I'm always making the best choice by doing what You say.

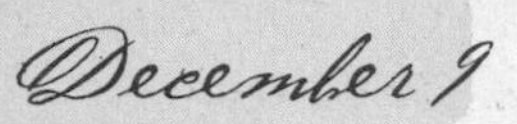

the serving absurdity

Your attitude should be the same as that of Christ Jesus: Who, being in the very nature of God... made himself nothing, taking the very nature of a servant, being made in human likeness...he humbled himself and became obedient to death—even death on a cross!

PHILIPPIANS 2:5–8

Serving others has got to be the greatest paradox of all time. I can remember riding in the car on the way to church and my mother asking us children why we went to church. Our response was as mechanical as it was routine; "To Serve others and Jesus." This was my mother's motto. Serve others here, serve others there. Quite frankly, I got sick of it all. "Can't a person just think about themselves once in a while?" I would ask in frustration. Her gentle answer to my harsh question was just absurd: "The joy comes in serving." This always confounded me. How on earth could anyone find joy in serving? Well, Christ did. He even found joy in dying because He gladly gave Himself up for us. If He could die for me, surely I could return some small service to Him. I found that by asking if I could help around the house, my days would pass ever so much more pleasantly. It was weird. Somehow I really was blessed by serving. It is the greatest inconsistency I have ever encountered. My normal mode is to get so wrapped up in myself, how I look and how I feel. Rarely do reach out to encourage and serve someone else. Yet every time, the most absurd thing happens. I am blessed and encouraged. The joy really does come from serving like Christ.

Caroline J. Hornok, 15, Veritas Academy, Texarkana, TX

God, I want to feel happy by making others happy. Show me today how I can help someone in need.

I am the way

"Good teacher," he asked,
"what must I do to inherit eternal life?"

MARK 10:17

Jesus is the one and only way! As teenagers, we want Jesus to fit into our way and our lifestyle and as long as He doesn't "conflict" with our lives, being a Christian is okay. We change His teachings to fit our needs and wants. Our lives control our faith and blind us from reality. God recently made me realize that I am too materialistic and concerned about money, and this attitude keeps me away from Him. I am guilty of changing the channel on the television when there is a commercial showing poverty-stricken countries and needy families. One phrase that stuck with me since church camp is that Jesus came to *comfort the disturbed and disturb the comfortable*! I'll admit I'm very comfortable. God is teaching me I can't simply sit here and pray for the needy and the troubled. I must put those prayers into action. Recently, my best friend and I adopted a Ugandan girl to support for the next several years of her life. I can't keep my money and possessions to myself anymore. I must reach out to those in need, just as Jesus did. God told the rich young man to sell everything and give it all to the poor and follow Him, and then he would have eternal life. Jesus said whoever has left everything for Him will not fail, but be rich in Him! When I am really trying to walk with the One "who is the way," the satisfaction is external. I pray that we all will find God's way and turn away from our own way.

Shelbie Lutz, 17, Seaman High School, Topeka, KS

I don't want to just sit around
while people suffer, Lord. I pray that I will not
just pray for them but actually go and help them today.

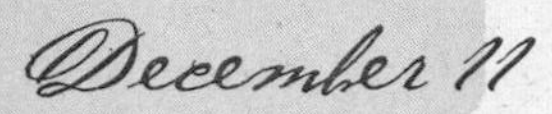

not my life

Naked I came from my mother's womb,
and naked I will depart. The LORD gave and the LORD has
taken away; may the name of the LORD be praised.

JOB 1:21

Sometimes, whether subconsciously or aware, I tell God what to do in my life. I pray, "Well, Lord, this situation isn't working out well, so if you could do something about it..." Or I pray, "God, it just makes sense that I should have this now." It's like I try to reason with Him. Last year I read Job, and I struggled with giving everything (yes, absolutely every situation!) to God. What scared me was that God could take it all away. Then I remembered that nothing is truly mine—everything I call my own is a gift from God. In Job 1, Job finds out that all his animals and servants were killed by raiders and fire and that his house collapsed on his children. Basically, all he had was lost. Although he was anguished, the first words out of his mouth were in praise and submission to God. Wow! Later his wife tells him to curse God and die, but Job replies, "You are talking like a foolish woman. Shall we accept good from God and not trouble?" So many times I have that wrong attitude. I want God to give me all I want, yet I grumble about even the slightest trials. I have been learning that giving up my life to God is a daily process. Each day, I need to make the decision to let go of my own desires and let God be in control.

Julia Postema, 16, Jonathan Edwards Academy, Erving, MA

Today, Lord, I want to make the decision to let go
of what I want and let You be in control. And I pray that I will
do the same thing tomorrow and the next day and forever.

the day Jesus came down

Today in the town of David a Savior has been born to you: he is Christ the Lord. This will be a sign to you: You will find a baby wrapped in cloths and lying in a manger.

LUKE 2:11–12

Whenever I think of Christmas, my mind automatically jumps straight to presents, shopping, and the things that I want to get. Who am I going to buy gifts for and what will they want? Will I have enough money? Okay, so yeah, Christmas may be about giving and not just getting, but THAT'S STILL MISSING THE POINT. Something else happened on that day, something *way* bigger than Christmas trees and wrapping presents. On that day, Jesus came down from heaven, to be fully God and yet fully man. Jesus was born to take away our sins. Jesus, our Savior, was wrapped in cloth (and we're not talking about silk here) and laid in a manger. Donkeys and cows ate out of mangers. They're *filthy*! But He loved us so much that He would do all of that for us. Just think about what Jesus had to go through later in His life. He was ridiculed and beaten and then put on the cross, and all of that was for us! Christmas day is so much more than just thinking of ourselves and our presents. It's about Jesus, His sacrifice, and the day He came down. He made us white as snow (maybe that's why it snows in December) and loves us *so* much! So please remember Jesus when you're opening your presents this year.

Kerstin Jones, 17, Stillwater Christian School, Kalispell, MT

Jesus, I don't want to ever forget what You went through for me. It's easy to get caught up in all the earthly Christmas stuff, but the only part of Christmas I really want to celebrate is the gift of You!

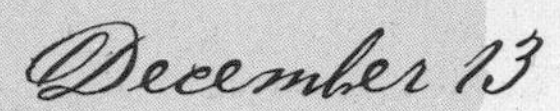

are you beautiful?

I am fearfully and wonderfully made.

PSALM 139:14

I enjoy eating so much that it's hard for me to imagine how anyone could be anorexic or bulimic. But when I think about how unsatisfied I feel with body sometimes, I can sort of start to understand. It's not fun to be on the receiving end of jokes about your appearance Maybe you have faced this torture and feel that you need to make yourself pretty by binging and purging. I hope not, but if you feel so unhappy with yourself that you would do such a drastic thing, please listen when I tell you that God thinks you are beautiful! You are "fearfully and wonderfully made" (Psalm 139:14). Nothing in this world can compare to God's affirmation of you. He holds you, His beloved daughter, tenderly in His hands and thinks you are absolutely lovely. The pressures of the world tell us that in order to be attractive we must be tall, thin, and acne free. This criteria falls short of God's qualifications of an attractive woman. "Your beauty should come from your inner self, the unfading beauty of a gentle and quiet spirit, which is of great worth in God's sight." (I Peter 3:3–5) Take care of your appearance, but do not become obsessive. As you allow Christ to work in your heart, you will become an even more beautiful person than you could have ever imagined. When you are confident in Him, nothing will shake you. You can hold your head high and revel in the fact that the Lord of all creation made you unique, and yes, even beautiful.

Jessica Runk, 19, Patrick Henry College, Purcellville, VA

Sometimes I really hate the way I look, Lord,
and I think I would do anything to change it.
Please help me not to get so obsessed with my looks
that I forget how much You love me.

thanks for bumps and bruises (part 1)

Consider it pure joy, my brothers,
whenever you face trials of many kinds,
because you know that the testing of your faith
develops perseverance. Perseverance must finish its work so
that you may be mature and complete, not lacking anything.

JAMES 1:2–4

A man at my church told me that he thanked God for bruises and bumps. I thought that was an odd thing to thank God for, but then he explained how the hard things in life are often the things that build our character. Sure, that makes sense…I believe that. But I still didn't get why I should thank God for them. I sure don't feel like thanking anyone when things are difficult. But then I thought about running cross-country. In athletics we are thankful for difficulty because it makes us better. We push our bodies through pain so that we can improve. Maybe, just maybe, this concept could apply in my personal life. At first I didn't like the idea, because no one want to experience pain, and we always think God is supposed to protect us from stuff like that. So could experiencing pain really make me a better Christian?

Carmen Dockweiler, 18, Nebraska Christian High School, Central City, NE

God, there is a lot of pain in my life
that I just don't understand. Please give me the
wisdom to see how hurting can actually help me.

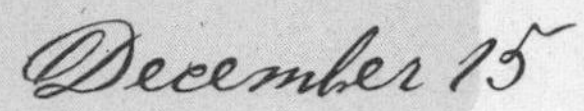

thanks for bumps and bruises (part 2)

Consider it pure joy, my brothers,
whenever you face trials of many kinds,
because you know that the testing of your faith
develops perseverance. Perseverance must finish its work so
that you may be mature and complete, not lacking anything.

JAMES 1:2–4

I started to make a list in my head of the things in my life that I originally regarded as curses that eventually became blessings. Getting teased on the playground taught me the importance of being sensitive to others' feelings. Having asthma taught me to never give up. Dealing with shin splints in cross-country taught me the importance of attitude over performance. Disagreeing with my parents taught me how to respect authority and still have my own opinion. My list kept growing, and I realized that I was thankful for these things. I have a long ways to go to be thankful *when* I am experiencing pain or difficulty, instead of just being thankful when I can look back and see the good that came from troubles. Now I would say that the man at church was not so odd in his statement about thanking God for bumps and bruises. And I hope I can be more like him.

Carmen Dockweiler, 18, Nebraska Christian High School, Central City, NE

I think being thankful for my pain
is too hard...at least for me. So I'm asking for
Your help, Father. I'll never succeed at this without You.

wisdom passed on

I have been reminded of your sincere faith, which lived in your grandmother Lois and in your mother Eunice and, I am persuaded, now lives in you also.

2 TIMOTHY 1:5

Today's younger generation is often known for disobedience and disrespect towards their elders. Many teenagers see their elders as boring and not understanding, but we have to remember that they were our age once and have gone through the same things we are, made the same mistakes, and learned from them. I've been fortunate to grow up in a solid Christian family and know both sets of my grandparents and two sets of great-grandparents. A favorite time is trail riding with my grandfather. He's a man after God's heart. I learn from him when we are riding. It's like having a living encyclopedia riding alongside you. It would be ridiculous for me to not listen to my elders when they are so wise. We should be proud to spend time with them and learn from them. In 2 Timothy 1:5, Paul is reminding Timothy of the lessons he learned from his godly grandmother and mother before he sets out to spread God's Word. Listening to those who have more experience in life is important, so instead of getting caught up in today's stereotype of teenager's, open your ears a little and learn something.

Claire Englehart, 17, Cedar Hall School, Bell Buckle, TN

Today, guide me to someone older who can teach me a good lesson about You, Father. I want to learn to listen to those who have more wisdom than I do.

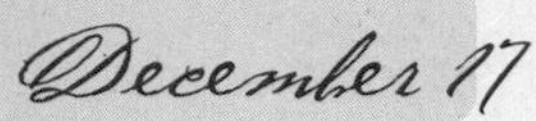

acting yourself

Then God said, "Let us make
man in our image, in our likeness."
GENESIS 1:26

There is a lot of focus today on being accepted by others, but what about accepting yourself? Most everyone, at some point in time, has struggled with being happy with the way they are. Girls have a tendency to be overly critical of themselves. How many times have you looked in the mirror and thought, *I wish I had better hair, my body is so ugly, why do I have so many zits?* Or when was the last time you thought, *I wish I were better at*...We forget that when we complain about the way we look or what we're not talented at, we are being discontent with the way God has made us—in the image of God fearfully and wonderfully. We are not perfect, even though we have unrealistic expectations of ourselves. Air-brushed models are our standard for beauty, and we always look to those who are better than us in a certain area, never satisfied with where we are at. 1 Samuel 16:7 says, "Man looks at the outward appearance, but the Lord looks at the heart." Why do we put so much focus one what we look like and how we appear to other people, when God is concerned with the attitude of our hearts? Before we can accept others, we need to take the vital first step of accepting ourselves and being content with the person he has especially designed us to be.

Julia Postema, 16, Jonathan Edwards Academy, Erving, MA

Father, You think so differently than me.
I can only see what people look like on the outside,
so I don't realize how important inner beauty is.
Give me new eyes to see more than just the physical.

the ultimate ruler

We do not dare to classify or compare ourselves with some who commend themselves. When they measure themselves by themselves and compare themselves with themselves, they are not wise.

2 Corinthians 10:12

Who are you comparing yourself to? Christ, who is the best measuring stick, or another imperfect human? If you're comparing yourself to other people, then you might end up like this girl I know about. She attended a local church with her parents and was involved in the youth group. She was blessed with Christian parents. She compared herself to girls who did not act like Christians and wanted to be like them. But her parents were very strict when it came to those things. This was torture for her because she wanted to be like all the "normal" girls. She ran away from home, rejecting her parent's instruction and grieving the heart of God because she chose to measure herself by the people around her. Another teen girl attends the same church, is homeschooled by parents who hold to the same standards, and is involved in the youth group, but she uses her time to encourage nursing-home patients or to assist young mothers with their little ones. She walks with the Lord, trying to please Him in everything she does. So much contrast: The second girl enjoys and embraces the same convictions the first girl felt were restrictions because she compares herself to Christ rather than the people around her.

Carrie Lewis, 14, home school with tutorial, Clemson, SC

God, I realize that I'm judging myself by the standards of the world rather than Your standards. Today, when I start to compare myself with some girl at school, help me to replace those thoughts with thoughts of You.

stress

And the peace of God,
which transcends all understanding, will guard
your hearts and your minds in Christ Jesus.

PHILIPPIANS 4:7

This is a very familiar passage, but I recently read it with new understanding. I was awed by the idea that peace can guard our hearts. The more I thought about it, the more it made sense. When I am stressed out or upset, I begin to question God, forget to read my Bible, and have negative attitudes. I can become so rundown and consumed by anxiety that I get sick. If I rely on God's peace, however, I am protected from these pressures. When my mind is going in a thousand directions at once, God's voice is crowded out. Once I realize that I am completely overwhelmed, I drop everything to reflect on the Lord. Time and again, He has gently reminded me that stillness is essential for my spiritual and mental well-being. My soul is calmed by His command to "be still and know that I am God" (Psalm 46:10). We would save ourselves from worry if we learned to rest in Him. You can dispel anxiety by setting aside a portion of every day for Bible reading, listening to uplifting music, and spending small amounts of time in solitude. Do you let anxiety and fear quench God's peace? Do you find yourself constantly frustrated and worn down? Trust in the Lord and believe that He will see you through. Do not rely on your own strength, but surrender yourself to His power. Surely the God who clothes the lilies and feeds the birds can calm your anxious soul.

Jessica Runk, 19, Patrick Henry College, Purcellville, VA

God, peace would be really nice.
Today when I'm stressed, please remind me
that peace in You is only a prayer away.

rejoice and be merry!

Today in the town of David a Savior has been born to you; he is Christ the Lord. This will be a sign to you: You will find a baby wrapped in cloths and lying in a manger.

LUKE 2:11–12

I love Christmas! It's definitely my favorite time of year. Wonderful food (what could be better than green bean casserole?), lots of family, and presents! Not to mention that all of the best songs are Christmas songs; the weather turns all nice and cold, with gray skies and the promise of snow; the house seems ever so cozy; and everything is in shades of white, silver, gold, green, and red. It's a cheerful time of year. Outshining all this, of course, is our Savior's birth. Every year, we get to celebrate the birth of the One who died for us to save us from our sins. It is an honor and a blessing to be able to do so. Everything (well, almost everything) is wrapped up in traditions that go back to Biblical times—which includes the giving of the gifts, of course. Okay, okay, I'll stop with the presents (even though I'm sure all of you don't mind getting and giving things on Christmas day). I love the tradition of a star or angel atop the Christmas tree. To me, it seems as if it is looking down on us, watching over us as we laugh and be merry. Christmas is a time of giving, and of celebrating our Savior's birth. It is a time to be cheerful, to have fun, and to be glad in our hearts. So, I have one more thing to say about Christmas: Rejoice and be merry!

Kelsie Nygren, 15, Covenant Christian Academy, El Paso, TX

Father, thank You for Christmastime
and all the traditions that I love,
especially getting to be with my family.

the best gift

For if the willingness is there,
the gift is acceptable according to what one has,
not according to what he does not have.

2 CORINTHIANS 8:12

One of the best gifts I ever received was from my little brother at Christmas. It was not because it was fancy or high tech or even very cool at all. I actually had helped him go shopping at Wal-Mart to get all his Christmas presents. I opened it and was greeted by a bright pink three-ring binder. But this was a very special binder. My brother was six, and he loved to color pictures for other people. This hot pink binder was covered in his drawings. The drawings were an expression of his personality right there on my notebook. It was filled with his smiling faces and the deformed looking bodies that only a six-year-old can draw. He's great. He didn't have any money to buy me anything, but he still wanted to get me something. I'd like to think that God's like that for me. I might not have a lot of money or talent or anything, but if I am willing to put the effort into whatever I do and embrace His promises to me, then I know God is smiling as He accepts my gift.

Calista Turner, 17, Donelson Christian Academy, Nashville, TN

Father, thank You for smiling down
at the work I do for You. My gifts to You
might not be much, but You love them anyway.

the christmas story retold

The virgin will be with child and will give birth to a son, and they will call him Immanuel—which means, "God with us."

MATTHEW 1:23

We have all heard the Christmas story a hundred times, and although it is wonderful, sometimes it is sort of boring because we have heard it so many times and could probably write it out from memory. At least that's how I felt until my volleyball coach shared a new perspective with me one night. Imagine that the room you are sitting in is the entire universe. That little speck of dust in the corner is a galaxy called the Milky Way. Now, in a tiny, tiny corner of the Milky Way is a little solar system. And in a little corner of that solar system is the planet earth. Sometimes the earth seems pretty big, but not when you think about it like this! Now, remember that God, who is bigger than the entire universe, with all its galaxies and solar systems and planets, looked down to miniscule earth and decided that we really needed help. So he sent his ONLY Son down to live and to die for us in this little corner of the universe. That really kind of gives the Christmas story a new twist! Immanuel: "God with us." Even though we are *so* small, *so* insignificant, He came down to be with us because His love is infinite!

Kimberlee DeGroot, 14, Petra Academy, Bozeman MT

Jesus, I want to really stop and think what Christmas means this year. This season goes by so quickly. I just want to slow down and think about how amazing it is that You came to earth to save me.

finding the heart of christmas

It is more blessed to give than to receive.

ACTS 20:35

Like many others, my favorite holiday is Christmas, with Christmas music playing on my radio, decorating a tree and loving the way that it makes the room smell, visiting family, eating big meals, and one of my favorites—helping my dad build a fire in the fire place so we can sit around and enjoy its warmth. The big reason I love Christmas is because of the presents. We all love getting something wrapped in pretty paper, don't we? I'm sure you've felt it just as I have. I always feel depressed when the sun sets on Christmas night. I sigh and then remind myself Jesus came on Christmas Day to give, not to receive. Looking back on Christmases past, the times I *gave* were my happiest times of the season. Last Christmas, my youth group made little treat bags to pass out, then we went caroling. I can't sing even if my life depended on it, and I really don't like to knock on people's doors. That night was dark and very cold, and it was raining as we shivered while one of us dared to knock and another one of us held the treat bag. When the door opened, we would start singing (very off-key) and hand the person the treat bag. Even though I was doing things I thought I hated, my heart felt happy and full because I was giving to someone else. Jesus came to give Himself to us. That's why Christmas is one of the best times for *us* to give. I always think of Jesus handing me the wonderful gift of salvation. It's what makes Christmas so special and unique, and it's the best gift I'll ever receive.

Rebecca Wilson, 18, Maranatha Christian Academy, Oakwood, GA

Jesus, please show me more ways to give this Christmas. When I think about how much You gave for me, I just want to give everything I can to those around me.

perfect like you

For all have sinned
and fall short of the glory of God.
ROMANS 3:23

Every year my church has a beautiful Christmas Eve service. There are decorations everywhere, and we sing carols, have special music, and hear about the birth of Jesus. I remember my sophomore year I was thrilled because my brother and my sister's families were there. I knew that we were going to have a great Christmas. We hadn't all been together for a long time. As the service was wrapping up, my pastor's five children, who were all home from various places in the U.S., went up and did special music, singing and playing different instruments. The song was very impressive; they all had a lot of talent. I listened intently and became very jealous. Questions were bouncing around in my mind: "Why wasn't I…why wasn't my family perfect like that?" I enjoyed my family, but after about a day of all of us being together, we would start to fight and I was ready for them to leave. I struggled with wanting so much to be perfect but never being able to. This summer a friend helped me see past not being perfect. She was someone I deeply respected and she told me what she had been struggling with in her faith that summer. She reminded me that we all struggle with things, and that is not always a bad thing. Christ teaches us through our weaknesses, and besides that, if we didn't struggle, we wouldn't need Him. I am learning, and am thankful, that God loves and uses imperfect people.

Lisa A. Osler, 18, Nebraska Christian High School, Kenesaw, NE

Thank goodness You use imperfect people, Lord.
I'm so glad that my flaws don't stop You for
using me for Your glory.

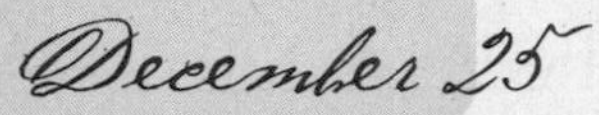

happy birthday!

The Word became flesh and made his dwelling among us.
We have seen his glory, the glory of the One and Only,
who came from the Father, full of grace and truth.

JOHN 1:14

Happy Birthday Jesus! How many of us on Christmas day "forget" about Jesus? I'm not saying we don't remember Him, but we don't really think about what He did for us. So many of us celebrate Christmas without celebrating the One Christmas is all about. When we celebrate Christmas we should always remember that Christ is at the center of our celebration. In the above verse it says that the Word, Christ, came to earth as a man. He set aside His deity and glory and came to die. Do you know what Christmas actually means? Christmas is Christ + mass. Mass means death, so Christmas means Christ's death. On Christmas, then, we should actually celebrate Christ's birth *and* death. Even though it sounds strange to celebrate a death on Christmas, Christ's death is the only way we can live. Isn't it incredible how even the name Christmas points to His death and our salvation?

Tiffany Heetderks, 15, Petra Academy, Bozeman, MT

Jesus, You came to this earth knowing
You would die. I really want to praise You
for loving me enough to come here and
face death on the cross.

mary, the Lord's servant

"I am the Lord's servant," Mary answered.
"May it be to me as you have said." Then the angel left her.

LUKE 1:38

Put yourself in Mary's situation. You're engaged (probably really excited about getting married), and your life is all set. Everything seems perfect. Then, suddenly, your whole world is turned upside down when an angel comes to you and tells you that you're going to have a baby, and not just any baby—God's Son. Wow! You try to process this information because it doesn't make any sense. "Uh, how is this possible?" you ask in confusion, "I'm still a virgin." The angel says that the Holy Spirit will make it possible. *No one will believe this*, you think. *Will Joseph? What will people think of me? Will I still get married?* If I were in that situation, I think I would have gone into shock and pleaded for God to choose someone else. I want God to use me, but not like this, please not like this. Mary's response to this life-altering news was, "I am the Lord's servant." Such simple words but spoken with such faith. I pray that I can have faith like that. I don't expect to be visited by an angel and get a direct message from God any time soon, but I know that there are things God wants me to do that I am afraid to do. The question is: Will you and I trust God? It seems so easy to say, but when the situation comes up, fear has a way of preventing us from obeying God. Mary is an outstanding example of extreme faith. She didn't doubt or question...she submitted. She trusted, truly trusted.

Julia Postema, 16, Jonathan Edwards Academy, Erving, MA

I want to trust, I mean truly trust,
You, Lord. When You come to me and
ask me to do something I think is crazy, I want
to have faith like Mary's. I want to say I am Your servant.

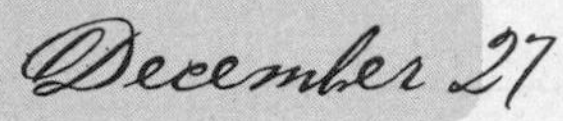

re-gifting

Not to us, O LORD,
not to us but to your name be the glory.

PSALM 115:1

Have you ever "re-gifted"? You know, given away a gift that someone else gave to you? Re-gifting may be considered rude by most people (and you'd probably be insulted if you knew someone re-gifted something you had given them), but the Lord actually wants you to give to others what He has given to you. God has given each one of us unique gifts. Some excel in academics, some in band, and others in soccer. Some are not exceptional at sports or other activities, but at reaching out to nonbelievers, listening to another's problems, or just encouraging someone else to do their very best. The reason God gives us these gifts is so that they will ultimately glorify Him. He wants His light to shine through our actions. It should be our goal to "re-gift": to take the gifts that God has given us, turn around, and give those gifts to others so that they might know Him.

Emily Wilkin, 15, Walnut Grove Christian Preparatory School, Carmel, IN

Father, I want to give the gift of You to everyone I meet.
It doesn't cost me anything, but it's worth everything!

seize the day

Be very careful, then, how you live—
not as unwise but as wise, making the most
of every opportunity, because the days are evil.

EPHESIANS 5:15–16

I try to make the most of every opportunity, but it is not quite as easy as I would like it to be. Sometimes I have disagreements with my best friend, and we both end up holding grudges. Through-out the day, we both think about the bitter words we exchanged and miss out on the good moments going on around us. It's hard for me to get past my selfishness so I can live in the moment and share it with the people I love and care about. Satan wants us to dwell on the negative parts of life, to stumble and wander and obsess. But instead we need to live joyfully, contented no matter what negativity we come up against. Life is precious and I don't want to waste a great day, a precious moment created by the most awesome God, by being negative or demanding that I am right in some stupid argument with my friend. Nothing is stronger than God's help when we let Him in on our trials and tribulations. He will always be there, helping us make the most of the opportunities in our lives, helping us delight in the moment.

Ashley Stone, 18, Nebraska Christian High School, Central City, NE

Father, help me to make the most of the time
You have given me and help me not to waste
that time being angry or selfish.

December 29

what's your new year's resolution?

Let us hold unswervingly to the faith we profess, for He who promised is faithful. And let us consider how we may spur one another on toward love and good deeds

HEBREWS 10:23–24

New Year's may be a secular holiday, but it can be a good holiday for Christians to celebrate. It is a good time to reflect on the past year, and it gives us a chance to think about how we should act in the coming year. We make resolutions to eat healthier or exercise more, but we should be applying New Year's resolutions to our Christian walk as well. Reflecting on the past year, you may recall things you are ashamed of. Don't worry, but repent, and our God, the God of second chances, will lovingly extend His forgiveness. As you look to the coming year, find ways to improve your walk with God by devoting more time to reading the Word. Consider how you treat your family. Be sensitive to their needs and make yourself a servant to your parents and siblings. As with dieting, these disciplines are not easy. It takes a lot of self-control and diligence to cultivate and maintain a healthy relationship with the Lord and the people around you. Many New Year's resolutions, like the latest fad diet, are forgotten before January ends, but do not let your spiritual resolutions slip. Instead, heed the exhortation found in Hebrews: "Let us hold *unswervingly* to the faith we profess."

Jessica Runk, 19, Patrick Henry College, Purcellville, VA

Father, my one and only New Year's resolution is to love and serve You more. Please give me the strength to stick with it all 365 days of the new year.

i want to be admired and praised

"There are many virtuous and capable women in the world, but you surpass them all!"

Charm is deceptive,
and beauty does not last;
but a woman who fears the Lord will be greatly praised.
Reward her for all she has done.
Let her deeds publicly declare her praise.

PROVERBS 31:29–31 (NLT)

A humble, lowly, contrite heart, believing, true, and clean,
which neither life nor death can part from Christ who dwells within.
A heart in every thought renewed and full of love divine,
perfect and right and pure and good, a copy, Lord, of thine.
Thy nature, gracious Lord, impart; come quickly from above;
write thy new name upon my heart, thy new, best name of Love.

Charles Wesley (1707-1788)

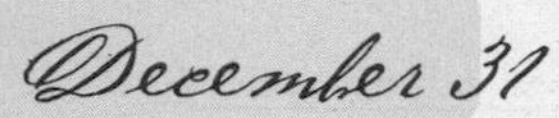

i am redeemed, restored, forgiven

Redeemed, restored, forgiven, through Jesus' precious blood,
Heirs of His home in heaven, oh, praise our pardoning God!
Praise Him in tuneful measures who gave His Son to die;
Praise Him whose sevenfold treasures enrich and sanctify.
Once on the dreary mountain, we wandered far and wide,
Far from the cleansing fountain, far from the pierced side;
But Jesus sought and found us and washed our guilt away;
With cords of love He bound us to be His own for aye.
Dear Master, Thine the glory of each recovered soul.
Ah! who can tell the story of love that made us whole?
Not ours, not ours, the merit; be thine alone the praise
And ours a thankful spirit to serve Thee all our days.
Now keep us, holy Savior, in Thy true love and fear
And grant us of Thy favor the grace to persevere
Till, in Thy new creation, earth's time-long travail o'er,
We find our full salvation and praise Thee evermore.

Henry W. Baker (1821-1877)

Grow in the grace and knowledge of our Lord and Savior Jesus Christ. To him be glory both now and forever! Amen.

2 PETER 3:18

biographies

KRISTIN ABERNATHY: 16; New Covenant Christian School, Pageland, SC; 3 sisters, 1 brother; enjoys playing on the varsity volleyball team, singing in the school chorus; active in her church's youth group.

JESSICA BAYLY: 17; Donelson Christian Academy, Donelson, TN; wants to be a preschool teacher and become involved in politics; 1 sister; color guard captain; plays the oboe; loves teaching children about Jesus and going to church.

BRITTANY BEHLER: 17; Chattanooga School for the Arts and Sciences, Hixson, TN; 1 sibling; loves to sing, dance, act, play volleyball, basketball, and softball, reading, and loves God; active in church (Bayside Baptist Church). God, family, and my friends are the things held dearest.

ERIKA BLACKMON: 16; New Covenant Christian School; Pageland, SC; 2 brothers; enjoys playing softball and sings in her high school choir.

MEGAN BORDENKIRCHER: 16; Nebraska Christian High School, Central City, NE; youngest of 3 kids; lives with a single parent.

SARAH BRAUTIGAM: 16; Houghton Christian Academy, Houghton, NY; 2 sisters; loves to play piano and likes to read; hopes to study piano next year in college and become a teacher.

GRACE BRICKER: 16; Jonathan Edwards Academy, Greenfield, MA; 3 siblings; loves playing soccer, acting, having sleepovers, and eating cereal; summa cum laude in school; plays piano for church and teaches two students.

REBECCA BRILL: 18; Nebraska Christian High School, Aurora, NE; 2 older brothers; loves to play volleyball, have jam sessions with friends, scrapbook; works in a nursing home, has a fetish for brushing dentures.

LAURA CAMPBELL: 17; Stillwater Christian School, Kalispell, MT; 1 sister, mom, dad, a dog, and 3 cats; loves to read and write; hopes to major in English and become an author.

MORIAH CAMPTON: 16, St. Ambrose Christian High School, Meridian, ID; 1st, 2nd, 3rd, 4th, Honorable Mention in Snake River Stampede Poster Contest, 1st place National Congressional Art Contest for Idaho, 1st, 2nd place in the Western Idaho Fair; loves painting, racing, basketball, lacrosse.

JENNIFER CAUDILL: 19; Hanover College, Hanover, IN; 2 siblings; loves theater, tennis, music, and reading; in HS earned an academic honors diploma and academic achievement award among other numerous awards.

HALEY CHEEK: 16; Oconee County Christian Academy, Seneca, SC; member of Drama Club, Beta Club, and VP of Student Government; enjoys reading, acting, and her 2 dogs, Malika and Luci.

BETHANY CHRISTENSEN: 18; Houghton Academy, Houghton, NY; missionary kid from the Philippines and Indonesia (where she was born); 3rd of 6 kids, loves to read, sew, play piano and violin, and loves sports.

LAUREN CHRISMAN: 18; Walnut Grove Christian Prep School, Sheridan, IN; 1 older brother and a younger sister; loves to shop.

RACHEL CRANE: 14; home school; Lewisburg, TN; 2 older sisters; loves horseback riding, playing with cat, writing a book, gymnastics. Helped with Good News Clubs in public schools; bowling awards.

CANDANCE KAMILLE CROSTON: 16; King's Fork High School; Suffolk, VA; member East End Baptist Church; mission trips: Antigua, Bahamas, Jamaica, St. Croix, St. Maarten, VA; Jubal Arts Center Star & Bible Challenge awards; Sunday school class president; drama, dance, choir, counselor.

CHANELLE 'NELL' DAVIS: 17; Houghton Academy, Cuba, NY; founder and president of the drama club; wants to be a professional actress someday.

KATIE DAVIS: 15; Jonathan Edwards Academy, Millers Falls, MA; 1 older brother, 2 younger sisters; enjoys listening to music, singing, and writing.

KIMBERLEE DEGROOT: 15; Petra Academy; Bozeman, MT; has awesome parents and 2 sisters; likes to play piano, read books, and hang out with friends; loves playing volleyball; honor roll student.

JUDELKISS DEMOSTENE: 17; Houghton Academy, Houghton, NY; 1 brother, 2 sisters; loves to read, play volleyball, and spend time with my friends/family; from the Dominican Republic and loves to travel there.

CARMEN DOCKWEILER: 18; Nebraska Christian High School, Central City, NE; 2nd of 4 children; loves running, scrapbooking, spending time with family; hopes to get EMT certification this year and get married next fall.

DANAE DOWNS: 15; home school; Grand Junction, CO; 3 sisters; loves all kinds of sports, mostly volleyball and basketball; loves hanging out with friends and attending Christian events.

RACHEL EGGENSPERGER: 19; Bethel Bible Village; Hixson TN; attending University of Tennessee at Chattanooga; mother of 1 precious son.

ALLISON ENGEL: 16; Wheaton North High School, Wheaton, IL; First Baptist Church, Geneva, IL; volunteer at Kline Creek Farm, an 1890s living-history farm; loves animals, playing violin and piano, talking with friends, and jumping on her trampoline.

CLAIRE ENGLEHART: 17; Cedar Hall School; Bell Buckle, TN; older brother who is a Marine, 1 younger sister; loves trail riding with grandfather; loves to paint and draw; loves TN; born again at 11 years old.

WENDI FERGUSON: 17; Metro Christian Academy; Madison, TN; 2 older brothers; tested and ranked third in district in chemistry; has huge passion for music.

SHANNON FITZGERALD: 17, Maranatha Christian Academy; Oakwood, GA; 3 siblings; enjoys friends, basketball, volleyball, long walks on the beach, mowing the lawn, music, black-and-white photos, and laughing.

KAITY FLYNN: 16; Nebraska Christian High School; Palmer, NE; 3 siblings, 4 nieces, & 3 nephews; loves animals; loves to sing and make music for the Lord; has been in many honor choirs; loves drinking coffee with friends.

AUDREY FOSTER: 19; Hanover College; Fishers, IN; twin brother; enjoys traveling, cooking, and being completely romanced by God.

ERICA FREEMAN: 17; Nebraska Christian High School; Central City, NE; active in youth group; loves hanging out with friends; plans to major in medicine and minor in Christian ministries during college next year.

JESSICA GORDON: 16; New Covenant Christian School; Pageland, SC; an only child; loves dancing and singing; listed in Who's Who of American High School Students; member, Senior National Beta Club and American Christian Honor Society.

DANSHELLE GUY: 17, New Covenant Christian School; Pageland, SC; bookkeeper, varsity volleyball team; cheerleader; school choir, ensemble, Beta Club, American Christian Honor Society; in Pageland's Youth Development and Coalition Institute, church choir, The Voices of Hope; employed by Hardee's.

HOPE HAMILTON: 17; Donelson Christian Academy; Donelson, TN; active in youth group Hermitage Hills Baptist Church; loves singing; in school choir and praise band; will attend Samford University majoring in family and child psychology.

TIFFANY HEETDERKS: 15, Petra Academy, Bozeman, MT; loves playing volleyball, going to camps, and hanging out with friends and family.

MELANIE HELM: 15; New Covenant Christian School; Pageland, SC; 1 older sister; plays volleyball, basketball, and softball; in the Beta Club, Who's Who, the high school chorus, ensemble, the choric speaking team, and sophomore representative on homecoming court.

BEKAH HENDERSON: 17; Oconee Christian Academy, Seneca, SC; attended the school since fourth grade; very active in The Rock Youth Ministry at the Mount Church

ANGELA HENDRIX: 15; New Covenant Christian School, Pageland, SC; an only child; on the varsity volleyball team, in the choir, the Beta Club, and on the homecoming court; loves spending time with friends.

CAROLINE J. HORNOK: 15; Veritas Academy, Texarkana, TX; 1of 7 children; loves to read old books, especially Jane Austen; likes to write, play piano, translate Latin literature, and eat omelets.

KARIS HORTON: 17; Houghton Christian Academy, Houghton, NY; has 3 brothers; enjoys reading, swimming, and playing volleyball; received the coach's award in volleyball in 2004.

HAILEY HOWERTON: 16; home school, Greenville, SC; minister father/mother; loves painting, soccer; desires to do missions after college; a favorite thing in the world is going on vacation with extended family.

HANNAH HOWERTON: 17; home school, Greenville, SC; minister father/mother, 3 younger sisters, 1 brother; student youth group leader, Alabaster Ministries; Shannon Forest Presbyterian Church; great-grandparents, grandparents, uncle, & aunt were missionaries to China and Indonesia.

KRISTIN HUMPHREY: 17; Houghton Academy; Warsaw, NY; 2 older siblings; loves to participate in musical events and sports; has earned awards in athletics, academics, and music.

KRISTEN ISAAC: 14; Covenant Christian Academy, La Union, NM; 1 brother and 1 sister; loves reading, playing piano, dance, karate; earned several awards for school and Awana (which is connected with church)

MEREDITH JANKE: 17; Houghton Academy, Houghton, NY; youngest of 4; loves reading, music, and having fun with friends; plays the flute and sings for a worship team; family used to be missionaries in Romania.

CHRISTINA JENSEN: 15; Dogwood Christian School, Asheville, NC; 1 sister, and a Shih Tzu; Enjoys oil and acrylic painting, handcrafting earrings, baking, and babysitting. Loves traveling and teaching kids at church.

MARYANNA JENSEN: 19; North Greenville College, Asheville, NC; 1 sister and many cousins; loves classes, musicals, jogging, and her Jeep. Kids' ministry is a big joy in my life.

KERSTIN A. JONES: 17; Stillwater Christian School, Whitefish; 2 sisters; numerous soccer and school awards; loves to read, listen to music, hear good jokes, and snowboard.

VICTORIA TAIMANE'IONA'A'AOALOFA (DIAMOND IN GOD'S LOVING HAND) KAOPUA: 15; Kealakehe High School, Kailua-Kona, HI; 1 brother; Polynesian dancer; loves high school, friends, youth group, learning to drive; Who's Who of American High School Students; Honors; will attend NYU and be a singer.

LA'NICE DOMINEK KIBLER: 17, Redemption Christian Academy, Troy, NY; daughter of Lee Kibler, 6 siblings; loves basketball, serving the Lord; MVP in sportsmanship; plans to study business at Villanova.

MEREDITH KOONTZ: 17; North Buncombe High School; Weaverville, NC; enjoys reading, writing, and spending time with family and friends; hopes to continue education and become an author.

STACEY KRIEGER: 16; Nebraska Christian High School; O'Neill, NE; farmer's daughter; 1 older and 1 younger sister; loves talking to and hanging out with friends; enjoys helping on the farm and hopes to become an RN.

JANA KROEKER: 15; home school, Medicine Hat, Alberta, CA; dancer; striving to become part of GX International, Impact World Tours; plans to attend discipleship training school, then missions; dad is police officer; 1 brother, 1 sister.

KATIE-LEE KROEKER: 16; home school, Medicine Hat, Alberta, CA; 2 siblings; loves to play the piano and guitar, singing, traveling, being with friends, talking to God, and shopping.

CARRIE LEWIS: 14; home school with tutorial, Clemson, SC; 4th of 8 children; hobbies are writing letters to pen pals, playing piano and bluegrass fiddle, and learning Spanish.

NINA LEWIS: 18; home school with tutorial, Clemson, SC; 2nd of 8 children; graduated in 2005; enjoys hanging out with friends and family and loves graphic design arts.

SARAH LEWIS: 14; Walnut Grove Christian Prep School, Sheridan, IN; dad is deceased; lives with my mom, brother, and sister; loves listening to music and hanging with my friends; winner of a Right-to-Life essay contest.

AMANDA LIEGL: 17; Nebraska Christian High School; Columbus, NE; 3 older siblings; lives with a single parent; helps with VBS; loves to play volleyball.

YUNJOO LIM: 17; Houghton Academy, Houghton, NY; from Korea; 2 older sisters; loves to converse with friends and play volleyball; grew up in a Christian family, but met God two years ago.

PAMELA K. LOCKE: 15; Walnut Grove Christian Preparatory School, Noblesville, IN; an only child; a recipient of the National Latin Exam, 2004; Principal's Award at Tabernacle Christian, 2002.

JESSICA LORD: 17; Houghton Academy, Houghton, NY; 2 brothers and 1 sister; loves to play basketball and soccer and help with youth group activities; NAIA Champions of Character Award in the eleventh grade.

SHELBIE LUTZ: 17; Seaman High School, Topeka, KS; plays varsity soccer and basketball; treasurer for Fellowship of Christian Athletes; loves God, family, attending church, and youth group.

EMILY MALONE: 15; Oconee County Christian Academy, Seneca, SC; 1 brother; on varsity basketball and soccer teams; member of Hepsibah Baptist Church; born in NY, but lived in many places; has a dog named Molly.

HALEY MARTIN: 17; New Covenant Christian School, Pageland, SC; 1 brother; in school chorus, ensemble, and is a Beta Club officer; VP, senior class; American Christian Honor Society; on homecoming court and is the school's Carousel Princess.

MARQUITA MASSEY: 17; Redemption Christian Academy, Guilderland, NY; daughter of a pastor and assistant pastor; church youth leader; likes basketball; recently engaged; plans to become a songwriter and professional musician.

LAURE P. MBIANDJA: 16; Redemption Christian Academy, Troy, NY; loves basketball, movies, music; awards: MVP basketball, English, math, Christian character, Christian service; plans to pursue a career in medicine.

WENDY MCCAIN: 17; Grace Academy, Asheville, NC; 3 brothers and 1 sister; became a believer at 4 years old; youth worship leader at church; enjoys music, reading, writing, drawing, shopping, and hanging out with friends.

VIRGINIA MACKINNON: 15, Jonathan Edwards Academy, Turners Falls, MA; senior brother also attends; loves reading stories about people in real-life situations.

AMY MCKOY: 18; Bryan College, Dayton, TN; 3 siblings; loves to work with kids, draw, talk, and act crazy; dean's scholarships for college; went skydiving for 18th birthday!

LARNIQWA MERRITT: 15; Redemption Christian Academy, Troy, NY; 2 Siblings; likes math, singing, playing basketball; plans to pursue a career in early childhood education.

SONJA MINDREBO: 17; Houghton Academy, Houghton, NY; youngest of 5 children; loves to read, run, sing, paint, and journal; works church nursery and is a part of school's NHS.

HOPE MINOR: 16; Veritas Academy; Texarkana, TX; 5 brothers; magna cum laude National Latin Exam; Silver Award in Girl Scouts; loves to hang out with friends, shop, cook, read, play with her dogs, and dance.

JANELLE NAOMI MITCHELL: 18; Siegel High School, Murfreesboro, TN (formerly Clinton, MS); youngest of 3 girls; loves soccer (awarded coach's award one year), rock climbing, running, play guitar, singing praise songs, laughing with sisters, hanging with friends.

SABRINA MONOSIET: 15; Redemption Christian Academy, Troy, NY; mother, Yolanda Summerset; 1 sibling; loves music, movies, and basketball; awards: math, science, Christian character, and Spanish; plans to be a pediatrician.

JESSICA MOREL: 17; Riverdale High School, Rockvale, TN; 1 younger brother; blessed to have 2 loving parents who are happily married; loves to sing, play softball, and read God's word.

HEATHER MORRIS: 15; Walnut Grove Christian Preparatory School, Carmel, IN; lives with mom and brother; loves music and swimming; attends Fisher's United Methodist Church.

BETHANY MUSGROVE: 17; home school; Christian Believers of Donelson Church; 2 sisters; loves photography; worked at a Christian camp one summer; wants to major in business and become a professional photographer.

ANNIE NICKEL: 17; Nebraska Christian High School; Cairo, NE; loves Jesus; favorite verse is Matthew 5:14.

KEEGAN NITZ: 15; St. Ambrose Christian High School, Meridian, ID; 1 younger sister and brother; competes in Irish dancing and piano; loves to read.

KELSIE NYGREN: 15; Covenant Christian Academy, El Paso, TX; an only child; loves reading and writing fantasy; "A" Honor Roll, Bible Writing; Best Supporting Actress in *Little Women*.

LINDSAY OLIVER: 15; Cedar Hall School, Nashville, TN; likes animals, doing crafts, making jewelry, bike riding, and cooking; would like to be a veterinarian; in church youth group.

LISA OSLER: 18; Nebraska Christian High School, Kenesaw, NE; 2 married siblings; an aunt of 2; enjoys discussing theology and philosophy with friends; wants to go into youth ministries.

KARI PAGE: 19, Hanover College, Hanover, IN; 2 brothers; loves tennis, reading, hanging out with people, movies, llamas, anthropology, Brazil, France, sponges, face wash, phone booths, skiing, dry weather, and her bad taste in music.

MICHELLE PALACIO: 15; Alpha Omega Academy, Charlotte, NC; raised in Africa; 4 siblings; the oldest at home; a student athlete who swims year round for Mecklenburg Aquatic Club.

GRACE PARK: 17; Houghton Academy, Houghton, NY; from Korea; Korean name is Kipeum; 1 brother. loves to sing in Italian; grew up in strict Christian family.

JAZMA PARKER: 16; Martin Luther King Magnet School, Nashville, TN; 3 sisters; runs track; president of Engineering Society; enjoys math and science; choir member; works in children's church and mime ministry.

COURTNEY PINTO: 15; Walnut Grove Christian Preparatory School, Fishers, IN; 3 older siblings; lives with mom and stepdad; has 2 beagles; loves to read and write; loves kids and teaches Sunday school.

BRITTANY PLYLER: 17; New Covenant Christian School, Pageland, SC; 1 sister; on the varsity volleyball team, in the school choir and ensemble; class officer; in the Beta Club and the American Christian Honor Society.

JULIA POSTEMA: 16, Jonathan Edwards Academy, Erving, MA; won the Jonathan Edwards Award; plans to apply for an all-summer ministry at a Christian camp. She loves little kids and hopes to combine that with a career in nursing.

ALLY POWELL: 17; New Covenant Christian School, Pageland, SC; 2 brothers and 5 sisters; plays volleyball, basketball, and softball; president, senior class; Beta Club officer, in the American Christian Honor Society and Who's Who.

LAYSHA POWERS: 17; Maranatha Academy, Oakwood, GA; likes volleyball, leadership, friends, church activities; words of wisdom to share: "We are only on this earth for a finger snap of time, so do something special with your life."

HANNAH REED: 16, Jonathan Edwards Academy, Greenfield, MA; 1 sister; loves Ultimate Frisbee, music, and being with the people close to her; academic and character awards at school; part of church worship team.

BETHANY PEARL REEVES: 15; home school, Central, SC; oldest of 7; enjoys doing things with family, spending time with other girls and little children.

HANNAH REEVES: 14; home school, Central, SC; 7 siblings; likes to read, play piano, and violin, writing long stories, and history, especially the Civil War.

LAURA REIMER: 17; Nebraska Christian High School, Central City, NE; loves to read, play sports, ride horses, travel (anywhere and any way); most importantly, loves eating home-made ice cream.

JESSICA KATHRYN RUNK: 19; Patrick Henry College, Purcellville, VA; was homeschooled and appreciates the values her parents taught her; loves spending time with family, playing music, and volunteering at church. Favorite activity: laughing.

LISSETE RUSSELL: 19; Redemption Christian Academy, Troy, NY; 5 siblings, loves basketball and math; enjoys writing short stories and poems, loves children and would like to be an educator after college graduation.

MARANATHA SCHULTE: 17; Ben Lippen School, Columbia, SC; younger brother and older sister; awarded Board of Trustees character-based scholarship at school; loves to sing, dance, act, and loves Jesus.

CHARICE SCHWEITZER: 18; Nebraska Christian High School; Cairo, NE; 2 older siblings; plays volleyball and coaches junior high volleyball; favorite pastime is shopping; loves working with kids and hopes to someday have a career involving children.

HOLLY SCOTT: 18; North Buncombe High School, Weaverville, NC; loves reading, making pottery, growing in God, volunteering, playing with kids, hanging out with friends, being outside, and sitting on the roof at night to look at the stars.

KIMBERLY SCOTT: 17; Oconee County Christian Academy, Seneca, SC; lives in Toccoa, GA; enjoys playing soccer; involved in youth program at First Alliance Church.

STEPHANIE SHERWOOD: 14; St. Ambrose Christian High School, Boise, ID; 1 older sister; dog named Princess; enjoys English, riding and jumping, composing music, and playing the piano, cello, and guitar. Hopes to be a pilot someday.

MOLLY JO SPATEHOLTS: 17; Houghton Academy, Houghton, NY; 3 younger brothers, 1 sister; likes tap dancing, volleyball, swimming, scrapbooking, reading, working with kids; awarded Christian Witness Award, NHS, Most Improved volleyball and softball; planning to study languages and/or psychology.

MARY KAYLIN STAUB: 16; Heritage Academy, Flowery Branch, GA; 4 siblings; frandfather, Chicago Bears, MVP National Champs; dad founded Eagle Ranch, home for troubled children; loves riding horses, reading, singing, acting, friends; National Beta Club.

ASHLEY STONE: 18; Nebraska Christian High School, Central City, NE; older brother and sister both graduated from NCHS. Favorite sport is softball and loves to play the drums.

ADRIAN THISTLE: 17; Houston High School, Willow, AK; 1 younger brother; loves to dance ballet, read, take pictures, and hang out with friends; active youth leader.

RACHEL THURMAN: 17; Cedar Hall School, Rockvale, TN; lives with her parents and younger sister; wants to become a nurse anesthetist; enjoys cooking, gardening, beading, and being outside.

JONI TIMMONS: 16; New Covenant Christian School, Pageland, SC; 2 older sisters; enjoys volleyball, basketball, and drag racing (in which she is ranked nationally); President of Beta Club; in American Christian Honor Society and Who's Who.

DONAE TOMAN: 17; Stillwater Christian School; Columbia Falls, MT; likes reading and music; loves hunting elk and deer, helping in father's auto shop; 5th of 6 children; would like to be a journalist or work in communications.

ALEXANDRA TRUEHL: 15; Adelaide, Australia; lived on houseboat with missionary parents on Purus River in Amazonas, Brazil; 2 sisters, 1 brother; loves art, acting, singing, drama; dreams of missions using her skills.

CHLOÉ TRUEHL: 18; Adelaide, Australia; moved from the Amazon, Brazil, where parents and 3 siblings were missionaries for 12 years; in 2005 traveled the world doing missions; loves the arts and cooking.

SASHA TRUEHL: 19; Concordia College, Adelaide, Australia; born in Minnesota; raised in the Amazon, Brazil; currently living in Australia when not traveling for missions; 2 sisters and 1 brother; enjoys watching movies, singing, and dancing.

CALISTA TURNER: 17; Donelson Christian Academy, Nashville, TN; all-year honor roll; Latin 1, best in class; National Junior Classical League Latin Honor Society; Distinguished Scholar; National Latin Examination-10th grade Maxima Cum Laude.

ALEXIS ELLEN VANMINOS: 15; Oconee County Christian Academy, Seneca, SC; 2 siblings; loves volleyball and riding her horse; A/B honor roll since 5th grade.

AMBER VAN OSDOL: 18; Hanover College, Hanover, IN; 1 brother; loves to have campfires and just hangout; finalist in "One Nation Under God" competition; plans to major in communication and minor in sociology.

STEPHANIE WARNER: 14; Walnut Grove Preparatory School, Carmel, IN; drama and creative writing is a passion; published in "Teacher's Selection: Anthology of 8th grade Poetry" and "Anthology of 8th Grade Short Stories"; plans to teach ancient history and literature and be a published writer.

KATELYN WESTFALL: 15; Dover High School, Dover, OH; loves to hang out with youth group, go line dancing; member of 4-H.

ANNA WHITE: 15; Walnut Grove Christian Preparatory School, Zionsville, IN; 7 sisters, 1 brother; awards: horseback riding and art; hobbies are horses, forensic science, criminal investigation, and self-defense; hopes to work for the FBI.

REBECCA WHITE: 16; Walnut Grove Christian Preparatory School, Zionsville, IN; born in Michigan; 2 years in IN; enjoys history, reading, and artwork; wants to major in Celtic studies and possibly be a professor.

EMILY WILKIN: 15; Walnut Grove Christian Preparatory School; Carmel, IN; aspiring journalist; student leader at church; lives with parents and younger sister; loves being with friends, playing piano, reading, and running.

REBECCA WILSON: 18, Maranatha Christian Academy, Oakwood, GA; 4 siblings; passions for writing, riding horses, reading, acting, volleyball, basketball, hanging out with friends; awarded Academic Scholar; saved at 5; life verse is 1 Corinthians 15:58.

DANICA WOODS: 17; Nebraska Christian High School, Central City, NE; aspiring Spanish teacher; enjoys playing basketball and hanging out with friends.

STEPHANIE (AMERICAN NAME) KI-YEON YOON: 18, Houghton Academy, Houghton NY; from South Korea; has twin sisters; an art major; loves to play volleyball.

SARA YORK: 16; Antioch High School, Antioch, TN; member of Gospel Chapel, Nashville, TN; 2 brothers, one sister, she is youngest; volunteers at Horton Haven Christian Camp in the summers.

CHARITY YOST: 17; Oconee County Christian Academy, Seneca, SC; stays busy with extracurricular activities; enjoys writing poetry and short stories in spare time; hopes to become a professor and novelist.

SAM YUN: 18; Houghton Christian Academy, Houghton, NY; 1 older sister; loves to read, watch sports, and sing; from South Korea; raised in a Christian family; 3rd year in America.